GREAT BRITISH GRAVEL RIDES

MARKUS STITZ

GREAT BRITISH GRAVEL RIDES

CYCLING THE WILD TRAILS OF ENGLAND, SCOTLAND & WALES

Vertebrate Publishing, Sheffield
www.adventurebooks.com

GREAT BRITISH GRAVEL RIDES

CYCLING THE WILD TRAILS OF ENGLAND, SCOTLAND & WALES

MARKUS STITZ

 First published in 2022 by Vertebrate Publishing.

Vertebrate Publishing, Omega Court, 352 Cemetery Road, Sheffield S11 8FT, United Kingdom.
www.adventurebooks.com

A CIP catalogue record for this book is available from the British Library.

ISBN 978-1-83981-126-5 (Paperback)
ISBN 978-1-83981-127-2 (Ebook)

Front cover   Grant Wildman and Dalila Lecky in the South Downs. © Maciek Tomiczek, *www.tommycheck.com*
Back cover (L–R)   Gail Brown and Josh Ibbett in East Anglia (route 16); Mark Beaumont in East Lothian (route 08); Jenny Graham in Glen Affric (route 01); Emma Osenton in the Calder Valley (route 14); Charlie Hobbs on the Isle of Purbeck (route 22); Aneela McKenna in the Scottish Borders (route 09); Rory Hitchens in the South Downs (route 20).
Opposite   Wide gravel path towards Pencil Crag in the Lake District (route 12).
Photography by Markus Stitz unless otherwise credited.

Mapping contains data from OS © Crown copyright and database right (2022) and © OpenStreetMap contributors, *Openstreetmap.org/copyright*
Relief shading produced from data derived from U.S. Geological Survey, National Geospatial Program.
Cartography by Richard Ross, Active Maps Ltd. – *www.activemaps.co.uk*

Edited by Helen Parry, design by Jane Beagley, production by Rosie Edwards
www.adventurebooks.com

Printed and bound in Europe by Latitude Press.

Vertebrate Publishing is committed to printing on paper from sustainable sources.

MIX
Paper from responsible sources
FSC
www.fsc.org   FSC® C106600

CONTENTS

Introduction – Why a book about gravel riding in Britain? ix
Acknowledgments xi
What is a Great British gravel ride? xii
Prepare your own adventure xii
The bike xv
Getting to a route xix
Prepare your bike xx
Choose your clothing xxii
Other kit xxiii
Safety xxiv
Legalities and access xxvi

SCOTLAND
01 Coast-to-coast gravel adventure JENNY GRAHAM 3
02 In search of gravel on the Monega Pass NAOMI FREIREICH 13
03 A tour of Highland Perthshire RICHARD PEARSON 21
04 Maelstrom gravel STEVEN GROOM 31
05 Lomond Hills gravel LOUISE CHAVARIE 39
06 Gravelfoyle KERRY MACPHEE 49
07 Clacks gravel WALTER HAMILTON 59
08 Explore Your Boundaries: East Lothian MARK BEAUMONT 69
09 Mòr Tweed Valley gravel ANEELA MCKENNA 79
10 Raiders gravel ESTHER TACKE AND WARREN SAUNDERS 87

NORTHERN ENGLAND
11 Tyne and Wear gravel OLLY TOWNSEND AND FRANCIS KING 97
12 Lakes gravel JAIMI WILSON 107
13 Buzzard loop GUY KESTEVEN 115
14 Packhorse gravel EMMA OSENTON 123
15 Pannier gravel STEFAN AMATO 131

SOUTHERN ENGLAND
16 Further East JOSH IBBETT AND GAIL BROWN 141
17 Windmill gravel GRANT WILDMAN 151
18 Cotswold gravel EMMA KINGSTON 159
19 London gravel DALILA LECKY 167
20 Not the South Downs Way! RORY HITCHENS 177
21 Mint Sauce gravel JO BURT 185
22 Jurassic gravel CHARLIE HOBBS 193
23 A taste of the East Devon Trail KATHERINE MOORE 203

WALES
24 Twmpa gravel tour ANDY DIX 215
25 A Gritfest in the Cambrian Mountains MATT PAGE 223

BONUS ROUTE
26 Deer Island gravel MARKUS STITZ 233

Reading list 242
Websites 242
Events 243
Guided gravel rides 243

Download the
Great British Gravel
Rides GPX files from
www.adventurebooks.
com/GBGR-GPX

INTRODUCTION — WHY A BOOK ABOUT GRAVEL RIDING IN BRITAIN?

'I've ridden many thousands of miles on my bike all these years and I can't say I regret anything … There were rough times but also good times. You just know it's a challenge that you've got to overcome.' Ron Bartle

One of the first articles I published about gravel bikes was titled 'Gravel joy'. Up until that point, my opinion about gravel riding was mixed. I had ridden 34,000 kilometres around the world on a rigid single-speed mountain bike. Before the summer of 2017 when I picked up a Surly Straggler, I didn't see the need for another bike and thought that gravel bikes were simply another marketing move from the bike industry. The bike, which I initially borrowed for mapping a network of routes in Glasgow's city centre and the Wild About Argyll Trail, stayed with me and became the stalwart in my collection of bikes. And while it has since been replaced by a Kinesis Tripster AT, it still serves me well as a single-speed gravel bike. My conclusion in 2017, and the reason why I was headlining the article 'Gravel joy', was: *'It's not just about the bike, it is also about what I am able to do with it. The nature of gravel riding, fast and adventurous at the same time.'*

When I wrote my first article, my opinion of gravel riding was still closely defined by the bike I rode. Gravel bikes had drop bars, 700c wheels and a geometry that was close to a road bike. Tyre clearance wasn't as big as it is now. Back then, the 41-millimetre tyres it had were much larger than those on my road bike, but still significantly smaller than my mountain bike would allow me.

By the time I was researching this book in the summer of 2021, my own definition of gravel riding had changed significantly. Gravel riding was no longer defined by a certain type of bike, but much more by the opportunities it offered and the community around it. Since I picked up my first gravel bike, I hardly touched another bike. I have successfully finished the Silk Road Mountain Race, which at times was much more intense than my round-the-world trip, on a fully-loaded drop-bar bike. When I look back on my round-the-world trip now, more than 5 years after completing it, I think that in the truest sense my longest ever journey on a bike was a gravel bikepacking trip.

For me, gravel riding isn't defined by the shape of bars or tyre width, nor by geometry or clothing style. The technological developments since the term was coined around 2012, when Kinesis introduced the Tripster ATR and Salsa introduced the Warbird, have been significant. Both tyres and bars have become much wider and bikes have become even more capable.

But the idea of gravel riding wasn't born with the Tripster or the Warbird. It didn't start on 29 May 1955, when 'forty members who, in pursuit of their pastime, traverse the rougher and less beaten ways' attended the inaugural meeting of the Rough-Stuff Fellowship.

What we call gravel riding has been around ever since people took their bikes off the beaten track, often in pursuit of adventure. As early as 1919, Wayfarer, as he was known to a large cycling audience, wrote scores of articles and gave lantern lectures about his cycling exploits.

SUNSET IN EAST ANGLIA (ROUTE 16).

From the cover of the 1933 *C.T.C. Gazette,* published on the Rough-Stuff Fellowship website, I learned that the moorland and valley roads in Wales were as popular then with cyclists looking for some peace as they are nowadays allowing them to get away from the 'sophisticated horrors' of the Devil's Bridge, a popular tourist attraction to this day. Wayfarer's passion for this type of cycling was infectious. A century later, this is exactly what was mirrored on my rides with the people who made this book happen.

'It is a convenience to be able to carry or push a bicycle six miles instead of retracing 40 or 50 miles of a roundabout route.' Harold Briercliffe

Gravel cycling also offers an insight into the history of Britain. When I picked up the three editions of Harold Briercliffe's *Cycling Touring Guides* from the 1940s, I found the wonderful quote above in there. While most of the road routes that Briercliffe describes in his book are no longer suitable for cyclists, much of the landscape in national parks like the Peak District described by him in the 1940s and the off-road routes have remained unchanged. And while 'Beeching's Axe' resulted in the closure of around 6,500 kilometres of railway branch lines, some of them have been converted to make excellent gravel routes.

After having spent most of 2020 in close proximity to my doorstep, I initially approached Vertebrate Publishing with the idea to write a book. I wasn't interested in just writing a guidebook. I wanted to write a book that portrays the huge variety of routes suitable for rough-stuffing in Britain. Even though we are often no longer able to enjoy the quiet and peaceful roads, we can still easily get away from the 'sophisticated horrors' as they were described in the early magazines. Even in a city like London, one of the most populated places in the world, there were times on my ride with Dalila when the noise of the city was drowned out by beautiful birdsong. I was curious about the places gravel bikes take us to, but I was even more interested in the people whose infectious enthusiasm makes gravel riding as vibrant as it is.

I am very grateful for the time and enthusiasm of the people who kindly shared their favourite gravel routes with me. Everyone I interviewed and photographed for this book, and captured in moving pictures for the documentary accompanying it, is representative of how colourful and diverse gravel riding in Britain is. While we still have a long way to go to make cycling more inclusive and diverse, I hope this book portrays the gravel riding community as one which has made a good start towards a journey in which neither race, gender or age present a barrier to participation.

Cycling's popularity has surged during the various lockdowns we have endured since a virus changed our lives. Before the Covid-19 pandemic, far-flung places like Kyrgyzstan, Morocco or Chile got me excited for gravel bike rides. The Silk Road, Atlas Mountains or the Carretera Austral provided not only dream routes, but also material for magazines and films. All of a sudden, my world became so much smaller, but it was my bike and the community of people around me that still made it richer. Even though most rides in 2020 started at my front door, I could still have adventures, no matter how small they were.

I used the journeys I undertook for this book to discover Britain from a different angle and understand better what connects us as human beings. I was warmly welcomed wherever I went, and discovered a country that has much more to offer than just good gravel riding. Researching the routes and speaking to people gave me a good insight into the country which I made my home in 2009, and personally I think I learned much more from this than any news programme would manage to teach me.

I tried to produce this book in as sustainable a way as possible. Most of the trips to research this book were done by train or bus. Due to time constraints, I couldn't research everything by public transport and bike, but I made sure that most of the routes in this book are accessible for people who choose not to own a car.

I am hugely grateful for the support from Schwalbe Tyres UK, who not only believed in my idea from the very early stages, but also produce sustainable and durable products with long service lives, and are a leader in the bike industry with their efforts to reuse and recycle. I am also grateful for the additional support from Kinesis UK, who provided me with the right bike to enjoy the gravel rides in this book.

I hope this book brings you as much joy as it has brought to me and that we can share our passion for

LUSH GREEN FORESTS AROUND HEBDEN BRIDGE (ROUTE 14).

not just for gravel riding, but for cycling in general, with the same enthusiasm as the early trailblazers did.

For me, there is nothing better suited to finish this introduction, and send you off on your very own journey, than with the words of Ron Bartle, whose remarks I included earlier. Now in his mid-eighties, over 60 years ago he was one of the members of the first-ever unsupported ride across the Sprengisandur in Iceland, a pioneering expedition inspired by the rough-stuff riding in Britain and presented in the film *The Further Away, the Better.*

'*It's a grand way to spend a life.*'

Markus Stitz
Edinburgh, December 2021

FEEDBACK AND UPDATES

For any feedback please contact me at **markus@bikepackingscotland.com** or on social media at **@reizkultur**

ACKNOWLEDGEMENTS

This book wouldn't have been possible without the great input from all the featured gravel cyclists who have dedicated their time and in-depth knowledge to make this happen, for which I am really grateful: Stefan Amato, Mark Beaumont, Gail Brown, Jo Burt, Louise Chavarie, Andy Dix, Naomi Freireich, Jenny Graham, Steven Groom, Walter Hamilton, Rory Hitchens, Charlie Hobbs, Josh Ibbett, Guy Kesteven, Francis King, Emma Kingston, Dalila Lecky, Kerry MacPhee, Aneela McKenna, Katherine Moore, Emma Osenton, Matt Page, Richard Pearson, Warren Saunders, Esther Tacke, Olly Townsend, Grant Wildman and Jaimi Wilson.

GRAVEL TRACK IN THE SOUTHERN CAIRNGORMS (ROUTE 02).

Big thanks also to Kirsty Reade at Vertebrate Publishing, Tim Ward at Schwalbe Tyres UK, Philipp Jahn at Schwalbe Tyres Germany, Rory Hitchens at Upgrade Bikes, Carron Tobin at RuralDimensions, Elaine Carmichael at East Lothian Council, Andrew MacNair at CalMac Ferries, Clare Cooper at the Cateran Ecomuseum, Mike Dennison at Sustrans, Gavin Morton at the Green Action Trust, Francisco Perez at Visit Falkirk, Neil Ramsay at Clackmannanshire Council, Grace Wilson and Kelly-Jayne Collinge at Komoot and Ben Hillsdon at Shimano Europe, who have directly or indirectly been involved in the making of this book. And special thanks to my partner Louise, my family and Mark Beaumont and his family, who have provided the framework that allowed me to make this book happen.

WHAT IS A GREAT BRITISH GRAVEL RIDE?

This book is neither meant to be a definitive guide to gravel riding in Britain, nor a definitive portrait of the gravel scene in the country. I see this book as a source of ideas to embark on your own journeys.

A Great British gravel ride is a cycling adventure, but it is not defined by a certain amount of elevation gain or distance. In my opinion, cycling should not be painful; it should be fun. I could try to use my own words, but Mark Beaumont, one of the riders featured in this book and a good friend of mine, described gravel riding perfectly.

'If I was to summarise gravel riding in a sentence, it would be: creating memories. I never come back from my gravel rides and define them by how far I went. I define them very much by moments in time. Gravel riding for me has been about redefining why I ride a bike.'

This is exactly what I want a Great British gravel ride to be. A ride that creates memories, a ride defined by moments in time, which redefines why you ride a bike.

PREPARE YOUR OWN ADVENTURE
HOW TO USE THIS BOOK

This book provides descriptions of 26 routes suitable for gravel bikes in England, Scotland and Wales and a portrait of the person who chose the route.

Each route provides you with the following information.

› An insight into why the route was chosen.
› A detailed route description, which includes information about interesting places passed on

solid earth with some flat roots and smaller rocks. The surface may become loose at times and periods of stand-up riding may be required to overcome obstacles. There are no sections without an obvious path, but there can be gates along the route.

Straightforward

These routes are suitable for riders with a good level of fitness and advanced riding skills. They are generally no longer than 30 kilometres in length and contain no more than 600 metres of ascent. The distance between services is no more than 20 kilometres. They might contain short sections of singletrack up to level S1, comprising mostly compacted gravel or solid earth with some flat roots and smaller rocks. The surface may become loose at times and periods of stand-up riding may be required to overcome obstacles. There are no sections without an obvious path, but there can be gates along the route.

Challenging

These routes are suitable for riders with a good level of fitness and advanced riding skills. They are generally no longer than 50 kilometres in length and contain no more than 1,000 metres of ascent. The distance between services is no more than 25 kilometres. They might contain short sections of singletrack up to level S2, comprising a looser surface, as well as many roots and rocks. Narrow curves and steeper gradients are to be expected. Readiness to brake at all times is required, as is the ability to shift your centre of gravity on the bike. They may include sections of up to 1 kilometre without an obvious path, which might require pushing the bike. There can be gates along the route.

the route with some historic background to add context, as well as details on terrain.
> Essential information to help you plan your ride including: route grade (see below); start/end locations; distance; ascent; maximum height; and the nearest bike-friendly public transport.
> A route profile.
> A summary of the types of terrain encountered, along with a bar chart showing the proportion of the route that is on different surfaces (singletrack, cycle path, path and road).
> Recommended tyres and best time to ride.
> Places to eat and details of nearby bike shops.
> Points of interest.
> Other routes nearby, which can inspire your own exploration.

ROUTE GRADES

Easy

These routes are suitable for all fitness and skill levels. They don't include any steep sections, either on or off the road. The distance between services (to stock up on food and water) is no more than 10 kilometres. They might contain short sections of singletrack up to level S1, comprising mostly compacted gravel or

Expert

These routes are suitable for riders with a very good level of fitness and expert riding skills. They are generally longer than 50 kilometres in length and may contain more than 1,000 metres of ascent. They may include steep sections with a gradient of over 20 per cent off-road and on-road, and there may be sections which are more than 20 kilometres away from the nearest public road. The distance between services can exceed 25 kilometres. They might

NAVIGATING WITH A MOBILE PHONE (ROUTE 01).

contain short sections of singletrack up to level S2, comprising a looser surface, as well as many roots and rocks. Narrow curves and steeper gradients are to be expected. Readiness to brake at all times is required, as is the ability to shift your centre of gravity on the bike. They may include sections of more than 1 kilometre without an obvious path, which might require pushing the bike, and can exceed an altitude of 650 metres above sea level. They can contain gates and stiles along the route, which may require lifting the bike over fences.

NAVIGATION AND ACCURACY

Alongside the route directions and maps, GPX files can be downloaded for all the routes (see page vii). You can sync the GPX files directly on to your GPS device, or use a route planning platform.

A separate GPS device and a mobile phone are highly recommended to ride the routes described in this book. Make sure you always have a back up available, so if one device stops working, you can rely on the other. Sync the route to both devices before the ride and, if possible, make the route available when offline, so you don't have to rely on a mobile phone signal.

If one of your navigation devices stops working or runs out of battery, it is advisable to cut the route short and finish the ride in the quickest possible way, especially in remote locations. Carrying a paper map, compass and cue sheets are a great back up too. Make sure to attach your navigation device to your handlebars or stem so it is clearly visible but doesn't obstruct your knees.

While every effort has been made to ensure accuracy within the directions and descriptions in this book, things change and we are unable to guarantee that every detail will be correct. Please treat stated distance and elevation as guidelines and exercise caution if part of a GPX file or some information in the text appears at odds with the route on the ground. A comparison between the GPX file and mapping should see you on the right track.

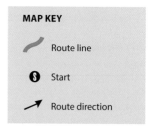

MAP KEY

Route line

S Start

Route direction

PICK YOUR ROUTE

This book offers a wide spectrum of routes. Take your time and choose the ride that's right for you. If you are in a particular region featured in this book, your choice might be influenced by the nearest available route. Please read the route descriptions carefully and decide if the route suits your expectations and riding ability. Most of the routes in the book are loops. There are two point-to-point rides included, which are both well served by public transport. For some routes, public transport can be used to shorten the routes. Wherever possible, this is mentioned in the route description.

Don't overestimate the distance that you want to tackle in a day. Gravel riding is meant to be fun. Plan enough time for stops, and allow time for when things go wrong. Fixing a puncture isn't a big task, but it takes time. You are likely to enjoy your gravel ride more if you have time to enjoy an ice cream on the beach, a hearty pub lunch or a coffee in a cosy cafe while you wait for the rain to pass.

THE KINESIS TRIPSTER AT OUTSIDE THE FOX GOES FREE (ROUTE 20).

GRAVEL WITH CHILDREN

If you are accompanied on a ride by children who are too young to cycle on their own, a tag-along bike (a bike that attaches to the back of another bike) may be a good alternative to a child seat or bike trailer, particularly for older children – some can be detached and cycled independently. There are also gravel bikes available in smaller sizes for kids.

THE BIKE
CHOOSE YOUR BIKE – SUPPORTED BY KINESIS

Kinesis G2 *(entry level)*

The G2 is offered as a complete bike and built on an aluminium frame with carbon fork and 700c wheels. The semi-sloping frame is a great feature, especially for smaller bikes as it reduces the stand over height. Short chainstays and the revised geometry give the G2 first-class road characteristics, while the low bottom bracket makes the bike very capable off-road. The bike has clearance for 700c x 45 millimetre tyres. It features internal cable routing and thru-axles on the front and rear. Flared handlebars, a short stem and full pannier rack mounts make this a very versatile gravel bike that can double up as a bikepacking, touring or commuter bike as well. It weighs about 10 kilograms as a complete bike.

Kinesis Tripster AT *(advanced)*

The Tripster AT was closely developed with the late Mike Hall and features a number of enhancements based on his input. These features make it not only a very capable gravel bike, but also a great choice for those multi-day bikepacking adventures Mike was well known for. It is different to the G2 as it offers additional mounts for a third bottle cage on the down-tube and a flattened edge on the top-tube to stabilise a filled frame bag. The flip-chip plates on the Columbus carbon fork can be adjusted to alter the rake of the fork between 47 millimetres and 52 millimetres. For smaller frames or longer bikepacking trips you will benefit from a longer wheelbase; for more technical day rides a shorter wheelbase is recommended. The bike has clearance for 700c x 45 millimetre tyres or 650b x 52 millimetre tyres. A complete bike with similar components as the G2 would weigh slightly less at 9.75 kilograms.

Kinesis Tripster ATR V3 *(enthusiasts)*

The Tripster ATR titanium bike was one of the first gravel bikes available the UK in 2012. It has since been refined a number of times to follow developments and is currently in its third incarnation (V3).

GRAVEL BIKES PARKED OUTSIDE A PUB IN EAST LOTHIAN (ROUTE 08).

A titanium frame along with a carbon fork makes this a very durable and comfortable bike for many uses. The Range fork features additional mounts for cages. Frame and fork are compatible with 700c x 45 millimetre tyres, or 650b x 50 millimetre tyres. Three bottle cage mounts, improved cable routing and flattened seat stays for greater comfort complete the package.

Kinesis Range Adventure E-Bike
The Range electric bike comes with drop bars or flat bars. The aluminium frame has a bigger tyre clearance for 700c x 50 millimetre tyres, using the same fork as the Tripster ATR with luggage mounting points. This is paired with a Fazua Evation drive system with a top-tube remote control and a removable 252Wh battery. The drive system has three different support modes, and the battery supports up to 1,000 metres of elevation with one charge (up to 55 kilometres using mixed modes). The frame has mounts for racks and mudguards and a complete bike weighs around 15 kilograms.

OTHER BIKES

There are loads of other options for what could be your gravel bike. Standard frame materials include steel, aluminium, titanium or carbon, with different wheel sizes and a wide variety of components to build the bike that best suits you. There are a number of other bikes that can be suitable for some routes, including tandem bikes, recumbent bikes, handcycles, tricycles or unicycles. Some routes have gates or obstacles that will make them unsuitable for bikes that cannot be lifted.

CHOOSE YOUR TYRE – SUPPORTED BY SCHWALBE TYRES UK

To guide your riding, each route has a recommended tyre choice to best suit the terrain. Tyre choice is very personal; it depends on your bike and wheel size, but also on your riding ability. As Schwalbe Tyres UK have supported the research of the book, the tyre choices are based on their extensive tyre range. Listed are specific gravel tyres, as well as tyres that are suitable alternatives from their mountain biking or touring ranges. In general, gravel tyres have a much more pronounced tread design than classic road or touring bike tyres, and are mostly lighter than mountain bike tyres.

KERRY MACPHEE TIGHTENING A CLEAT BOLT (ROUTE 06).

A minimum width of 40 millimetres is recommended. As some older frames won't be able to accommodate that width, especially on the rear, there are also some skinnier choices listed. The same applies to the other end of the spectrum, with some gravel bikes able to accommodate much wider tyres, especially on the front. Fast-rolling and light mountain bike tyres can often be a good choice for more technical and challenging terrain. It is also possible to mix different tyres; for example, using a more pronounced tyre on the front and a faster rolling tyre on the back. In general, back tyres wear more quickly than front tyres, and will need replacing more often.

Most modern tyres and rims support a tubeless set-up. The biggest advantage of tubeless tyres is that they allow for much lower tyre pressures, which in return improves comfort and grip in critical situations and poor road or trail conditions. Tubeless systems also provide higher puncture protection, as the risk of a sudden loss of air pressure, caused by burst tubes or a valve tear off, is significantly reduced.

Setting up a tubeless tyre requires airtight rim tape (often already standard on wheel sets), valves and the use of puncture protection liquids, which are able to reseal small cuts in the tyre within seconds. Tubeless tyres can be run with tubes, but will often be more difficult to fit, as they sit together on the rims to seal. Mounting fluid (such as Schwalbe Easy Fit), a good track pump and the Schwalbe Tyre Booster will help inflate the tyre and seat it properly on the rim, so no air can escape. If you are not confident with tubeless set-ups, please consult your local bike shop.

Minimum pressures depend on the individual tyre and are displayed on the sidewall. When out riding, it is always recommended to carry a repair system to fix bigger cuts with a plug (such as the Dynaplug Micro Pro). You are also advised to always carry a spare tube, for the scenario that the tyre cannot be sealed with plugs or puncture protection liquid.

Tubeless tyres also need to be properly seated on the rims. A small puncture will often not result in the tyre popping off the rim, but if it does and reseating fails, a spare tube will come in handy as well.

Most bicycle tubes are made of butyl rubber. A Schwalbe tube is 100 per cent recyclable. Used tubes provide the raw material for the recycling process. In Great Britain you can return used tubes to your local bike shop free of charge, and the recycled

GRAVEL TYRES IN ACTION – CROSSING A SMALL RIVER IN THE LAMMERMUIR HILLS (ROUTE 08).

butyl rubber is used in the production of new tubes without any loss of quality.

Much more expensive than butyl are thermoplastics, like Schwalbe's Aerothan. Those tubes are extremely light and pack very small. They offer puncture protection close to a tubeless set-up and allow for running low pressures. On the flipside, they are much more expensive and harder to repair, but can also be fully recycled.

The last consideration when it comes to bicycle tyres is whether to buy a folded or a wired tyre. Most modern gravel tyres only come folded, where the wire bead is replaced by a bead of kevlar strands. This enables the tyre to be folded up and, depending on the tyre size, makes it approximately 50 to 90 grams lighter. Wired tyres are heavier, but less expensive.

GRAVEL-SPECIFIC TYRES
G-One Speed
This tyre has a homogeneous round knob profile for optimal rolling on the road and safe grip on gravel. It is not suitable for most routes in the book, except in very dry conditions.

G-One Allround
The versatile tread of this tyre rolls easily and with low vibration, but grips safely and reliably on gravel tracks and smoother, dry trails.

G-One Bite
The open tread design and strong outer blocks give stability when cornering and provide this tyre with the perfect grip. This is the most universal gravel tyre, which still feels good and rides reasonably fast on roads, but its true strength shows off-road, in both wet and dry conditions.

G-One Ultrabite
The aggressive tread design of the tyre makes it best suited for use on gravel roads, forest tracks and trails in challenging conditions. The compact tape knobs in the middle of the tread provide full grip and traction, while the strong outer blocks provide safety when cornering. It's a slower tyre on roads, but still runs fairly smoothly. This tyre offers great performance as a front tyre in combination with the G-One Bite or G-One Allround on the rear wheel.

G-One R
The G-One R is predominantly a race gravel tyre, made for use on light terrain, gravel roads and asphalt. The angled side lugs create great cornering grip in

conjunction with the Super Race carcass, which offers a particularly smooth ride with low rolling resistance and high impact protection. It combines *souplesse*, speed and control at the highest level. This is the most expensive tyre in the range.

OTHER TYRES SUITABLE FOR GRAVEL RIDING
X-One Allround/X-One Bite
Designed for cyclo-cross use, these tyres can be a great alternative for frames with smaller tyre clearance, which can't accommodate wider tyres. The X-One Allround has pronounced side studs for high cornering speed in dry and wet conditions, while the X-One Bite has coarse, round studs for the optimal 'bite', even in the poorest conditions.

CX Comp
At a lower price point, this is an easy rolling tyre with good cornering grip.

SCHWALBE G-ONE R GRAVEL TYRE.

Smart Sam
This is a very durable mountain bike tyre which is well suited for gravel riding. The dense centre lugs provide comfortable rolling with low vibration and long durability, and the edged outer blocks simultaneously provide safety and optimum off-road grip.

Thunder Burt
The low weight and rolling resistance make this a good choice if a wider tyre fits your bike. The tyre has multiple small, flat studs for fast and quiet rolling, numerous grip edges for hard ground and edged shoulder studs for good grip and control on curves.

Marathon Mondial
Designed as an extremely robust cycle touring tyre, the Marathon Mondial is also suitable for some of the easier routes in this book. The tread pays homage to its legendary Marathon XR predecessor, which has been the tyre choice for many off-road bike expeditions.

Winter tyres
Some of the routes described can be ridden in winter conditions. Especially in icy conditions, a studded tyre is recommended, such as the Marathon Winter

Plus or Marathon Winter. For modern frames with big clearances, the Ice Spiker Pro on 650b wheels might be another option for more aggressive riding. In snow, the G-One Ultrabite and Marathon GT 365 offer much greater traction than a normal gravel tyre.

GETTING TO A ROUTE

To facilitate people who don't own a car, or to encourage you to leave your car at home if you do own one, the routes in the book have been chosen with bike-friendly public transport access in mind. Around 60 per cent of the routes start and finish at either a railway station or a ferry or bus service that offers bike transportation. Roughly another 20 per cent start and finish less than 10 kilometres away from the nearest bike-friendly public transport. For the remaining 20 per cent, you can combine the route with other routes to get to some appropriate public transport. The train, bus or ferry services that take you to the starting point will transport bikes free of charge, but pre-booking is often essential, normally up to two hours before the departure time. Make sure to either lock or supervise your bike on the whole journey and it's best keep all bags normally mounted on the bike with you.

When booking train tickets in advance, you will

THE BIKE YOU OWN IS THE BEST GRAVEL BIKE – FROM WIDE TO SKINNY TYRES, FROM DROP TO FLAT BARS.

often benefit from a better price. Splitting up longer journeys is usually cheaper than booking a ticket for the whole distance. There are a number of websites that can help with that. Where needed, bus and ferry options are listed in the route descriptions.

PREPARE YOUR BIKE

Make sure you clean and service your bike at regular intervals. How often depends on your bike, the amount of riding you do and the conditions you ride in. Be careful when using a pressure washer for cleaning your bike. If you are not confident in maintaining your bike, it is best to book a service at your local bike shop well in advance. Don't rush to the bike shop on the day before you want to set off.

It's worth learning the basics of maintenance, as some of the routes are remote and require you to perform the following basic fixes yourself if needed.

> Check and lubricate the chain
> Remove front and rear wheel
> Replace or repair an inner tube
> If tubeless: plug a small hole in the tyre
> Place a tyre boot

> Fix a chain with chainlinks (unless you are using a carbon belt)
> Replace brake pads
> Carry out basic gear adjustments (manual or electronic)
> If using non-hydraulic brakes: adjust brakes
> If using cleats: tighten or replace a cleat
> Tighten bolts properly (not overtightening them)

Being able to do these things will help you to fix common problems yourself and prevent you from having to walk a long way. Local bike charities often offer bike maintenance courses, which will help you to learn the skills if needed. Otherwise, online tutorials are a good idea too.

Checking your chain regularly for wear will potentially save you a lot of money. A worn chain, which is not replaced in good time, will wear out your drive train, and will result in much higher repair costs.

Especially in autumn and winter, mudguards will protect you from the worst of the spray from the tyres. Most gravel bikes have fittings for them, but they will impact the maximum tyre size you can fit.

FRAME
top tube
down tube
seat tube
seat stay
chain stay

SADDLE AREA
saddle
seatpost

FRONT SET
handlebar grip
headset
fork
front brakes

rear brakes
cassette
rear derailleur

WHEEL
valve
spokes
hub
rim
tyre

front derailleur
chain

pedal
crank arm
chainrings

FIGURE 1 THE M-CHECK AND PARTS OF A BIKE. © SHUTTERSTOCK/ROBCARTORRES

THE M-CHECK

Before setting off on each ride, you should always perform the M-check to check everything on your bike is working properly. Check your bike in the following steps, starting at the rear wheel and finishing at the front wheel. *(Figure 1)*

Rear triangle (frame) and wheel

Check that the thru-axle, quick release or bolts are tight and in a secure position. Check the rear wheel for play or cracks in the rim. Check all spokes by plucking each one with your finger – the sound should be similar. Check the tyre tread, sidewalls and pressure. Recommended tyre pressures are normally engraved on sidewalls. Check seatstays and chainstays for visible cracks.

Seat tube and saddle

Check the saddle, attachment and seatpost. Normally you don't need to tighten the saddle clamp or adjust the saddle height. If you do, make sure you don't exceed the limit marked on the seatpost and be careful not to overtighten the saddle clamp.

Chain, crankset and pedals

Check the chain for wear and lubrication. There are different lubes for various conditions; your local bike shop or online tutorials can help. Check for any cracked or stiff links. Check the crankset and pedals for loose bolts or play. Both cranks and pedals should spin smoothly.

Main triangle (frame), headset, stem and bars

Check for any play in the headset and make sure that bolts on the stem or handlebars are tightened properly. Check the down tube, head tube and top tube for cracks; check bottle cages or top tube bag fittings (if applicable) for loose bolts.

Brake and gear levers

Check brake and gear function. Hydraulic disc brakes normally adjust themselves; cable disc brakes need manual adjustment. If you have hydraulic brakes and you can pull your brake lever too close to the bar, your pads might be worn or the brake needs bleeding. If you have cable breaks and you can pull your brake lever too close to the bar, the pads might need replacing or adjusting or the cable tension might need adjusting. Manual gearing systems might need an adjustment of cable tension; electronic systems can normally be adjusted via an app. For other brake and gearing issues, it is best to consult your local mechanic or bike shop.

Fork and front wheel
Check that the thru-axle, quick release or bolts are tight and in a secure position. Check the front wheel for play or cracks in the rim. Check all spokes by plucking each one with your finger – the sound should be similar. Check the tyre tread, sidewalls and pressure. Check the fork and any cages or racks for loose bolts.

KIT LIST – BIKE REPAIRS
> At least one spare tube
> Box with multiple patches (check if usable with tube)
> At least two tyre levers
> Multi-tool
> Chainbreaker (can be part of multi-tool)
> Spare mech hanger (if applicable)
> Tubeless repair kit with sufficient plugs
> CO_2 cartridge (to reseat tubeless tyre if needed)
> Chainlink (correct size for the chain)
> Pump (with some duct tape wrapped around it)
> One spare cleat and bolts (if riding clipless)
> At least one set of brake pads
> Cable ties and tape
> Small bottle of lube
> Toothpaste wrapper or tyre boot

REPAIR HACKS
If you are out on a ride having forgotten something, here are a couple of hacks for trailside repairs using basic items.
Gel wrapper
Keep your used energy gel wrappers close at hand, as they make a great tyre boot if your sidewall is pinched. If needed, a bank note will work as well.
Fix a cleat with your bike's 'back-up bolts'
If you are losing a cleat bolt, you can replace that with a bolt from the brake rotor. To mitigate risk, take a rotor bolt from the rear wheel, and practise

clipping in and out a few times before you start riding again to ensure there are no interference issues between the new bolt and the pedal.

CHOOSE YOUR CLOTHING
With the rise of gravel biking in recent years, many bike clothing manufacturers have added gravel-specific collections to their range. A quick browse online will make the choice easy. Often gravel apparel is a mixture between tight-fitting road bike kit and more comfortable and loose-fitting mountain bike gear. Recommending specific clothing is beyond the scope of this book. Wear what you are most comfortable in, and be prepared for the weather you are likely to encounter.

Check the weather forecast before you head out and base your kit choice on how likely you are to encounter a variation of temperatures and weather conditions. The longer the ride, the more likely you are to face changing conditions. Britain enjoys a wide range of weather conditions, but you are unlikely to experience extreme heat or arctic cold. Wearing multiple layers gives you much greater flexibility to adapt to various weather conditions.

In all seasons try to avoid getting wet, either by sweating too much or from precipitation. Should you get wet, especially in colder conditions, make sure to protect yourself from losing too much body heat. As a rule of thumb, synthetic clothing will dry quicker than wool-based clothing, but will also start to smell more quickly than natural fabrics.

CLOTHING HACKS
If you are out on a ride and have forgotten something, here are some hacks which may help if you get cold.
Newspaper
A newspaper can act as a windproof layer if stuck under your jersey.
Single-use gloves
These disposable gloves can act as liner or waterproof gloves if your hands get cold or wet.
Aluminium foil
If you have cold feet, aluminium foil under your insoles reflects the heat from your feet.

KIT LIST – CLOTHING

Essentials
> Shoes (comfortable, ideally waterproof)
> Socks
> Suitable cycling shorts/skorts, bib shorts, leggings or bib tights
> Fast-wicking base layer
> Jersey (short or long sleeve)
> Windproof and waterproof jacket
> Gloves
> Helmet

Extras – useful in some conditions
> Shoe covers
> Knee or leg warmers
> Waterproof legwear
> Arm warmers
> Additional gloves (liners or outers)
> Headwear
> Buff (which can double up as face mask)
> Sunglasses
> Gilet

KIT LIST – SAFETY
> Basic first aid kit
> Emergency blanket
> Mobile phone

KIT LIST – EXTRAS
> Sufficient lights, with a back-up for front and rear (such as a head torch with red light function)
> A dynamo and charger fitted on the bike and/or a powerbank and cables to charge phone or GPS, or spare batteries
> Trowel and toilet paper
> Down jacket and beanie
> Spare socks
> Extra tubes
> Sunscreen
> Chlorine tablets or water filter

OTHER KIT

In addition to a working bike and suitable comfortable clothing, you should always carry some basic safety equipment – see the list above.

A long day in the saddle is best enjoyed if you are prepared. If you carry the items in the extras list, you should be able to enjoy a spontaneous meal in a pub or a side trip to visit a castle.

FOOD AND WATER

Nutrition is as individual as what you wear, so giving specific tips would be well beyond the scope of this book. Check your route before you set off, and don't completely rely on services, especially in rural areas. Either bottles or a hydration bladder can provide you with sufficient water for a shorter ride. For longer rides, it's usually possible to fill up bottles or bladders at pubs or cafes. Water purification (chlorine dioxide) tablets can help to sterilise water from natural water sources, but it will be around 30 minutes before you can drink the water. There are also water bottles and hydration bladders with water filters included – a good solution for more remote rides. Whatever you eat or drink, make sure you leave no trace and carry out all packaging.

BAGS AND RACKS

Additional clothing, spares and food can be carried on a variety of bags, either attached directly to your bike frame, handlebars, saddle, seatpost or forks, on a rack or in a backpack or hip belt. As with anything else, there are no rights or wrongs. Try out any bags or additional equipment before you go on a long ride. Some fittings and closing mechanisms of road-specific bikepacking bags might not be suitable for gravel riding, especially if you choose a very bumpy route. Most mountain-bike-specific bags will be just fine, as they have been designed with rough tracks in mind. Be aware that most bikepacking bags will rub on the frame and fittings. Self-fusing silicone tape will help you to preserve the paintwork.

Racks, either on the front or rear of the bike, have become popular again. Modern carbon racks weigh less than traditional aluminium racks and can increase the luggage carrying opportunities on smaller bikes, which often don't have enough

NAOMI FREIREICH CHANGING TUBES IN THE CAIRNGORMS (ROUTE 02).

clearance between the bars or seatpost and the tyres.

A lightweight hydration pack, either in the form of a backpack or hip belt, can be useful for longer rides.

TEST YOUR KIT

Small changes can make a big difference to your comfort on any cycling adventure. Find the saddle that suits you best; discover the food that makes you happy; check that your waterproofs keep you dry; work out what is missing from your toolkit. Try to find out what suits you best, not what others prefer. The more you ride, the more you know what works for you – don't expect your first gravel adventure to be perfect!

SAFETY

Do not rely on a single form of navigation (see **Navigation and accuracy** (page xiv) for more advice). Always carry a mobile phone in order to alert the emergency services in the event of an accident. Be aware that phone signal may be intermittent or non-existent, particularly in remote or mountain areas. A satellite GPS messenger will be a valuable addition if you are planning to ride in very remote regions. When buying the device, it is worthwhile considering additional costs such as annual subscriptions.

IN THE EVENT OF AN ACCIDENT

If you do get into difficulties and require help, dial **999** or **112** and ask for the **Police** and then (if you are in a remote location) **Mountain Rescue**. Calls are free from any public or private phone, but they should be made only in real emergencies.

MARK BEAUMONT SYNCING HIS PHONE AND GPS DEVICE IN EAST LOTHIAN (ROUTE 08).

Another option is to contact the emergency services by SMS text – useful if you have a low battery or intermittent signal. Texts can often get through when a call cannot. Register your phone first by texting '**register**' to **999** and following the instructions. Do it now – it could save your or someone else's life. This should only be used when voice call contact with emergency services is not possible. **www.emergencysms.net**

Mountain and other countryside rescue services in Great Britain and Ireland are provided as part of national emergency services by voluntary organisations. Charitable organisations such as Mountain Rescue and the Royal National Lifeboat Institution are financed by public donations and reliant on volunteers.

Mobile phones let you store a medical ID, which will help emergency services with basic information. Make sure it is up to date.

In the event of needing to call for rescue, prepare the following information.

Your name – normally you are asked your full name, and sometimes your address, to identify you. Your mobile number will show on the emergency operator's screen, but you may be asked to confirm it.

Where you are – make sure you know how to locate your UTM coordinates using your mobile phone or smartwatch. The free app OS Locate is a fast and highly accurate means of pinpointing your exact location anywhere in Great Britain.

Phone number – if you are low on battery, tell the operator and provide an alternative phone number of another group member.

What occurred – detail the event that occurred in terms of numbers involved, their ages, and injuries and how they were sustained. Provide any detail you feel pertinent, such as fractures, medication, or the time elapsed since the accident.

JENNY GRAHAM ON THE SHORES OF LOCH AFFRIC, SCOTTISH HIGHLANDS (ROUTE 01).

Rescuer details – you may be asked various details that the rescue teams might require, such as local weather conditions.

Try and remain calm when providing this information, as your clarity and quality of the information is of vital importance to the rescue team.

LEGALITIES AND ACCESS

Routes in this book have been researched to respect the current legal frameworks in Britain. Please note that they can change.

ROAD CYCLING

In Britain, cyclists are obliged to adhere to the Highway Code. Although no speed limits are applicable to cyclists, you may be charged with cycling carelessly or furiously. Cycling on pavements is illegal, unless it is also a cycle path. Helmets are not mandatory. At night, your bike must have a white front and red rear lights (flashing lights are permitted), and also needs to be fitted with a red rear reflector

and amber pedal reflectors. You can be charged with cycling under the influence of drink or drugs.

OFF-ROAD CYCLING

For off-road cycling, access to the countryside is different in England and Wales from the access rights in Scotland.

ENGLAND AND WALES

In England and Wales, bikes are permitted only on the following public rights of way:

> bridleway
> byway open to all traffic
> restricted byway (not for use by mechanically propelled vehicles)

There are also other routes with public access, like cycle routes or permissive bridleways, where landowners have permitted public use. These are not rights of way. All the above are liable to change and may not be clearly defined on the ground. Please check with the relevant local authority for the latest information. It is trespass (currently a civil offence, although this is under review) to cycle on footpaths in England and Wales, unless the landowner gives permission.

SCOTLAND

In Scotland the Scottish Outdoor Access Code gives people the right to access most land, including private roads, tracks and paths, for recreation and to get from place to place. This right is conditional on people acting responsibly. The main exceptions to the new right are: people's gardens, farmyards (although access is often possible – if in doubt, ask), and land in which crops have been sown or are growing (but you can use field margins as long as you avoid unnecessary damage to the crops). You can access golf courses (except greens and tees), but only to cross the area and without interfering with play. On golf courses, cyclists need to keep to paths at all times. You are also allowed to cycle off-path, but are encouraged to avoid going on to wet, boggy or soft ground, and churning up the surface. Take care not to alarm farm animals, horses and wildlife and do not endanger walkers and horse riders: give other users advance warning of your presence and give way to them on narrow paths. More information can be found at **www.outdooraccess-scotland.scot**

BE RESPONSIBLE

Leave only tyre prints, take only photos and leave a positive impact on the communities you travel through.

Keep it clean – clean your bike and shoes before travelling to another region to avoid transporting weeds and diseases such as Phytophthora ramorum, which attacks larch trees, and is present in South West England, Wales and Scotland.

Pack it out – do not leave any rubbish on trails. Take it with you and, where available, use recycling facilities.

Toilets – plan your day to take advantage of public toilets or facilities in cafes and so on. If necessary, do your business well away from waterways and bury your waste and toilet paper with a trowel.

Share with care – be mindful that you share the routes with walkers, drivers, horse riders, wildlife

PUBLIC BRIDLEWAY SIGN IN YORKSHIRE (ROUTE 13).

and livestock, and show respect. Never ride towards stock; instead pause and give them time to get out of your way. Give any cows with calves a wide berth, or change your route if necessary. Always leave gates as you find them.

Respect our cultural heritage – many places in Britain have special spiritual and historical significance. Treat these places with respect.

Climate change – reducing carbon dioxide emissions is the most critical challenge of our time. You can play your part by taking public transport, sharing cars with others and avoiding flights.

SCOTLAND

SCOTTISH HIGHLANDS

01 COAST-TO-COAST GRAVEL ADVENTURE

99KM   JENNY GRAHAM

This coast-to-coast expedition through one of Scotland's most scenic glens offers a long day in the saddle or the perfect opportunity for a weekend adventure, with local beer, a bothy and one of Scotland's most photographed castles along the way.

ABOUT JENNY

Gravel riding for Jenny in three words
all-round journey

'I was born and bred in the Highlands of Scotland – being out on our bikes and exploring on foot is in our DNA up here.'
Riding a bike has been part of Jenny Graham's life since she was a kid, either for travelling to various places or playing around the Scottish city of Inverness. It was when her son Lachlan started school that Jenny used her spare time to take up cycling as a sport, mountain biking in particular. Back then, a three-hour ride was a pretty big deal for her, but Jenny was drawn to the wild places the bike took her. As her son got older and more independent, they spent a lot of time cycling together. She gained a number of national qualifications, started guiding young people from the Highlands and created bespoke trips for people to show them around the Highlands.

'It was never about getting fit enough to go around the world, it was always this curiosity of how far I could travel on my bike.'
When her son became a teenager, Jenny could spend even more time on gathering experience and being out on the bike. What first started as a hobby, became a career. While getting the miles in, she found herself questioning how many miles a day she could do. Things had fallen into place in her life and, at the age of 38, she was confident that she would be capable of breaking the women's round-the-world record.

'There was no one at home sorting things for me. Keeping on top of my timings became more and more difficult when I was out there. It's difficult to

keep that at the forefront of your mind, because you're so busy looking after yourself and making sure that your basic needs are being met.'
When Jenny arrived at the Brandenburg Gate in Berlin on 18 October 2018, she had completed her unsupported circumnavigation of the globe by bicycle in 124 days, 10 hours and 50 minutes, setting a new world record. Although she missed the target of averaging 290 kilometres per day she had set herself, mainly due to fatigue and weather conditions in Australia and New Zealand, she averaged an impressive 254 kilometres per day. And her last leg involved an all-nighter. Cycling for 30 hours straight and covering over 482 kilometres, Jenny made it to the finish in Berlin to complete her cycling mission.

'Getting to the start line of that trip was probably the hardest thing that I've ever done.'

PREVIOUS PAGE THE MAJESTIC MOUNTAINS OF KINTAIL (ROUTE 01).   **OPPOSITE** CAMBAN BOTHY IN THE KINTAIL MOUNTAINS.

SCOTTISH HIGHLANDS   01 COAST-TO-COAST GRAVEL ADVENTURE   3

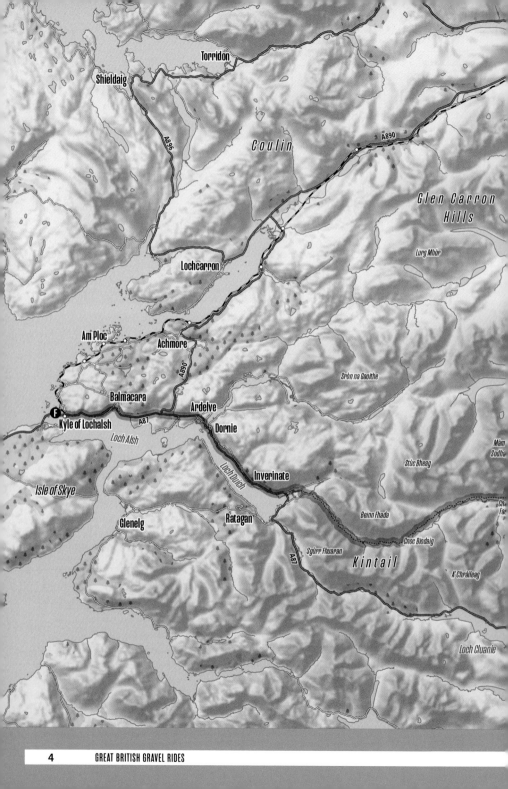

Torridon

Shieldaig

A896

Coulin

A890

Glen Carron Hills

Lurg Mhòr

Lochcarron

Am Ploc

Achmore

A890

Sròn na Gaoithe

Balmacara

Ardelve

F

Kyle of Lochalsh

A87

Dornie

Loch Alsh

Loch Duich

Inverinate

Stùc Bheag

Màm Sodhe

Isle of Skye

Beinn Fhada

Cnoc Biodaig

Cn' Fa

Glenelg

Ratagan

Sgùrr Fhuaran

A87

Kintail

A' Chràileag

Loch Cluanie

Dingwall

A835

Muir of Ord

Beauly

Wester
Balblair

Orrin Reservoir

Strathfarrar
Hills

Loch Monar

A833

Strathglass

Glen Cannich
Hills

A831

Cannich

A831

Milton

Loch Mullardoch

Lewiston

Toll Creagach

Glen Affric

A82

B852

Loch Beinn a' Mheadhoin

Loch Affric

ffric Hills

Loch Ness

A887

Fort Augustus

N

0   10 Kilometres

THE AFFRIC KINTAIL WAY IN GLEANN LICHD.

While Jenny's experience at the finish was a mixture of exhaustion and shock, the real accomplishment for her was getting the start line. When she was greeted by friends and family in Berlin it was hard to process what had just happened, but looking back she is incredibly proud of making the decision to set off and putting so much effort into making the trip a reality. After months and months of talking about the trip, and the battles she came across to make it happen, she felt a huge euphoria and a whoosh of emotions when she was finally on her way.

'We need to see that there's a place for everyone in this world. Having a variety of faces, colours, shapes and voices out there is hugely important. I think it can only inspire more and can create content for everyone, and make the world a little bit fairer.'

At the beginning Jenny doubted whether she was educated enough or had enough money to be an adventurer. She couldn't see anyone like her doing those things; adventuring seemed to be the domain of the wealthy. For Jenny, representation of minority groups, so people can picture themselves doing it, is key to get a more diverse group of people into cycling. As is hearing those stories of people that come into cycling and adventuring through another field.

'We could get on these bikes and travel fairly fast. It was really good fun, just coming on and off roads into wild places, then cycling down glens. That bit captured me – the journey aspect is what makes me reach for the gravel bike each time.'

Jenny's journey into gravel riding was slow to start with. She wasn't a fan at the beginning, as the gravel bike didn't go on the road as fast as she wanted, and it also didn't do what was expected of a mountain bike.

It was a joint trip with Lee Craigie from the Adventure Syndicate, crossing Scotland from north to south, that finally changed her mind. The variety of terrain that gravel bikes could cover was what triggered Jenny to rethink, and since then a gravel bike has become a stable companion on her adventures.

ABOUT JENNY'S ROUTE

This is one of only two point-to-point routes in this book. Often logistics make it difficult to complete a coast-to-coast journey but, as Jenny's favourite route starts and finishes at a train station, it is possible to ride this route in one day without the need for a car. However, taking you through one of Scotland's most beautiful glens, past a pretty unique hostel and a bothy, which provide valuable shelter from the elements and midges, this route would also make a great multi-day trip.

Tapping into the wealth of other routes that Jenny's itinerary passes, this journey can easily be extended and provide the backbone to a longer adventure. For Jenny, this is the gravel riding she can easily find when she leaves her house in Inverness. This route gets her to the other side of Scotland, travelling through the most incredible places. It reminds her how lucky she is to call the Highlands her home.

ROUTE DESCRIPTION

People have been living in the area around Beauly from around 2000 BC, but the origins of the town trace back to the founding of the priory in the early thirteenth century. Local legend says that Mary, Queen of Scots stayed overnight in Beauly in 1564 and that the town's name is credited to her reaction: '*C'est un beau lieu*' (what a beautiful place). While Mary's reaction might have given the town its name, it more likely that it originates from the French monks who founded the priory at Beauly. The monks were of the Valliscaulian order from Val-des-Choux.

This coast-to-coast gravel adventure starts at Beauly railway station, which is connected to Inverness by the Far North Line, with around ten services per day. Only the abbey church remains of Beauly Priory, but the town has a good variety of places to eat and stay and is located on the popular North Coast 500 route, an 800-kilometre scenic route around the coast of Northern Scotland. From the station the route follows the A862, part of the North Coast 500. The route meets the A831 east of Wester Balblair and follows this road for a short while. Near Kilmorack the route joins a quieter road on the left and crosses the River Beauly. The bridge crossing the river is one of three bridges spanning this 25-kilometre-long river. The route continues on a road to the south of the River Beauly towards its source near Struy.

The first climb of the route takes you to Fanellan, from where the road undulates through the valley to Struy. The village of Struy is the gateway to Glen Strathfarrar and the surrounding Munros; it lies near the confluence of the River Farrar and the River Glass, where the rivers join to become the River Beauly.

LOCH BEINN A' MHEADHOIN.

A visit to Struy Church is worthwhile, and the nearby Eagle Brae Log Cabins offer mountain bike hire for those travelling without their own bike. The route continues on the road following the River Glass to Cannich through a mixture of beautiful, lush woodlands and more open stretches. This part of the route follows the Great North Trail and An Turas Mor, two long-distance bikepacking routes which ultimately lead to Cape Wrath in the far north-west of Scotland.

The route crosses the River Glass at Comar Bridge and continues on the A831 into Cannich. This small village is sandwiched between the River Cannich in the north and the River Glass in the south, and is surrounded by beautiful woodlands. Comar Bridge is where the route meets the Affric Kintail Way, a long-distance walking and mountain bike route connecting Drumnadrochit, on the shores of Loch Ness, to Morvich in Kintail. Once you reach the village, the route leaves the Affric Kintail Way again. For those wanting to add more climbing and gravel to the itinerary, you can continue to follow the signposted Affric Kintail Way; it meets our route again near Dog Falls.

Cannich is the last stop for food and supplies for the next 50 kilometres. If you want to taste

HEADING TOWARDS THE HIGHEST POINT OF THE ROUTE AT BEALACH ALLT GRANNDA.

the craft beers of the Glen Affric Brewery, a stop at the Slaters Arms is recommended. Be prepared to be turned away when it's busy. If this is the case, the well-stocked Cannich Stores and Post Office provide takeaway food as well.

Cannich also marks the eastern end of Glen Affric, which is often described as the most beautiful glen in Scotland. The glen, which is surrounded by moorland and mountains, contains two large lochs and the third-largest area of ancient Caledonian pinewood in Scotland. The area was first colonised by Scots pine trees around 8,000 to 10,000 years ago, after the last ice age. However, even the older trees in the glen which have survived tree felling are not that old, as for many years tree growth was hampered by the high populations of deer and sheep. These older trees have a gnarled appearance and are known as 'granny trees'. After many decades of careful management to encourage the native forest, biodiversity has improved and the glen now supports a wide variety of birds including capercaillie, black grouse, crested tits and Scottish crossbills, along with golden eagles and ospreys. Scottish wildcats and otters also reside in the glen.

Taking you into this scenic haven, the route follows the GB Divide trail for a short while, although it goes in the opposite direction from the standard one for the GB Divide. From Cannich the environment becomes increasingly remote; the upper reaches of Glen Affric being among the most isolated in the Highlands. The route follows the Glen Affric Road to Dog Falls,

pipes from Glen Cannich, just to the north, into Loch Beinn a' Mheadhoin, which is dammed to raise the water level. From there, the water flows on to a power station at Fasnakyle, near Cannich. The route travels on the road along the lochside, with great views on to some of the islands and peninsulas. A small car park on the left provides a good opportunity for a stroll through the Scots pine and birch woodland or a picnic on the shores. There is another good spot right at the end of the public road, where short waymarked trails provide for stunning views of Loch Affric and the surrounding mountains.

The end of the public road marks the start of a great gravel track to Affric Lodge. This route keeps mostly well above the loch and passes through both fine pinewoods and moorland scenery, with views of the mountains high above. Now used as private accommodation, the four walls of the drawing room within the lodge were painted with sporting scenes by Sir Edwin Landseer, whose painting *The Monarch of the Glen*, which is now exhibited in the National Gallery of Scotland, is one of the most popular paintings of the nineteenth century.

Affric Lodge marks the point in the route where scenic tarmac roads give way to off-road trails. A wide gravel track continues on the northern side of Loch Affric, climbing first and then descending to Cnoc Fada, where the Affric Kintail Way is joined once again. A few fords need to be negotiated on this section, which can become dangerous after prolonged spells of rain. The River Affric is followed westwards on a wide gravel track, which undulates on the northern side of the river. The scenery here is some of the finest that Scotland has to offer. Glen Affric Youth Hostel, housed in a former stalking hut on the Affric Estate, is a good stop for those doing the route over 2 days. You'll get a warm welcome at this friendly eco-hostel; there is also a small hostel shop which sells basic food and soft drinks, if your supplies need topping up. Please be aware that the hostel is only open from April to September (double check opening times with the hostel before you set off).

a series of waterfalls on the River Affric within the Glen Affric National Nature Reserve. There are several waymarked paths to the falls, which are just a short detour off the route from a car park on the left. This is also the point where the route meets the Affric Kintail Way again. At this point, for those wanting to add more gravel to the itinerary, you can follow the Affric Kintail Way on the southern shores of the River Affric and Loch Beinn a' Mheadhoin – this is also the route of the Highland Trail 550.

Our route follows the tarmac a bit longer, climbing steadily uphill. Soon Loch Beinn a' Mheadhoin is reached. The loch looks very much at home in the glen, but it is not quite as natural as it looks. In the 1950s an ambitious hydroelectric project was undertaken in the area: water runs in

From the hostel, the riding continues on a grassy track with a few fords to reach Camban Bothy. A very basic unlocked shelter, maintained by volunteers from the Mountain Bothies Association, Camban is

nestled in the beautiful surroundings. A few ruins around the bothy provide signs that there might have been a settlement here once. Please help by carrying out any rubbish you find here, and always follow the Bothy Code when visiting **www.mountainbothies.org.uk/bothies/bothy-code** From the bothy the riding becomes much more technical – be prepared to push on this section and allow plenty of time for this part of the route. The next 8 kilometres will feel like a proper expedition.

Bealach Allt Grannda is the highest point of the route at 348 metres; a small cairn marks this point on the watershed of Scotland between the headwaters of the Allt Grannda and the Allt Cam-bàn. From here, a well-maintained but very technical path leads downhill, first gradually, and then very steeply. The steep section continues for around 2 kilometres – you'll be pushing or carrying your bike. While the terrain is exceptionally tough, this part of the route is really dramatic as the path contours round the slopes high above a deep basin. This is one of the toughest sections of the Highland Trail 550; at least you'll get to descend instead of pushing uphill, while waterfalls tumble down into the depths. Once you have reached the Edinburgh University Mountaineering Club hut at Glenlicht, you'll be back in the saddle.

The route continues along the southern side of Gleann Lichd. Bounded in the north by Beinn Fhada and in the south by the Five Sisters of Kintail, the route continues on a well-graded gravel track through this wild and dramatic treeless glen, with the beautiful River Croe meandering between the steep mountainsides. The legend of the Five Sisters of Kintail actually involves seven sisters: the youngest two sisters of the seven fell in love with two Irish princes, who had been washed ashore during a storm. However, the sisters' father would only allow the two youngest sisters to marry once the older sisters were married. The princes and the father came to an agreement that, if they could marry the two sisters and return to Ireland, they would send their other five brothers to marry the remaining five sisters. The five sisters waited, but the five princes failed to appear – they eventually turned into mountains to wait into eternity.

There is usually a herd of Highland cattle grazing in Gleann Lichd, so ensure that you leave all gates as you find them. The gravel track continues to the Kintail Outdoor Centre, from where a tarmac road leads to Morvich, which marks the end of the Affric Kintail Way.

From Morvich the route continues on a smaller road and then joins the A87 along the shores of Loch Duich. Please take care on this part of the route (especially in summer, when traffic can be an issue), as the A87 is the main road from Fort William to the Kyle of Lochalsh. Along with the neighbouring sea lochs of Loch Long and Loch Alsh, Loch Duich forms a Marine Protected Area to conserve the lochs' burrowed mud and their flame shell beds. A small petrol station on the left provides the first resupply point after the long and remote section. If you have plenty of time, the smaller road on the right shortly after Inverinate is a great alternative, but be prepared for more climbing in exchange for great views over the loch.

One of Scotland's most visited and iconic visitor destinations is next. Eilean Donan is a small tidal island situated at the

---

DISTANCE **99km/62 miles** 〉 ASCENT **979m/3,212 ft** 〉 GRADE **Expert** 〉 START **Beauly railway station** 〉 FINISH **Kyle of Lochalsh railway station** 〉 START GRID REF: **NH 520458** 〉 FINISH GRID REF: **NG 762272** 〉 BIKE-FRIENDLY PUBLIC TRANSPORT **At the start and finish** 〉 HIGHEST POINT **348m/1,142 ft** 〉 TERRAIN **Very remote on alpine terrain which requires a long hike-a-bike. The second most difficult route in this book** 〉 RECOMMENDED TYRES **Schwalbe G-One Bite**

BEST TIME TO RIDE

| JAN | FEB | MAR | APR | MAY | JUN | JUL | AUG | SEP | OCT | NOV | DEC |

SINGLETRACK **10%**   PATH **20%**   ROAD **70%**

LOCH BEINN A' MHEADHOIN WITH THE MOUNTAINS OF KINTAIL IN THE BACKGROUND.

confluence of three sea lochs about 1 kilometre from the village of Dornie. The island and its picturesque castle are connected to the mainland by a footbridge. There has been a castle on the island since the thirteenth century; it was rebuilt in the early twentieth century by John MacRae-Gilstrap. Probably the most photographed castle in the whole of Scotland, it has featured in movies such as *The World is Not Enough* and *Highlander*. Eilean Donan Castle is open to the public from March to December.

The route passes the village of Dornie and crosses Loch Long, then a smaller road with a pizza place and a cafe on the left provides a shortcut before the A87 is joined again. The route continues on the main road arriving in Kyle of Lochalsh, finishing at the railway station, from where services leave around four times a day to Inverness.

If you have travelled from the south of Scotland to get to Beauly and bike spaces on the train for the way home are booked during peak times, you can extend the trip to Armadale on the Isle of Skye, about 35 kilometres away, and take the ferry to Mallaig, which has frequent train connections to Fort William and on to Glasgow or Edinburgh.

OTHER ROUTES NEARBY
> Affric Kintail Way
> An Turas Mor
> GB Divide
> Great North Trail
> Highland Trail 550
> North Coast 500

WHERE TO EAT
> Corner on the Square, Beauly
> Cannich Stores and Post Office
> Slaters Arms, Cannich
> Glen Affric Youth Hostel
> All The Goodness Coffee & Bakeshop, Ardelve
> The Lighthouse Coffee, Kyle of Lochalsh

BIKE SHOPS
> OrangeFox Bikes (servicing and sales), Muir of Ord
  (T 01463 870 346)
> Eagle Brae Log Cabins (mountain bike hire), Struy
> Ticket To Ride (mountain and hybrid bike hire), Inverness

WHERE TO STOP
> Beauly Priory, NH 528465
> Dog Falls, NH 287283
> Loch Beinn a' Mheadhoin, NH 244262
> Loch Affric, NH 199233
> Glen Affric Youth Hostel, NH 080202
> Camban Bothy, NH 053183
> Bealach Allt Grannda, NH 045176
> Eilean Donan Castle, NG 882259

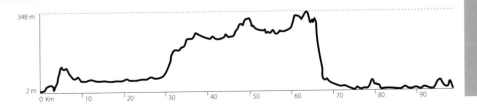

02 IN SEARCH OF GRAVEL ON THE MONEGA PASS

42KM   NAOMI FREIREICH

The toughest and remotest gravel ride in this book, travelling over two ridges in the superb surroundings of the southern part of the Cairngorms National Park with 360-degree views over mountains and deep glens.

ABOUT NAOMI

Gravel riding for Naomi in three words
versatile; escape; fun

'I was just amazed at how capable it was: on the rough stuff, and then on the smoother sections it was just so fast. And I think that versatility is what got me into doing a bit more gravel riding.'

Naomi Freireich has seen many podiums in her career as a mountain bike racer – she is a three-times UK 24-hour mountain bike champion and the 2018 European 24-hour mountain bike champion. She tried gravel riding when a chance opportunity through one of her sponsors left her following Ness Knight, an explorer, conservationist and ocean advocate, on a tour of Scotland. As she only had a mountain bike, she borrowed a gravel bike and instantly fell in love with it on the coast-to-coast crossing from Ullapool to Ardgay.

'I think the beauty of cycling is that you can do quite a lot, or most things, on most bikes.'

As a 24-hour mountain bike champion she is used to riding fast, and trains a lot to ride fast. Gravel cycling has ultimately made her a better rider on the mountain bike as well. She loves how capable gravel bikes are, even on the more challenging stuff. And, if required, gravel bikes are that little bit faster on the sections that are not off the beaten track.

'I think it's that beautiful mix between riding away from traffic out in the wilds, or exploring lesser ridden paths. Maybe they are not quite gnarly enough for your mountain bikers, or they are viewed as tame, but it is still off-road and away from people.'

Based in Edinburgh, she lives at the foot of the Pentlands Hills, which in winter become, in her own words, a 'bog-fest'. Gravel bikes extend

the reach from her front door significantly and allow her to skip the muddy paths in the Pentlands and ride further afield. There are more gravel tracks to enjoy, with the additional benefit of some road training as well. Or to say it in the words of one of her sponsors: faster, further.

'What I think is beautiful about gravel riding is that it's not considered to be completely hardcore; you don't have to throw yourself off rocks to fit in, which mountain biking has always had this persona of. I think it's far more accessible to the slightly more risk-conscious females.'

Naomi has a wealth of knowledge from years of racing, and loves to share that, especially with women, who are still under-represented in the world of cycling. Her social media channels are one way of sharing her expertise. In addition, she set up the Edinburgh

THE DESCENT FROM MONEGA HILL WITH THE RIVER ISLA BELOW.

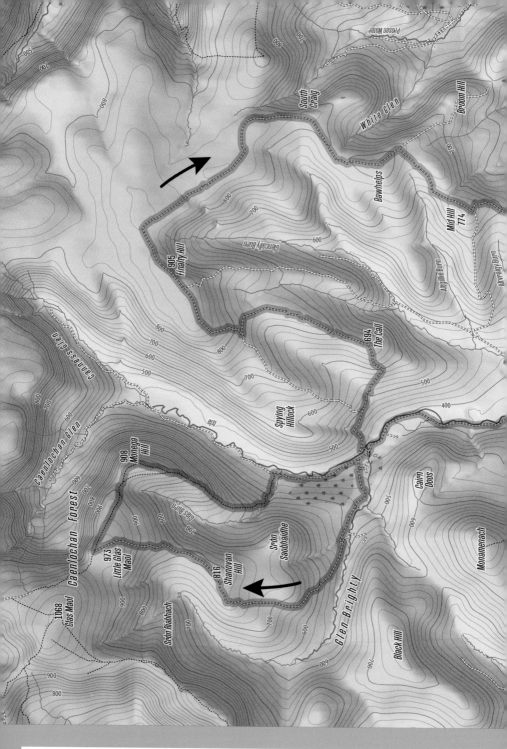

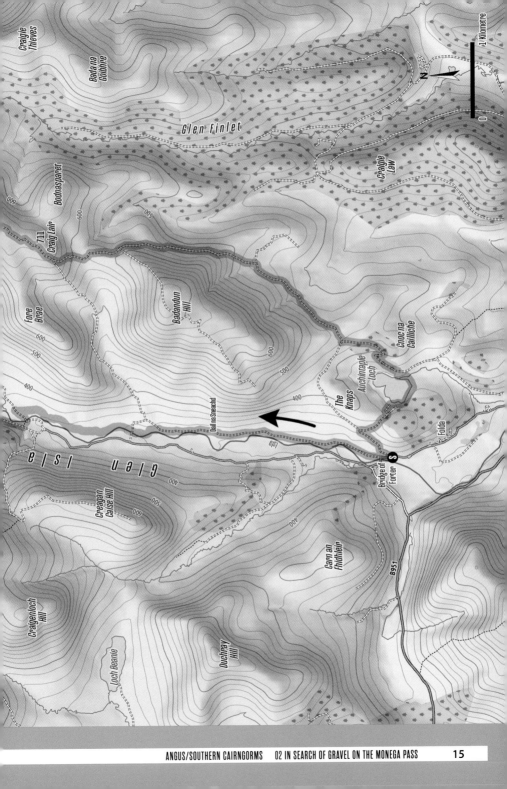

Creagie Thieves

Bad a na Goibhre

Glen Finlet

Craigie Law

Bodnaspaner

Craig Lair

711

Fore Brae

Badandun Hill

Choc na Cailliche

Auchintaple Loch

The Knaps

Dal na Sheachd

Folda

Isla

Glen Isla

Bridge of Fortew

Creagan Caise Hill

Carn an Fhidhleir

Craigenloch Hill

Loch Beanie

Duchray Hill

B951

1 Kilometre

N

0

campus of the School of Rocks – a woman-led community offering a toolkit to empower everyone to find joy in off-road cycling. Through this initiative Naomi aims to build other women's skill, confidence and community by organising a curriculum of rides over six-week terms. Especially in the last year she has met a lot of women who don't want to ride on roads anymore, and feel empowered to make the switch to gravel riding.

And does a multiple 24-hour champion think there will be 24-hour gravel races in the future? No – they exist already. It's called bikepacking, and in her opinion is even more fun than gravel riding!

ABOUT NAOMI'S ROUTE

Naomi's route fits her favourite bike – the Mason InSearchOf. A mix between a gravel and a mountain bike, it features wider tyres and allows for enjoying the chunkier and steeper gravel routes in Scotland. This loop in the Southern Cairngorms, which is also one of the Cateran Ecomuseum cycling routes, is one of Naomi's favourites; it is a miniature version of a proper adventure cycling route, with some lovely smooth sections, some narrow trails and steep descents and, of course, some hike-a-bike.

ROUTE DESCRIPTION

In the eighteenth century, particularly after the Union of Parliaments in 1707, droving became a significant feature of the Scottish economy. Robust Highland cattle were assembled from farmsteads and settlements across the north of Scotland and walked along drove roads heading south to 'trysts', or markets. At these markets, the most sizeable of which were at Falkirk and Crieff, the cattle were fattened and sold.

Many of the drove roads followed gentle gradients and suitable terrain so that the cattle could walk them easily. In the seventeenth century, drovers often used the Monega Pass to get from Badenoch to the market in Bridgend of Lintrathen. This route was the last section of a group of well-known drove roads, which passed through Glen Feshie to Braemar and on to Glen Clunie, from where the drovers faced the choice of traversing the shorter, but riskier, Monega Pass or the longer, but safer, Cairnwell Pass.

Although droving has long since ceased, both the Monega Pass and the Cairnwell Pass provide excellent crossings over the mountains of the Southern Cairngorms. With a summit altitude of 665 metres, the Cairnwell Pass is the highest main road in the United Kingdom and a very challenging climb for road cyclists. The Monega Pass, reaching just over 1,000 metres near the summit of Glas Maol, is the highest pass to cycle off-road in Scotland.

The many necessary qualities of a drover, as discussed in ARB Haldane's excellent book *The Drove Roads of Scotland,* including endurance, the ability to face great hardship and good judgement are also needed to tackle this ride, which is the most challenging route in this book. On a clear and calm day, the Monega Pass can be Scotland at its very best. If the weather changes, it will become one of the most demanding rides you'll ever do.

Be aware that mobile coverage is sparse and there are no resupply points on this route. It mostly travels on exposed mountain terrain, and at times over boggy ground, which will make navigation challenging. The gradients of climbs and descents are the steepest you will find in this book. For most, there will be some hike-a-bike involved. The rugged gravel paths require wider tyres. The reward for all the hardship? Panoramic 360-degree views in a quiet part of Scotland's second national park and some mind-blowingly-fast descents that will leave lasting memories.

THE CLIMB UP GLEN BRIGHTY.

The route starts at the Bridge of Forter, which crosses the River Isla north of Folda. Getting here by public transport with a bike is a challenge, but the Cateran Ecomuseum and Perthshire Gravel websites list a range of road and off-road cycling routes, which can be combined with this ride. The nearby Glenisla Hotel provides affordable accommodation and meals, and is the only place for food close to the route.

Following the eastern banks of the river, a 4x4 track heads north after a gate, passing a few houses along the way to Linns. Here, you cross the river on a bridge just north of Auchavan, then follow a short section through a woodland before continuing on a gravel path heading north. The first part of the route can get muddy after prolonged rainfall; an alternative is the quiet road that runs on the opposite side of the river and meets the route after Auchavan. From here, a very smooth gravel track climbs gently towards Tulchan Lodge. The route then follows the northern bank of the Glenbrighty Burn on an estate track, with a few fords along the way. The route climbs gradually, with some steep sections, heading towards Little Glas Maol. This is the highest point of the route at 973 metres; the highest point of the Monega Pass can be seen from here. The route meets a track and

turns right. If you want to cycle on the highest part of the Monega Pass, it's possible to continue on the rough track that leads past Glas Maol and (leaving the Monega Pass) on to Cairn of Claise, at an altitude of 1,064 metres, and return the same way.

The crossing point is a perfect place for a rest. The views from here into Caenlochan are worth the effort of getting here. The glen is a Special Area of Conservation, incorporating plant communities found nowhere else in the United Kingdom, and a Special Protection Area for birds, specifically the dotterel.

Our route follows the ridge to Monega Hill, with more breathtaking views into the glen and a 360-degree panoramic view across the Cairngorm Mountains. Deer densities in the Caenlochan area are among the highest in Scotland and deer herds of over 1,000 animals can be seen throughout the year. Extra care is needed on the downhill from Monega Hill, which can be very slippery in wet conditions and has very steep gradients. The path leads back on to a smooth gravel road to Tulchan Lodge. If you want to cut short the route at this point, you can simply follow the outward route or the tarmac road from Auchavan back to the start.

After a bridge over the River Isla, which provides

ON A GOOD DAY THIS ROUTE OFFERS AMAZING VIEWS ACROSS THE SOUTHERN CAIRNGORMS.

another excellent opportunity to stop, a gravel track climbs, at times steeply, to The Call and on to Finalty Hill and Dun Hillocks. The views from this track are stunning. At Dun Hillocks, the route continues on the ridge heading south-east past Mayar and the Corrie Fee National Nature Reserve. A visit to Corrie Fee is a worthwhile excursion if the route is split over 2 days as an overnight trip. The route continues on the tops past Bawhelps and Mid Hill, and then descends past Badandun Hill. After an abandoned quarry on the left, the route joins the Cateran Trail towards Auchintaple Loch. The woodland it passes

has been largely clear-felled, although a few trees remain. A small track on the right leads down towards the man-made loch into a native woodland, which provides shelter and another great place for a rest. Bob Ellis, founder of the Cateran Trail, who knows this area of Scotland like no other, counts Auchintaple Loch among his favourite places; you'll understand why when you sit on the shores marvelling at the beautiful mountains of the Cairngorms reflecting on the water. On a low rise just above the loch there is the site of an early chapel; it is identifiable by a turf-covered stony bank which encloses a shallow hollow

DISTANCE **42km/26 miles** ⟩ ASCENT **1,375m/4,511 ft** ⟩ GRADE **Expert** ⟩ START/FINISH **Bridge of Forter** ⟩ START/FINISH GRID REF **NO 187648** ⟩ BIKE-FRIENDLY PUBLIC TRANSPORT **Pitlochry railway station (39km from the route)** ⟩ HIGHEST POINT **973m/3,192 ft** ⟩ TERRAIN **Open moorland and exposed mountain ridges; very remote** ⟩ RECOMMENDED TYRES **Schwalbe Thunder Burt or G-One Ultrabite**

BEST TIME TO RIDE

| JAN | FEB | MAR | APR | MAY | JUN | JUL | AUG | SEP | OCT | NOV | DEC |

SINGLETRACK **15%**   PATH **75%**   ROAD **10%**

A RIVER CROSSING IN GLEN ISLA.

containing several stones. Nearby is the Lady Well, also known as Virgin Mary's Well, which still has an ample flow of clear water. In the past, the wells in the area were known for their therapeutic properties.

The route continues along the dam and shortly afterwards a gate is reached. It passes a private boat house and descends on a great gravel track with more breathtaking views into Glen Isla. For the last section, the route rejoins the Cateran Trail back to the start.

OTHER ROUTES NEARBY
> Cateran Trail
> Routes on Cateran Ecomuseum website
> Perthshire Gravel trails

WHERE TO EAT
> Glenisla Hotel, Kirkton of Glenisla

BIKE SHOPS
> Alyth Cyclery, Alyth (**T** 07871 309 900)

WHERE TO STOP
> Caenlochan, NO 181758
> Auchintaple Loch, NO 196648

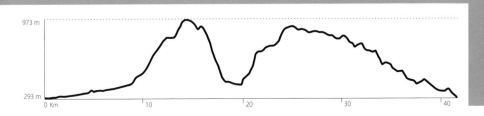

03 A TOUR OF HIGHLAND PERTHSHIRE

99KM RICHARD PEARSON

A long and demanding Highland adventure in the Southern Cairngorms and the Cateran Ecomuseum, which offers you some of Scotland's finest scenery in the shadow of Beinn a' Ghlo.

ABOUT RICHARD

Gravel riding for Richard in three words
escapism; health; well-being

'I have always had a fascination with events since the early days of the London Marathon and Great North Run, which I competed in on a number of occasions. I always thought: how on earth does all this come together?'

Richard Pearson runs his own events company, Still Going Strong, in Aberfeldy, Highland Perthshire, organising multi-sports events like open water swimming events, triathlons and road races. It was by accident that he got into the events industry.

'I came to Highland Perthshire as a Sports Facility Manager, managing a cluster of sport and recreation facilities across the area. A number of the facilities had events as part of their programme including triathlons, half marathons and mountain bike events, amongst others.'

Richard started organising these events as part of his job and loved it. He then got involved with a number of commercial event companies on a freelance basis, with more jobs coming forward as he progressed. And back in 2017 he finally took the leap and started his own events company. As an events organiser he has seen the gravel bike market growing, and is now breaking into it, adding gravel events to his portfolio in 2022.

'I've cycled all my life, and I am really enjoying getting off-road for a change. Most of my cycling has been on the road. Just getting off-road has opened up a whole new world of cycling to me.'

He is in the best place in Scotland, as he has a 'playground' with multiple opportunities right on his doorstep. He doesn't have to drive anywhere. Richard can leave the house for a run, cycle or an open water swim, and within a few minutes he is on forest trails, riverbanks or paths. Some of them even inspired the mighty Robert Burns. And if he goes a few minutes further, he is in the mountains.

'I think in 10 years' time, it'll still be booming.'

For him, especially as an events organiser, gravel riding is anything but a short-term trend – it is here to stay. It's the perfect opportunity for people to get away from busy roads and to explore the traffic-free, off-road paradise that gravel riding opens up. And nothing could be more inspiring for future gravel events than the Perthshire mountains he calls home.

A WIDE TRACK IN KINDROGAN WOOD IN THE CATERAN ECOMUSEUM.

A WIDE GRAVEL TRACK IN TUMMEL FOREST, WITH LOCH TUMMEL IN THE BACKGROUND.

ABOUT RICHARD'S ROUTE

Pondering about a potential route for an event, Richard and I started to look into a good location in Highland Perthshire. A location that would be unique – with something that you wouldn't find anywhere else in Britain. This route is what we jointly came up with. This loop gives you the sense of remoteness for which Scotland is so well known, somewhere where you can dig deep into Scotland's history and somewhere where you can not only enjoy the amazing landscape, but also great food. After we had ridden the route together on a nice day in May, we both agreed that this adventure would tick all of these boxes, and many more.

ROUTE DESCRIPTION

Highland Perthshire is a great hub for gravel riding in Scotland. In 2020, Highland Perthshire Cycling, a charity with the aim to promote cycling in this area, published a network of gravel routes for riders of a variety of different abilities: the Highland Perthshire Gravel Trails. The routes start and finish in Aberfeldy, Blair Atholl, Comrie, Dunkeld, Rannoch and Pitlochry, and range from very short rides to adventurous, long rides; this ride falls in the latter category. And with more gravel trails ready to be explored in the neighbouring Cateran Ecomuseum, the aim of this route is to give you a sense of both areas.

Pitlochry is the base for this ride. The largely Victorian town developed into a tourist resort with the arrival of the railway and became even more of a destination after Queen Victoria and Prince Albert visited the area and bought a Highland estate at Balmoral. A good railway connection still exists, with trains from Perth and Inverness a number of times a day, and Pitlochry remains a popular tourist resort today. For culture buffs, the town is particularly known for its Pitlochry Festival Theatre, which produces original work, despite its rural location. Each May thousands of cyclists flock to the town for the Etape Caledonia, one of the few closed-road sportives in Britain.

The Moulin Hotel on the outskirts of the small town is the start and finish point for this ride; the hotel has its very own brewery. You'll pass another brewery, Wasted Degrees, further along the route at Blair Atholl, so there is no shortage of craft beer along this route. Some sections of the early part of the route overlap with the Highland Perthshire Drovers Trail, a 300-kilometre bikepacking route designed for more adventurous gravel riders, and also with the Cairngorms Grand Tour. This 70-kilometre tour, which takes a different route through Glen Tilt to Blair Atholl, can also provide a shortcut for the return to Pitlochry if needed.

Given its length, this loop is best ridden from early summer to early autumn, but beware of the midges, which can make any ride in the Scottish Highlands fairly unpleasant. A light breeze and sunshine help to keep them away. If the length of the route is too much for a single day, this loop can easily double up as a weekend bikepacking route as well, with plenty of fresh water and good spots to camp along the way.

From the Moulin Hotel the route follows the A924 to Kinnaird. Edradour Distillery, the smallest traditional distillery in Scotland, is just a short detour off the route. The route climbs steadily on tarmac, with great views back to Pitlochry and towards the mountains ahead. The road reaches its highest point near a transmitter mast on the left, and then descends into Glen Brerachan, following the Brerachan Water on its way down. This is among the best road cycling you can find in Scotland, but it can get busy in summer. Just before Straloch, the route follows a gravel track and crosses the river on an old stone bridge at West Lodge. This is the entrance to Kindrogan Wood. This area of coniferous forest is part of the Cateran Ecomuseum and provides fantastic trails at the head of Strath Ardle. It is a commercial forest, so be prepared for temporary restrictions and to slow down for forestry vehicles. Shortly after Balnald, the route climbs on a wide trail steeply into the forest. The views from the top into Gleann Fearnach, where the landscape is more open, are worth the effort, before the route descends around Kindrogan Hill to meet another gravel track that leads back to the road. At Enochdhu, there is the opportunity to connect to the Cateran Trail and other gravel routes starting in nearby Kirkmichael.

SINGLETRACK WITH BEINN A' GHLO IN THE BACKGROUND.

The route passes the early-nineteenth-century Kindrogan House and rejoins the road at West Lodge. This 10-kilometre loop can be skipped if necessary, but is a great addition if you have the time and legs for it.

The route continues on the road, passing a standing stone in a field to the right, just opposite the entrance gate to Straloch House. The stone is by the river and not clearly visible from the road. There are many more standing stones and ancient sites across the nearby Cateran Ecomuseum www.cateranecomuseum.co.uk/site After Straloch, the route follows a private road on the left into Gleann Fearnach (Valley of the Alder Trees). This is an old drove road that was used to get cattle to the tryst at Kirkmichael, which was reputed to be one of the biggest cattle markets in Scotland by the middle of the eighteenth century. The single-track road climbs steadily into this beautiful valley, lined by mountains on either side. You'll shortly be entering Scotland's second national park, the Cairngorms National Park. At Daldhu, the route takes a left fork and follows the Cairngorms Loop until Bridge of Tilt. As the gravel track becomes steeper and more

THE SCENIC ROAD INTO GLEN BRERACHAN.

technical, Beinn a' Ghlo dominates the view ahead. The 'Hill of the Mist' is a huge and complex hill with three Munros: Carn Liath, Bràigh Coire Chruinn-bhalgain and Carn nan Gabhar. Heather grows quite profusely on the lower slopes of the mountain, while higher up there is a mixture of grey scree and grass. You are also likely to find patches of snow on the mountain into early June.

The track follows the Allt Glen Loch upstream into this wide open and very remote Highland landscape. It's worth stopping to enjoy the views looking back into Gleann Fearnach. On a good day, this is some of the finest off-road riding to be found in Scotland. The route takes a left fork towards the shieling at Bothan Ruigh-chuilein (the right fork leads to Loch Loch). From the junction, a further 2.5 kilometres of climbing takes you to the highest point of the route at 589 metres. What follows is a stunning descent on singletrack through the heather, which will test your riding skills at times. Carn Liath, the 'Grey Rocky Hill', dominates the view as the valley opens up while you descend.

The route fords a river and shortly afterwards the singletrack becomes a wide gravel path again. At Loch Moraig the route joins a single-track road. Just to the north of the loch are the remains of prehistoric hut circles; these circles were formed by banks of earth which have eroded over time. The route follows the road for a while, but shortly before Fenderbridge it diverts on to a gravel track on the left to stay on the Cairngorms Loop into Bridge of Tilt. The last descent is on tarmac through a beautiful woodland, providing fabulous views towards Blair Atholl and Bridge of Tilt.

The villages of Bridge of Tilt and Blair Atholl are bounded on their southern sides by the River Garry and bisected by

the left through some woodland and rejoining the road at Old Bridge of Tilt. Here the route takes a left turn, crosses the river and passes under a beautiful stone bridge. The car park which follows on the left is the official start and finish of the Cairngorms Loop, which is once again joined from here. After Old Blair, the tarmac once again becomes a gravel path while the route passes the grounds of Blair Castle, where visitors can see some of the country's finest and tallest trees within a fairly small area. Diana's Grove is home to a number of impressive specimens including a grand fir, the UK's second tallest tree measuring over 62 metres, a Japanese larch, measuring 44 metres, and a red fir, measuring 39 metres.

The castle and the beautiful views to the left are worth a stop. The route leaves the Cairngorms Loop just as it is about to join the road, taking a wide gravel track to the right to climb steeply at first, and then more moderately, through Baluain Wood towards the Falls of Bruar. This series of waterfalls on the Bruar Water were celebrated in a poem by Robert Burns and have been a tourist attraction since the eighteenth century. This route provides a great viewpoint of the falls away from the crowds. Care is needed when descending on the track down to the railway, which has sections of very loose gravel. The route crosses under the railway and joins Sustrans National Route 7 on the road.

the southerly flowing River Tilt, a tributary to the River Garry. Blair Atholl's most notable feature is Blair Castle, which is open to the public and one of Scotland's most impressive stately homes. It was besieged in 1746 during the last Jacobite rising, reputedly the last time a castle in Britain was besieged. There are a couple of good places to stop and eat in the villages, or you could stop and taste the great beers and ales at the taproom at the Wasted Degrees brewery (limited opening hours). Blair Atholl has a train station with regular connections back to Pitlochry to shorten this loop if needed. Another shorter alternative is to follow the route of the Cairngorms Grand Tour from Blair Atholl railway station, or Sustrans National Route 7, which both lead back to Pitlochry.

The route continues on the road on the eastern side of the River Tilt before following a small track on

Shortly afterwards, The House of Bruar is a popular stop for local food produce and, possibly less interestingly if you are travelling on a bike, Scottish country clothing. This is the last food stop until Pitlochry if the nearby Struan Inn is closed. The route follows Sustrans National Route 7 to Calvine and continues on the B847 on the left. The combination of a road bridge and a railway viaduct across the River Garry is an interesting feature, before the route continues through Struan into Glen Errochty. The road climbs very gradually while it follows the Errochty Water upstream. Shortly after Kinaldy, the route follows a forestry road on the left to cross the river and zigzag up into Tummel Forest. Reaching the highest point of the climb, the forest thins out and the route descends on a fantastic gravel track towards Bohally Wood. The views from here over Loch Tummel and, in the distance, towards Loch Rannoch

CORONATION BRIDGE.

and the mountains of Rannoch Moor are amazing on a good day. You can enjoy the same views as from the nearby Queen's View, but without the crowds. Farragon Hill and more mountains are visible looking across Loch Tummel to the south, which host an abundance of gravel tracks that can be accessed from Pitlochry or Aberfeldy.

The route continues through Tummel Forest, with two last big climbs while it passes Loch Bhac. This popular fishing loch is a short detour off the route – the views across the loch towards the mountains near Blair Atholl are great, and it's a fantastic spot for a rest on a long summer's day. The route continues through the forest and then descends towards Edintian and into Glen Fincastle. A few farms are passed to the left and, shortly after the first house on the right, a tarmac road then Glenfincastle Road provide a fast descent. The route continues on to the B8019, which can get busy at times, and follows a gravel track on the right after passing Bonskeid House.

This section of the route passes a great woodland and follows singletrack underneath pylons to reach Coronation Bridge. This very distinct footbridge crosses the River Tummel and commemorates the coronation of King George V in 1911. The next short section requires you to push the bike, before the road is followed, giving views of the Linn of Tummel waterfall.

The route follows the western shores of Loch Faskally, a man-made reservoir forming part of the Tummel Hydroelectric Power Scheme. The scheme was constructed in the 1940s and 1950s; there are now several reservoirs and power stations covering the area bounded by Pitlochry in the east, Rannoch Moor in the west and Dalwhinnie in the north. Loch Faskally is

DISTANCE **99km/62 miles** 〉 ASCENT **1,716m/5,630 ft** 〉 GRADE **Expert** 〉 START/FINISH **Moulin Hotel, Pitlochry** 〉 START/FINISH GRID REF **NN 944592**
BIKE-FRIENDLY PUBLIC TRANSPORT **Pitlochry railway station (2km from the route)** 〉 HIGHEST POINT **589m/1,932 ft** 〉 TERRAIN **Roads and forest trails, with a large section on open and exposed moorland** 〉 RECOMMENDED TYRES **Schwalbe G-One Bite**

BEST TIME TO RIDE

| JAN | FEB | MAR | APR | MAY | JUN | JUL | AUG | SEP | OCT | NOV | DEC |

SINGLETRACK **5%**   PATH **50%**   ROAD **45%**

OTHER ROUTES NEARBY

> Atholl Estates Cycle Trails
> Cairngorms Loop
> Cateran Ecomuseum Trails
> Cateran Trail
> Highland Perthshire Gravel Trails
>> Blair Atholl Bothy Trip
>> Blair Atholl Gravel Adventure
>> Cairngorms Grand Tour
>> Drovers Trail
>> Duntanlich Weekend Grinder
> Sustrans National Route 7

WHERE TO EAT

> Moulin Hotel, Pitlochry
> Escape Route Cafe, Pitlochry
> Atholl Arms Hotel, Blair Atholl
> Wasted Degrees Brewing, Blair Atholl
> The House of Bruar, Pitagowan, Blair Atholl

BIKE SHOPS

> Escape Route, Pitlochry (**T** 01796 473 859)
> Blair Atholl Bike Hire, Blair Atholl

WHERE TO STOP

> Kindrogan Wood, NO 036618
> Straloch standing stone, NO 038637
> Bothan Ruigh-chuilein, NN 993718
> Loch Moraig, NN 906671
> Blair Castle, NN 866662
> Diana's Grove, NN 865664
> Falls of Bruar viewpoint, NN 820666
> River Garry viaduct, NN 802657
> Loch Bhac, NN 820622
> Coronation Bridge, NN 903602
> Linn of Tummel, NN 910600
> Clunie Memorial Arch, NN 915595
> Pitlochry Boating Station, NN 929587

the last reservoir in the scheme, with water flowing from Loch Tummel passing through a tunnel to the Clunie Power Station before reaching the Pitlochry Power Station on Loch Faskally. Close to the road is the Clunie Memorial Arch; the arch has the same diameter as the tunnel that carries water between Loch Tummel and the Clunie Power Station.

A small footbridge, the Clunie Bridge, is clearly overshadowed by the road bridge, which carries the A9 across Loch Faskally. After crossing the footbridge, the route continues past Pitlochry Boating Station on Clunie Bridge Road, crosses the A924 and carries on along Cuilc Brae, which is the last spicy uphill to test your legs before the finish. Passing The Cuilc, a small lochan, the route continues past the golf course to return to the Moulin Hotel, where a cold beer and tasty pub food are the best plan to end a very long day in the saddle.

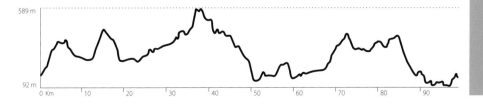

04 MAELSTROM GRAVEL

19KM   STEVEN GROOM

This loop takes you to a foaming whirlpool on Scotland's west coast, with only a few off-road sections and good options to stop and eat halfway through.

ABOUT STEVEN

Gravel riding for Steven in three words
tough; fun; wet

Britain's cycling clubs are well-established institutions, which are gradually getting their teeth into gravel cycling too. Cycling clubs flourished in the nineteenth century, a time when there were no commercial cars available, and the principal mode of transportation was horse-drawn vehicles. Formed in 1878 and among the oldest was the Bicycle Touring Club; it later changed its name to the Cyclists' Touring Club and then to Cycling UK.

The success of those clubs depends, in recent and modern times, on the people that spent many hours as volunteers. Steven Groom is one of the many, often unsung, heroes of the British gravel scene. It's almost impossible to find him without a grin on his face. Steven's name is very closely connected with the North Argyll Cycle Club, a friendly and inclusive interdisciplinary cycling club based in Oban.

The club runs group rides and organises time trials and APRs from spring to early autumn, when the weather on Scotland's west coast is the most favourable for cycling. Steven is also heavily involved in the annual Oban Sportive cycling weekend (which includes the Ben Cruachan hill climb). It is the highlight of the busy events calendar of the cycling club, and perhaps the only sportive in Britain that starts and finishes at a distillery.

'The facilities we have locally are fantastic: the scenery, and also the courses and terrain. There is always a new corner to find and look for.'

Jointly with other club members, Steven contributed a number of routes to the Rail&Trail website, which highlights a great variety of cycling routes that start from stations on the West Highland Railway Line.

This railway line can easily boast to be Britain's most cycle-friendly, as its trains carry up to 20 bikes at once.

'There is nowhere special, because everywhere is special.'

Steven's gravel cycling journey started with road cycling first, then mountain biking. He wanted to add another dimension to his cycling and was impressed by the versatility of gravel bikes. With such spectacular trails close to his home in Benderloch, it is no wonder that he is proud to call the west coast of Scotland his home.

ABOUT STEVEN'S ROUTE

Steven's route takes you across some of the most spectacular back roads around Oban. With the weather on the west coast best described as unpredictable, this loop is fairly sheltered and can be ridden in most weather conditions. It is also a great loop

ON THE ROAD TO CONNEL.

Connel

A85

North Connel

A828

Ledaig

Lusragan Burn

Camas
Bruaich
Ruaidhe

A85

Ardmucknish
Bay

Eilean Mòr

Dunstaffnage
Bay

Dunbeg

Lochan
Dubh

Ganavan

Ganavan Bay

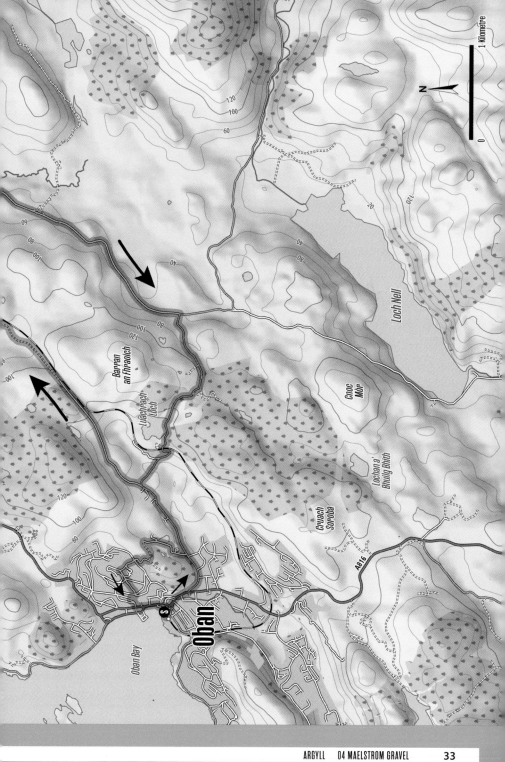

Oban

Oban Bay

Loch Nell

Croc Mòr

Barran an Fhraoich

Luachrach Loch

Lochan a' Bhuilg Bhith

Cruach Soroba

A816

120
100
60
20
40
80
100
120
80
100
120
80
100
120
80
100
80

1 Kilometre

0

N

LOOKING TOWARDS CONNEL WITH BEN CRUACHAN IN THE BACKGROUND.

for new gravel cyclists that have made the transition from road cycling. The route doesn't feature any technical sections, but it does have a fair number of climbs. If you want a great warm-up ride for the Oban Sportive, Steven's favourite event, this loop is perfect, and leaves enough time to sample some delicious seafood afterwards.

ROUTE DESCRIPTION

Oban, which sits on the shores of the Firth of Lorn, is best known as 'Scotland's Seafood Capital'. However, it is not just the supreme seafood that attracts visitors from around the world to the town – it is also one of the best places in Scotland to take a bike to. This has become much easier recently with the introduction of ScotRail's Highland Explorer trains, Britain's first active travel carriages, which run from Glasgow to Oban. Each carriage has a total of 20 individual bike racks, as well as designated seating for 24 people. The racks are designed for bikes with tyres of up to 14 centimetres wide (when inflated), and can also accommodate some larger bikes, such as tandems.
www.scotrail.co.uk/scotrail-highland-explorer

Oban is also a busy port, with regular ferries to Barra, Coll, Colonsay, Mull, Lismore and Tiree, all operated by CalMac. Oban Distillery, which offers tours and tastings, was founded in 1794; the town grew around the distillery. The town hosts the annual Oban Sportive, one of the most scenic road cycling events in Britain. For something different, the waters around Oban and the Firth of Lorn offer awesome sea kayaking.

The route starts at Oban railway station and follows the Caledonia Way along Glencruitten Road. Be aware that the sign-posting for the Caledonia Way

A HIGHLAND EXPLORER TRAIN.

can be confusing at times. On the parts where it is classified as a Sustrans route, you can follows signs for *Sustrans National Route 78;* on other sections, you can follow a round Caledonia Way symbol.

The route climbs gradually out of town on residential streets. At Glencruitten, the route leaves the Caledonia Way and the town to follow a small road parallel to the West Highland Railway Line. After a few private properties and a gate, the route travels on a small tarmac road, which at times becomes a gravel road as it hasn't been maintained. This is a beautiful ride with great views towards Ben Cruachan on a clear day; at 1,126 metres, this is the highest point in Argyll and Bute. The mountain also gives its name to the Cruachan Power Station, a pumped-storage hydroelectric power station; the turbines are located in a cavern inside the mountain. An annual hill climb event, run as part of the Oban Sportive

weekend, runs on the closed roads that lead up to the Cruachan Reservoir.

There are some short, steep sections but, overall, this is a gentle ride. The route gradually descends towards Connel, a small village where the main road splits into the A828 (the coastal road to Glencoe) and the A85 (to Tyndrum), almost marking the halfway point of the route. Situated on the southern shore of Loch Etive, the most noticeable feature in the village is Connel Bridge, a large cantilever bridge that spans the Falls of Lora, a foaming maelstrom which is popular with adventurous kayakers and divers.

The Falls of Lora, which sit at the narrow entrance to Loch Etive, are also a stunning sight for tourists and photographers. They form on the ebb tide when the water level in the Firth of Lorn (to the west of the falls) drops below the water level in Loch Etive (to the east of the falls), making the water in Loch

MCCAIG'S TOWER ON BATTERY HILL.

Etive pour out through the narrows. The currents and waves produced by the rising tide are also well worth seeing. There are always strong currents here, but the tidal range varies a lot, so sometimes they are really dramatic and at other times there isn't much to see. The best place to witness this natural spectacle is from a viewpoint on the southern shore of Loch Etive.

Connel also has a railway station and places to eat. After a short section on the busy A85 and A828, where extra care is needed, the route follows a minor road, signposted as the *Caledonia Way*, which gradually climbs up to the top of Glen Lonan. The road dips in and out of some smaller stretches of woodland. Stopping and taking in the view towards the coast is highly recommended, and a detour into Glen Lonan, with a prehistoric cairn, standing stones

and a Neolithic stone circle, is worthwhile.

At a crossroads the route follows the Caledonia Way towards Oban and reaches its highest point shortly afterwards. While this climb is steep, you'll eventually be rewarded with a cracking descent towards Glencruitten. The last climb of the day leads to Battery Hill and McCaig's Tower; this can be avoided by using the outward route to return to Oban if preferred. McCaig's Tower, also known as McCaig's Folly, is a striking, listed structure overlooking the town. The tower has two tiers of lancet arches and a circumference of around 200 metres.

In the late nineteenth century, John Stuart McCaig, a philanthropic, wealthy banker, wanted to provide a permanent monument to his family along with supplying work for the local stonemasons

DISTANCE **19km/12 miles** 〉 ASCENT **333m/1,093 ft** 〉 GRADE **Easy** 〉 START/FINISH **Oban railway station** 〉 START/FINISH GRID REF **NM 858299**
BIKE-FRIENDLY PUBLIC TRANSPORT **At the start** 〉 HIGHEST POINT **106m/348 ft** 〉 TERRAIN **Gentle cycling through urban environments and open countryside; mostly sheltered** 〉 RECOMMENDED TYRES **Schwalbe G-One Speed**

BEST TIME TO RIDE

| JAN | FEB | MAR | APR | MAY | JUN | JUL | AUG | SEP | OCT | NOV | DEC |

PATH **20%**   ROAD **80%**

GLENCRUITTEN ON THE OUTSKIRTS OF OBAN.

during the quieter winter months. An admirer of Roman and Greek architecture, he had designed an elaborate structure, based on the Colosseum in Rome. His death in 1902 brought construction to a halt – only the outer walls had been completed. The structure dominates the Oban skyline; it is now a public garden with magnificent views out to sea at to the islands of Kerrera, Lismore and Mull.

From Battery Hill it's all downhill back to the station, where the Green Shack is a favourite of locals and travellers alike to sample the finest seafood the west coast has to offer.

OTHER ROUTES NEARBY
> Bikepacking Argyll's Islands
> Caledonia Way
> Wild About Argyll Trail
> Rail&Trail routes

WHERE TO EAT
> Oyster Inn, Connel
> Green Shack, Oban
> Markie Dans, Oban

BIKE SHOPS
> Rusty Cycle Shed, Oban (T 07791 974 152)
> Oban Cycles, Oban (T 01631 566 033)

WHERE TO STOP
> Falls of Lora viewpoint, NM 910344
> McCaig's Tower and Battery Hill, NM 861302
> Oban Distillery, NM 860301

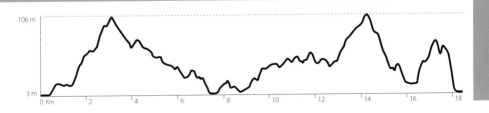

05 LOMOND HILLS GRAVEL

59KM   LOUISE CHAVARIE

The strangely eroded features on the slopes of the Lomond Hills and the historic village of Falkland provide the fabulous setting for this fast-flowing gravel adventure.

ABOUT LOUISE

Gravel riding for Louise in three words
slow; fast; wild

Louise Chavarie is an associate professor at the Norwegian University of Life Sciences in Ås, Norway. Before moving to this small town to the south of Oslo, she spent about 2 years researching salmon on the shores of Loch Lomond. She enjoyed her transition into gravel riding and bikepacking in that time, using her Surly Disc Trucker for a number of day and overnight trips exploring Scotland off the beaten track.

'I was bikepacking without even knowing it, and it was really great. It was something that I will remember for the rest of my life. That was my first exposure to cycling.'

Louise made the most of her time before defending her PhD thesis to celebrate this landmark with a cycling trip to Peru with her brother. It was *'unexpectedly off-road'.* They didn't want to face the heavy traffic on other roads, so let themselves be guided by other people's journeys, and quickly found out that secondary roads in their native Canada are different from those in South America. What was planned as a cycling trip on roads, turned out to be an off-road touring adventure instead.

'Just do it. If you want it, you can do what you want. And if you want to cycle or if you want to do anything in your life, you should never wait for someone else to do it for you. There is nothing like taking on a new adventure ... for you, by yourself.'

Louise was a relative newcomer to cycling and bikepacking. She hadn't done anything of a similar scale before she went on her bikepacking trip in Peru. Her advice for people new to gravel cycling is never to limit yourself. Her trip in Peru got her accidentally into gravel riding, and her cycling story continued in Scotland. To others she would

recommend not starting too big and going on rides in smaller groups. But the most important thing for her is to start and then give the other things a chance to fall into place.

'I was not scared. There are not a lot of things that scare me. But I said "no" many times at the beginning, because I knew that I was not there, or I was reaching my limits, or I was respecting the feeling of that day.'

Improving her riding skills was a gradual process. Louise respected what she was able to ride and what she was not able to ride. Before she came to Scotland she did a lot of cycling on roads, and her drop-bar bike was designed for that. But with a set of wider tyres, the bike could be turned into a gravel bike, which enabled her to do more adventurous routes off-road. Gravel cycling in Scotland was a new adventure for her: something to embrace and learn, with plenty

CLIMBING UP GLEN VALE.

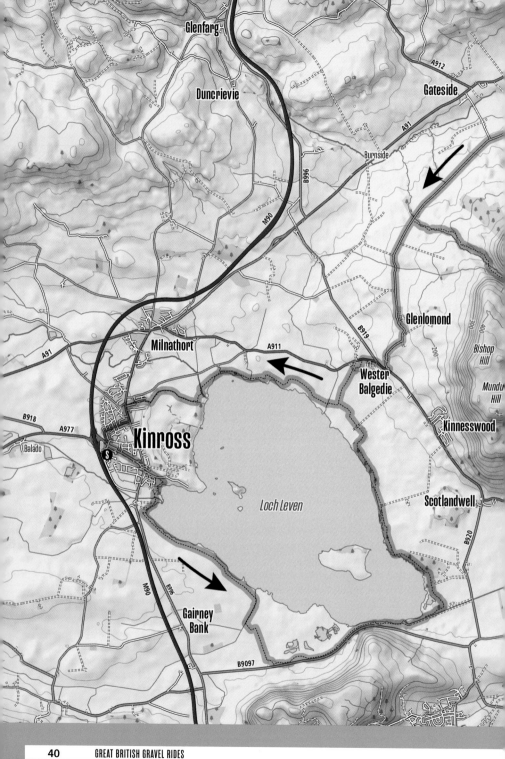

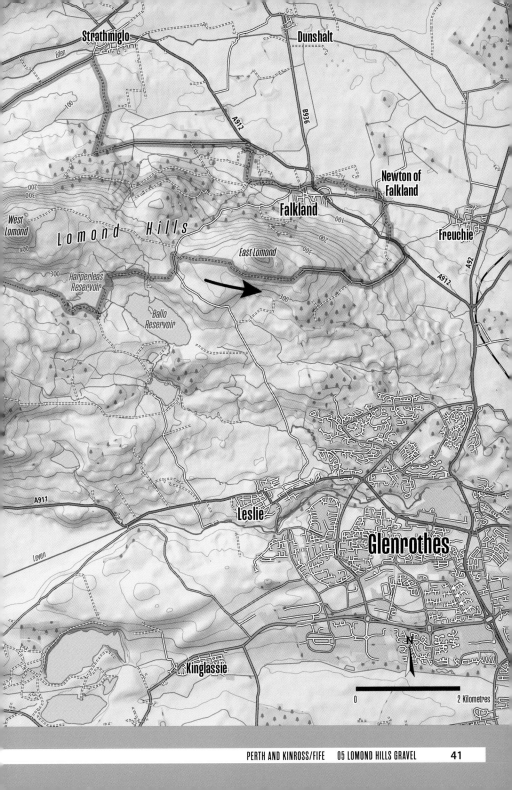

of rewards. As getting into cycling was in the first instance, coming to Scotland and riding more off-road was not necessarily a step that Louise was foreseeing – it naturally happened.

'Like in any sport there's always a steep learning curve. You get better really quickly.'

It was the riding on singletrack first, then the riding in snowy conditions, but Louise realised that it's fun to push her limits and to improve her technique. Cycling is no different to any other sport in that aspect for her. Having grown up in Canada and having done research in far flung places such as the Arctic helped her, as the remoteness of some Scottish cycling routes and the self-supported aspect of bikepacking weren't an issue.

'I will keep cycling for work and I actually do enjoy cycling in the snow more than I expected. It was a nice surprise.'

While she wouldn't have considered riding her bike in winter in Canada, boosting her confidence with off-road riding and getting good tyres have encouraged her to keep cycling in Norway, even in much colder temperatures.

ABOUT LOUISE'S ROUTE

The Lomond Hills offer a great playground for gravel riding in close proximity to Edinburgh. The introduction of a frequent electric bus service from Edinburgh to Dundee has opened up a new way to reach Kinross, the starting point of this route, by bike-friendly public transport. This loop is a great choice if you want to try different aspects of gravel riding and enjoy the stunning landscape of the Lomond Hills at the same time.

From faster sections on rural roads and the cycle path along the shores of Loch Leven to more technical off-road passages, this route combines a variety of gravel riding surfaces with amazing views across the surrounding countryside.

The many listed buildings in the village of Falkland, picturesquely situated at the foot of East Lomond, are well-preserved and were used as backdrops for the TV series *Outlander*. In addition to beautiful cycling and historic buildings, the Pillars of Hercules cafe has a great garden to enjoy tasty food and drinks. This is one of Louise's favourite places in Scotland – listening to the birds and enjoying the beautiful countryside of rural Fife with a cafe latte.

ROUTE DESCRIPTION

Kinross, where the route starts, is a town in the local council area of Perth and Kinross. The town sits on the shore of Loch Leven, the largest loch of the Scottish Lowlands. In fact, the name Kinross means 'Head of the Point' and stems from to the original location of the local church overlooking the loch. Lochleven Castle, which is on an island in Loch Leven and accessible by a small ferry service in summer, has achieved

fame through the imprisonment of Mary, Queen of Scots, and her successful escape after almost a year on 2 May 1568. However, King Dongart of the Picts had a fortress on the island as early as AD 490, so the ruins visible today are just the last in a long line of defensive structures built there.

Getting to Kinross by train

GRAVEL TRACK FROM CRAIGMEAD TOWARDS EAST LOMOND.

was once very easy. In the nineteenth century three independent railway companies served the town: the Devon Valley Railway from the west, the Kinross-shire Railway from the south and the Fife and Kinross Railway from the east. Kinross Junction railway station stood on the line between Perth and Edinburgh, before it was closed to make space for the M90 motorway. Kinross is now a popular commuter town, due to its central location and good local amenities. While there have been ambitions

to reopen the railway line between Perth and Edinburgh, the best way to get to Kinross by public transport is by using the Ember electric bus service, which runs several times a day between Edinburgh and Dundee and takes bikes for free.

The route starts at Ember's stop at Kinross Park and Ride and follows Station Road southbound through town, and then continues on a number of smaller streets to Kirkgate Park, where it joins the Loch Leven Heritage Trail. This 21-kilometre path,

HEATHER SPANS FIFE'S LOMOND HILLS.

which in parts follows the line of a former railway, circumnavigates the Loch Leven National Nature Reserve. Loch Leven is a haven for wildlife – thousands of migratory ducks, swans and geese pass through in the autumn and winter.

The trail is a well-graded gravel path and mostly flat – it makes for a great riding experience. Care is needed though, as it is very popular with other users during peak times. Shortly after joining the Loch Leven Heritage Trail, you pass the terminal for the ferry to Lochleven Castle, which is open to the public from April to October. The route offers great views over the loch and towards the Falkland Hills, and leaves the shore for a short while at the Waterbutts Plantation. The route passes the mouth of the River Leven, where the distinctive Sluice House still looks much as it would have done when it was constructed in the 1830s. This remarkable building contains the original cast iron mechanism which is still used to operate the sluice gates in order to control the flow of water into the River Leven. From here, the trail runs through a beautiful woodland, the Levenmouth Plantation, with a bird hide just a few metres off the trail at Levenmouth Pool.

The trail exits the woodland shortly before it joins Sustrans National Route 1 to Channel Farm. The farm hosts Loch Leven's Larder, a well-known shop and cafe with fresh local produce, and Loch Leven Cycles, who offer bike repairs and hire. The route follows Sustrans National Route 1 on the A911 for a short section, and then continues on a much quieter road to Glenlomond. Just before Glen Burn and Glen Vale car park, the route leaves the tarmac behind for a while. This is where the more demanding gravel riding starts. This part of the route also features in The Central Belter, a 1,200-kilometre bikepacking route from Bikepacking Scotland.

Crossing a woodland first, the trail climbs through dense ferns, which soon give way to a great view towards a prominent rock outcrop, known as John Knox's Pulpit. There are a number of strangely eroded features in the Lomond Hills; the grey sandstone outcrop John Knox's Pulpit was formed from desert sand dunes in the Late Devonian period (this part of the Earth was closer to the equator at that time). There are thin layers visible in the rock called pin stripes – these are a typical feature when sand is deposited by wind in an arid environment. There is a cave at the foot of the cliff, but it is now much smaller than it was due to a major rock fall in 2004. As the area around John Knox's Pulpit is prone to rock falls, the singletrack directly below it has been closed for public safety.

The route follows the track near the burn and meets a closed track at the top, and then climbs gently over open moorland towards the highest point of the route at 338 metres. The last section of the track, in particular, to the so-called Three-Shires Stone can be boggy. Soon after a gate the route enters a woodland, where the path becomes a wide gravel track. It follows the shores of Harperleas Reservoir and crosses its dam. Bikes need to be lifted over a gate here, as the pedestrian opening is too small. From the dam, the route climbs gently and joins another well-graded farm track. Watch out for livestock here, as there is a resident herd of cows who like to congregate around the gate. The track provides great views on to Ballo Reservoir. Shortly after Ballo Craigs, the route joins the road for a short while to reach Craigmead car park.

From Craigmead car park, which also provides water and toilet facilities, the route continues on an old drove road. This is another great gravel track, which takes you towards East Lomond, the second of the steep-sided peaks in the Lomond Hills. East Lomond and West Lomond are volcanic in origin; the hills are often referred to as the Paps of Fife. After a short section through woodland the route continues on a grassy gravel path over open moorland to where a walking path leads to the top of East Lomond.

FERNS LINE BOTH SIDES OF THE PATH UP GLEN VALE TOWARDS HARPERLEAS RESERVOIR.

Taking a bike to the top is not recommended but, if you have enough time for a walk, the views from the top are stunning. Another worthwhile short excursion by foot is a small path to the right. This leads to a really well-preserved limekiln at the former East Lomond Quarry. Probably dating from the late eighteenth or early nineteenth century, structures such as this with so little alteration are becoming increasing rare; the former lime pits are now home to an abundance of pond life and are perfect to catch a glimpse of the resident dragonflies.

The route continues to the East Lomond Mast car park and descends steeply on tarmac down Purin Den to meet the A912. This is a popular car park, so care is needed on the downhill when approaching oncoming traffic. After a short section on the main road, a gravel track on the right takes you to Newton of Falkland, where the route meets Sustrans National

WEST LOMOND AND BISHOP HILL AS SEEN FROM THE TRACK UP GLEN VALE.

Route 1 for a very short section, before it continues on Laich Road to Falkland. This historic trail is another great gravel path, which provides lovely views towards East Lomond and across the open countryside of Fife.

The route meets Sustrans National Route 1 at the A912 in Falkland. The village of Falkland is Scotland's first conservation area and is famous as the location of Falkland Palace. The palace, which is one of the finest examples of French-influenced Renaissance architecture in Scotland, was built for the royal court, including Mary, Queen of Scots, to use on hunting trips in the nearby forests. The east range was destroyed in 1654 when a fire broke out while Oliver Cromwell's troops were occupying the building; the court never returned to the palace after this time. After a period of neglect, extensive rebuilding and restoration work began in the late nineteenth century; today the palace and gardens are open to the public.

American country and western singer Johnny Cash traced part of his family ancestry to this district of Fife, and Falkland was used to portray the city of Inverness in the TV series *Outlander*. The Covenanter, a pub and hotel, is a great place to stop for food and drink, and there are several other cafes and small shops in the village. The route continues along West Port out of the village and follows Sustrans National Route 1 into a small woodland. The route then leaves the Sustrans route, following a track and crossing a small bridge, before rejoining the Sustrans route again to reach the Pillars of Hercules, an excellent place for coffee and cake. The organic farm also offers very basic camping pitches for cyclists and has a well-stocked farm shop. The route continues on Sustrans National

DISTANCE **59km/37 miles** 〉 ASCENT **516m/1,693 ft** 〉 GRADE **Challenging** 〉 START/FINISH **Kinross Park and Ride bus stop** 〉 START/FINISH GRID REF **NO 112025** 〉 BIKE-FRIENDLY PUBLIC TRANSPORT **At the start** 〉 HIGHEST POINT **338m/1,109 ft** 〉 TERRAIN **Hilly terrain; at times very exposed. Well-surfaced and mostly rideable paths, except for a short boggy section** 〉 RECOMMENDED TYRES **Schwalbe G-One Bite**

BEST TIME TO RIDE

| JAN | FEB | MAR | APR | MAY | JUN | JUL | AUG | SEP | OCT | NOV | DEC |

SINGLETRACK **45%**   PATH **10%**   CYCLE PATH **10%**   ROAD **35%**

MEADOW NEAR LOCH LEVEN.

Route 1 into another woodland. At the end of this tarmac road, which typically has virtually no traffic, a gravel path on the right takes you through the Barrington Muir Plantation and over open farmland towards Strathmiglo.

The route follows a quiet country road from Strathmiglo to Loch Leven's Larder, where the Loch Leven Heritage Trail once again provides for another great gravel section (still signposted as Sustrans National Route 1). At the Ury Burn, the route leaves the Loch Leven Heritage Trail and follows a cycle path towards Kinross. It meets Sustrans National Route 775 and follows Springfield Road back to Kinross Park and Ride. If you are looking for a coffee and cake after your ride, then continue along High Street to Unorthodox Roasters. It's easy to spot – look for the yellow bike on blue walls. From here, Station Road takes you back to Kinross Park and Ride.

OTHER ROUTES NEARBY
> Loch Leven Heritage Trail
> Sustrans National Route 1
> Sustrans National Route 775
> The Central Belter

WHERE TO EAT
> Loch Leven's Larder, Channel Farm
> The Covenanter, Falkland
> Pillars of Hercules, Falkland
> Unorthodox Roasters, Kinross

BIKE SHOPS
> Loch Leven Cycles, Channel Farm (**T** 01577 862 839)

WHERE TO STOP
> Lochleven Castle, NO 128018
> Loch Leven bird hide, NT 176998
> John Knox's Pulpit, NO 189058
> Harperleas Reservoir, NO 213051
> East Lomond limekiln, NO 238058
> Falkland Palace, NO 253074

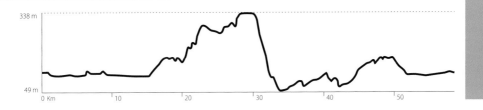

TROSSACHS
06 GRAVELFOYLE
67KM   KERRY MACPHEE

This loop around Gravelfoyle offers a seemingly endless amount of wide gravel roads, nestled in the beauty of Scotland's first national park.

ABOUT KERRY
Gravel riding for Kerry in three words
cathartic; escapist; peaceful

'When I first came, I thought it was humongous. It's not at all, now that I've lived in the mainland for a long time.'
Kerry MacPhee hails from the Outer Hebrides and is a native Gaelic speaker. She didn't learn English until she went to school on the island of South Uist. As a lot of the place names in Scotland are either Gaelic or derived from Gaelic, going on a gravel ride with Kerry is much more than a cycling adventure.
'I race mountain bikes predominantly and didn't start gravel riding properly until 2018.'
Racing is in Kerry's blood. To date she is the only Hebridean athlete to ever represent Scotland at the Commonwealth Games; she is also a Scottish cross country and cyclo-cross champion and has also recently moved into adventure cycling. In 2021 she cycled the 154-kilometre West Highland Way, setting the fastest known female time of 11 hours and 46 minutes.
'I didn't realise that there was so much of it on my doorstep in the Trossachs. There's a really nice number of riders in this tiny little village and there's always someone around for a ride. And if they're not riding, there's always someone around for an ice cream. And if they're not into ice cream, there's always someone around for coffee and cake.'
It was actually an invitation from the organisers of the Dukes Weekender to come and participate in the event in 2018 that got Kerry involved in gravel riding. She had a cyclo-cross bike and had raced a lot on it, so she gave it a go. While the racing was fun, it was the community around gravel cycling that drew her back to the Trossachs time and time

again. Close to her home in Stirling, the sheer number of enthusiastic riders is something that is unique about Aberfoyle.
'A bike is a bike. And if it moves, it will eat up the gravel just fine. If you've got a bike, you can ride it on gravel.'
You would expect someone who has raced at an international level to be fussy about bikes, but Kerry is as far away from that attitude as it gets. For her, there's nothing that's special about a gravel bike. What makes it different from a road bike is that the tyres are a bit wider. What makes it different from a mountain bike is that it's maybe a little bit quicker, more charged and a little bit slimmer. For Kerry, all bikes have something in common: they are awesome. It doesn't really matter how and where you ride them, as long as you ride them.

A LUSH GREEN FOREST ALONG THE SHORES OF LOCH VENACHAR.

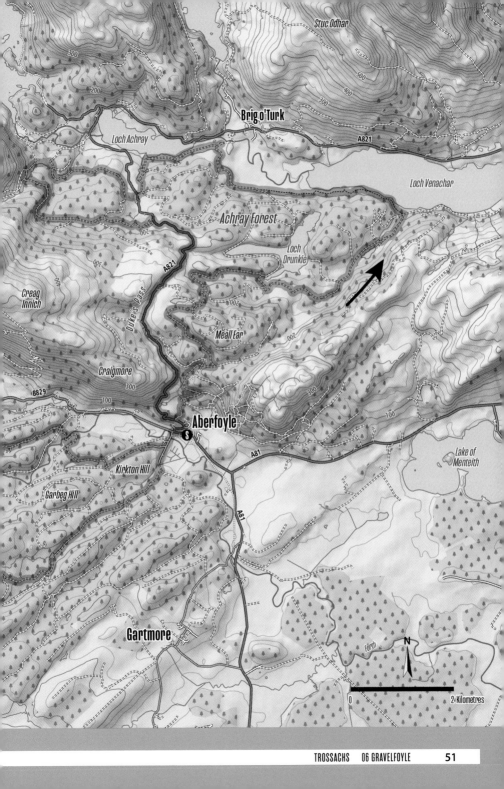

ON A GRAVEL TRACK IN LOCH ARD FOREST.

ABOUT KERRY'S ROUTE

The sheer number of trails and route options around Aberfoyle, Scotland's self-proclaimed gravel capital, is almost overwhelming. Gravelfoyle is one of the few places in Britain that is right in the heart of a great area to cycle. This ride takes in some excellent trails both to the north and the south of Aberfoyle; it can easily be ridden as two separate loops. If you ride it in one day and have a big day out, make sure to stop for an ice cream at Achray Farm and for one of the famous scones from Liz MacGregor's Coffee Shop in Aberfoyle. On a good day you can sit outside; the chances are that someone will come along to either join you for a chat or to tackle the second loop with you. This route also gives you a taste of the event that got Kerry into gravel riding: the Dukes Weekender.

ROUTE DESCRIPTION

Thanks to a very engaged group of people from the community, the village of Aberfoyle – which is better known to the cycling community as Gravelfoyle – has been at the forefront of developing gravel cycling in Scotland for a number of years. The Dukes Weekender celebrates gravel cycling annually in September. There is no shortage of bikes leaning on the walls of various cafes, shops and pubs at weekends. You'll find amazingly smooth gravel trails off the beaten track at Aberfoyle and, except for that one weekend in September when the Dukes Weekender takes place, there will be very few people on them. There are ample opportunities to extend this loop, or to try the other trails in the area on another day.

Nestled in the Queen Elizabeth Forest Park, which ranges from the eastern shores of Loch Lomond to the mountains of Strathyre, Aberfolye also marks the start of the Lomond Trossachs Loop, a 300-kilometre bikepacking loop for experienced mountain bikers. The Great North Trail from Cycling UK,

THE CLASSIC GRAVELFOYLE PICTURE – CASTLE BURN AQUEDUCT WHICH SUPPLIES GLASGOW WITH FRESH WATER.

the Lochs and Glens Way from Sustrans and two of Scotland's Great Trails, the Rob Roy Way and the Great Trossachs Path, connect the Aberfoyle area with other destinations. The town is located on the River Forth at the foot of Craigmore. Craigmore appears prominent, although it is not particularly high, due to its situation on the edge of the Trossachs range and its southerly slopes which drop steeply down to the valley of the River Forth and the Scottish Lowlands beyond. The Duke of Montrose constructed a road over the eastern shoulder of Craigmore in 1885, which joined an older road at the entrance of the Trossachs pass; this made Aberfoyle an alternative route to the Trossachs and Loch Katrine. This road, which became known as the Duke's Pass, was opened to the public in 1931 once the Forestry Commission had acquired the land.

Major industries in and around Aberfoyle included slate quarries and an ironworks, along with wool spinning and a lint mill. The village was also served by a railway to Glasgow but, as the industries have died out and the railway has been shut, Aberfoyle is now mainly supported by forestry and tourism. Aberfoyle and the surrounding area became popular with visitors after the publication of *The Lady of the Lake* by Sir Walter Scott in 1810; the poem describes the beauty of nearby Loch Katrine.

The route is divided into two loops, both of similar length and difficulty, starting and finishing at the bike hire and cafe in the heart of Aberfoyle. The route starts with the northern loop. Follow Main Street then pick up the Lochs and Glens Way (Sustrans National Route 7) and follow this up the hill on the right. This long-distance cycle touring and bikepacking route connects Glasgow in the south with Inverness in the north and provides a great itinerary for a longer gravel cycling adventure. The biggest climb of the route starts here – follow the small tarmac road and then continue on a cycle path on the right (the entrance is marked by two purple bikes that act as gates). The route climbs on a paved path through the beautiful woodland, passing near the Lodge Forest Visitor Centre, where there is a variety of walking trails which invite people to explore the area further. The paved path turns into a gravel path and, after crossing a river, becomes a wider gravel forest track, all signposted as *Sustrans National Route 7*.

The climbing gets steeper where the path widens. The following section has risen to fame among gravel riders, as it was used in 2021 for the Endura Gravel Hill Climb. This individual time trial is part of the annual Dukes Weekender, which features a number of activities for gravel cyclists spread over the second weekend in September. The route continues through tall trees, where you can spot the Go Ape ropes and structures, passing Meall Ear on the right. The gradient of the climb improves towards the top as the woodland thins out, giving way to beautiful views across to the Duke's Pass and the Trossachs. The route follows a track to the left, descending on this alternative gravel path to soon meet the Sustrans route again at the shores of Loch Drunkie. As this picturesque freshwater loch is enclosed on all sides by high hills, it is difficult to access and less commonly visited than other Trossachs lochs. The route continues on wide gravel tracks, first on Sustrans National Route 7 and then on a forest track, past another small loch to Invertrossachs.

At Invertrossachs the route joins the Lochs and Glens Way again, this time travelling on a smaller forest trail on one of the most picturesque sections of the route along the shores of Loch Venachar, with great views to the north towards Ben Ledi and Stuc Odhar. Take care on this section of the route, as it's very popular with walkers. Where the track widens, the route leaves Sustrans National Route 7 and joins the Three Lochs Forest Drive. This is one of only a few off-road routes for cars in Scotland. It is open to vehicular traffic between March and October; walkers and cyclists are welcome at any time of year. The route continues on a wide gravel track across a more open landscape to Achray Farm, a great first stop for a rest to marvel at the scenery. From late May to October this small farm, which also offers accommodation, is a top place for artisan ice cream, made in the Trossachs from goat's milk using seasonal ingredients and foraged flavours. There's seating at the farm and you might see the goats out in the fields or grazing on the forest drive.

From Achray Farm the route continues on the forest drive and the Great Trossachs Path, another long-distance route connecting Callander in the east and Inversnaid at Loch Lomond in the west. After a picturesque section along the shores of Loch Achray the route crosses the Duke's Pass road and continues on the Great Trossachs Path into another forest. The first section after crossing the road is on singletrack. Make sure to switch into the easiest gear you have, as the small ramp at the top on to the next wide gravel track is really steep. After busting the lungs, the route continues on wide gravel tracks around Gleann

Riabhach, with another short section of singletrack. The terrain is best described as undulating. The route joins tarmac for a while from here, climbing uphill on the Duke's Pass road. The road heads east first, with fantastic views over Loch Drunkie, and then continues southwards to the top of the pass at 238 metres. From here it's all downhill towards Aberfoyle to tackle the southern loop, after a

SMOOTH GRAVEL ON THE FOREST DRIVE PAST LOCH ACHRAY.

stop for lunch or coffee and cake.

Start the southern loop in Aberfoyle, following the route of the Great North Trail (not signposted) and the Rob Roy Way (signposted) south across Aberfoyle Bridge. This fine stone bridge was built in the eighteenth century and carries Manse Road over the River Forth. The Rob Roy Way is one of Scotland's Great Trails, running from Drymen in the south to Pitlochry in the north. It takes its name from Rob Roy MacGregor, an eighteenth-century outlaw and Scottish folk hero. The trail is suitable for cycling in parts; it is waymarked with blue and white signposts

that bear its name. The Great North Trail was recently designed by Cycling UK as an adventure mountain biking and bikepacking route running from the Peak District to Cape Wrath and John o' Groats. Be aware that this southern loop takes you through a working forest, so be prepared to stop for forestry vehicles and watch out for temporary diversions.

Where the tarmac ends, shortly after Aberfoyle Cemetery, the route climbs steadily into the forest on a wide gravel trail. At Dungarrow the route descends for a short section, and then forks right to leave the Rob Roy Way. After more climbing the track descends,

BEAUTIFUL CYCLING ON SUSTRANS NATIONAL ROUTE 7 ALONG LOCH VENACHAR.

following a concrete aqueduct for a short while. Afterwards a number of shafts appear along the route. Both the aqueduct and the shafts are unique features of two aqueducts that still supply the city of Glasgow with fresh water from Loch Katrine. During the nineteenth century the need for Glasgow to have a supply of clean water became apparent: Scotland's first cholera epidemic in 1832 killed over 3,000 people in Glasgow alone; further epidemics in 1848 and 1853 finally led to action. In 1856 work commenced on a 55-kilometre aqueduct from Loch Katrine to the city. The scheme was operational by 1860. Work started on a second aqueduct in 1885, as the supply was no longer sufficient.

The track crosses underneath the Castle Burn Aqueduct Bridge, an iconic sight on the Gravelfoyle trails, and continues to Duchray Cottage, from where it takes a track on the left to follow the river on its

southern bank for a while. This section of the route is sheltered and a good option for cloudy and rainy days. The route gets more exposed as it climbs on forest tracks towards Beinn Bhan, with Loch Lomond providing a stunning backdrop as you climb. The climbing gets steeper towards the top, and the route reaches its highest point at 301 metres before it crosses the Bruach Caorainn Burn. A long descent follows into Gleann Dubh to Duchray Water, with a short climb sandwiched in, all on very good, rideable gravel tracks.

Where the route crosses the river you can spot Loch Dubh, the 'Black Loch', to the left – this lovely lochan is nestled in a wooded valley. At Stronmacnair there is another short climb as the route takes a left to follow the slopes of Stob a' Bhlàir Bhàin, and then descends towards the Water of Chon. The views towards Loch Chon are great from here. The

DISTANCE **67km/42 miles** ⟩ ASCENT **1,131m/3,711 ft** ⟩ GRADE **Expert** ⟩ START/FINISH **Aberfoyle Bike Hire & Cafe** ⟩ START/FINISH GRID REF **NN 523010** BIKE-FRIENDLY PUBLIC TRANSPORT **Dunblane railway station (29km from the route)** ⟩ HIGHEST POINT **301m/988 ft** ⟩ TERRAIN **Mostly well-graded and wide gravel tracks, with some exposed sections** ⟩ RECOMMENDED TYRES **Schwalbe G-One Allround**

BEST TIME TO RIDE

| JAN | FEB | MAR | APR | MAY | JUN | JUL | AUG | SEP | OCT | NOV | DEC |

SINGLETRACK **5%**   PATH **80%**   ROAD **15%**

track follows the route of the signposted Statute Labour Road from here, running parallel to the Water of Chon, to reach Loch Ard. Reputed to be one of Scotland's most picturesque lochs; it is ideal for kayaking and other water sports due to its sheltered location.

The route continues to undulate along the shore of Loch Ard through the forest and joins the Eight Mile Loop, another signposted trail, and just before Creag Bhreac it continues on the Loch Ard Sculpture Trail. The trail leads to a car park, and from here a short section of singletrack follows, crossing the Duchray Water and leading to Lochan Spling – this is a great place to take a short rest while admiring the salmon sculpture in the water. The gravel soon turns into tarmac as the route follows Duchray Road and then Manse Road towards Aberfoyle for a well-earned coffee and cake.

OTHER ROUTES NEARBY
> Eight Mile Loop
> Great North Trail
> Great Trossachs Path
> Loch Ard Sculpture Trail
> Lochs and Glens Way (Sustrans National Route 7)
> Lomond Trossachs Loop
> Rob Roy Way
> Statute Labour Road
> Three Lochs Forest Drive

WHERE TO EAT
> Aberfoyle Bike Hire & Cafe, Aberfoyle
> Aberfoyle Delicatessen, Aberfoyle
> Liz MacGregor's Coffee Shop, Aberfoyle
> The Station Coffee Shop, Aberfoyle
> Achray Farm Ice Cream, Brig o' Turk

BIKE SHOPS
> Aberfoyle Bike Hire & Cafe, Aberfoyle (**T** 01877 382 023)

WHERE TO STOP
> Loch Drunkie, NN 538039
> Loch Venachar, NN 559054
> Achray Farm, NN 530063
> Loch Achray, NN 521061
> Duke's Pass viewpoint, NN 525045
> Aberfoyle Bridge, NN 520009
> Castle Burn Aqueduct Bridge, NS 470988
> Salmon sculpture at Lochan Spling, NN 505005

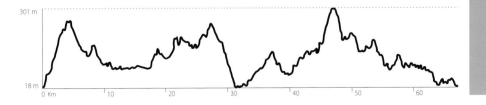

CLACKMANNANSHIRE

07 CLACKS GRAVEL
29KM   WALTER HAMILTON

The zigzag gravel tracks in the Ochil Hills offer not only great views across the Forth Valley, but also some of the best gravel riding close to Scotland's capital city, Edinburgh.

ABOUT WALTER
Gravel riding for Walter in three words
not just fun

'I got injured playing impact sports, so a friend got me into cycling just as an alternative. There was that new kind of freedom. You could go a lot further than if you went for a run, and you could explore lots of different terrain.'

Walter Hamilton runs Velow Bikeworks, a small independent bike shop in Portobello, who specialise in vintage bikes. It was only in his early thirties that he got into cycling. But as soon as he started, Walter was hooked. It was the quick advances he enjoyed with cycling, and that he was able to track his progress easily. And very shortly after his initial dabbles into the sport, it completely took over.

'I loved recycling and I loved riding. But I also loved bikes – the technology, and playing with them. I taught myself to fix my own bike and then quickly realised that there was maybe a business to be started.'

Walter started Velow Bikeworks in 2015, the same year he became Scottish hill climbing champion. His ethos of reusing old bikes has stuck with him since then – he loves fixing up old bikes and beautifully restores them to their former glory, or adapts them for new uses.

'Gravel biking has become a big thing for me since I've moved away from the competitive side of cycling. I am just trying to get the most out of the more limited time that I have to cycle. I would much rather go and explore off-road away from traffic and into different terrain.'

Although Walter is a very social person, he loves the me time that gravel cycling gives him. And that he has the terrain all to himself. The extra freedom that comes with gravel riding is what he values, especially as his time is sparse – running a bike shop and, more recently, becoming

a dad. Cycling for him has become about exploring and having fun rather than pure fitness, speed and competition.

'You weren't going gravel riding; you were literally just riding your bike. But there's only so far the tarmac can take you.'

Walter started riding a mountain bike at the age of 14. These days, he sees a lot of bikes from the early 1990s to refurbish in the shop. In his opinion, mountain bikes from 30 years ago were built for gravel tracks. There weren't any downhill trail centres then. Mountain biking was just about getting out into the hills on forest paths and trails and exploring. For him, gravel riding has taken up the space that mountain biking did in its early days.

'We've almost come full circle again back to steel, because people understand that it's a great material to build a bike. It's a bit like vinyl

CLIMBING INTO THE OCHIL HILLS NEAR MENSTRIE.

Mickle Corum

Glentye Hill

Big Hunt Hill

Loss Hill

Lossburn Reservoir

Loss Burn

Cocksburn Reservoir

Waltersmuir Reservoir

Sheriffmuir Big Wood

Dunblane

A9

Ashfield

B8033

B8033

Allan Water

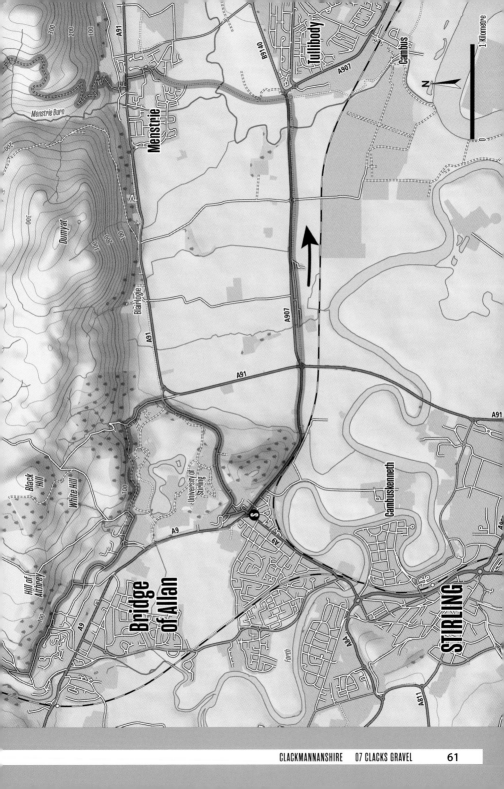

CYCLING TOWARDS MYRETON HILL WITH DUMYAT IN THE BACKGROUND.

records. You can't replicate the sound quality of a viral record and you can't replicate the ride quality of a steel frame.'

Walter admires the Rough-Stuff Fellowship, whose members rode their touring bikes in extreme terrain as far back as the 1950s. Especially looking at their efforts and what they achieved on seemingly simple bikes, there is nothing new about gravel riding. But there's a real synergy with what people are doing now: using cycling for adventure and exploring while pushing their boundaries. Even though modern bikes are a lot more advanced and specific, for him there's something nice about an old steel-frame touring or mountain bike – robust and designed for exploring.

'With modern bikes there's not really the opportunity to cobble things together and make them work.'

Walter likes the simplicity of vintage bikes and the flexibility that comes with fixing them. While modern bikes are technologically much more advanced, they lack the versatility of vintage bikes. For Walter, there is technology, like integrated lever shifters for drop bars, which has certainly advanced cycling. At other times though it just feels like everybody's trying to develop something new to some sort of new standard, which makes things more difficult than is worthwhile.

'It's still got its place in the line-up.'

Steel is where Walter's cycling heart lies. While there are no major factories building steel frames, certainly not in Britain, there are now artisan builders and small companies that are specialising in steel. This makes steel bikes a highly sought-after, premium product. Steel is still the base for many of the beautiful bikes Walter gets in his shop on an almost daily basis, and some will certainly go on their fair share of gravel adventures in the future.

ABOUT WALTER'S ROUTE

There are two key moments of Walter's life in this very personal choice of route. When we rode the route on a nice early summer's day it took Walter straight back to the days when he first explored off-road, with the mountain bike he got as a teenager, a Raleigh Montage. Many times he went up the zigzag gravel track behind Menstrie with a bunch of friends – wearing tennis shoes, shorts and a t-shirt – before 'bombing' back down with nothing but a Vetta helmet and borrowed ski goggles for protection.

And even with a pair of fresh eyes, those tracks from his youth are still as good now as they were back then. The route also passes Logie Kirk, which marks the start of the iconic hill climb where Walter earned his Scottish Cycling National Hill Climb Championship title in 2015. Being a big fan of Robert Millar (now Philippa York), it makes him proud that Millar once won that title before becoming one of the most successful British cyclists of all time. For Walter, this is not the wildest, the most extreme or the longest gravel route, but a lovely, very accessible route, hidden away in Scotland's Central Belt.

ROUTE DESCRIPTION

The route starts at Corrieri's Cafe in Stirling, one of the most popular cafes for cyclists in the area. The start is accessible by train; it is a short bike ride on Sustrans National Route 765 from Stirling railway station or following the same route from Bridge of Allan railway station in the opposite direction.

The route begins by following a short section of road and then joins Sustrans National Route 76 while

THE ANCIENT WOODLAND IN KIPPENRAIT GLEN.

it passes Abbey Craig, a volcanic crag rising above the River Forth and Cambuskenneth Abbey. The iconic 67-metre, Victorian-Gothic-style Wallace Monument sits on top of the hill and is clearly visible from all directions. It is said that Sir William Wallace watched the English army of King Edward I assembling from this hill just before the Battle of Stirling Bridge in 1297.

After Abbey Craig a cycle path on the left runs parallel to the road to reach a busy roundabout, where extra care is needed when crossing the road. The next section of the route is the old Alloa Road, now a wide, traffic-free cycle path, passing Manor

SUSTRANS NATIONAL ROUTE 768 WITH DUMYAT IN THE BACKGROUND.

Powis and Manor Steps as well as a petrol station. Shortly afterwards, the route leaves Sustrans National Route 76 and joins Sustrans National Route 768, another traffic-free cycle path heading north towards Menstrie.

The small village of Menstrie stands on the flood plain of the River Devon. The village extends across the Ochil Fault; the movement of which created the dramatic southern edge of the Ochil Hills. Menstrie sits to the south of two of the most westerly summits of the Ochil Hills: Dumyat and Myreton Hill reach around 400 metres in height. Menstrie

Glen divides these two hills: Menstrie Burn emerges from Menstrie Glen and runs through the village, before it joins the River Devon to the south of the village.

The route covers the western side of the Ochil Hills. Historically the Ochils were important as a main gateway to the Highlands,

takes a few roads through Menstrie, with Menstrie Castle, a three-storey manor house, just a short detour away. It was home to Sir William Alexander, the first Earl of Stirling; the earl was involved in founding a colony in Nova Scotia in Canada. After a twentieth-century restoration, the castle won a Civic Trust award.

Leaving Menstrie, the route climbs very steeply on a zigzag gravel trail up the scarp face of Myreton Hill. This trail was originally built to access mine workings which produced calcite during the Napoleonic Wars. This is where the route overlaps with the Explore Your Boundaries Clackmannanshire route from Bikepacking Scotland, which provides another, but much more demanding, gravel ride in this part of Scotland. The track is perfect for testing your climbing skills on a gravel bike and provides fantastic views south over the Forth Valley.

The route climbs uphill along the Menstrie Burn, with great views towards Dumyat. To the west of the summit of Myreton Hill, the path starts descending towards a burn, from where another steep climb takes you to the highest point of the route at 442 metres. While this gravel track is well maintained, some of the gravel can be quite chunky, and those sections might require pushing for less experienced riders. It's worth stopping at times on both climbs, as the views across the Firth of Forth and the Ochil Hills are stunning.

Once the highest point is reached, the route descends through woodland on the slopes of Big Hunt Hill and Little Hunt Hill and reaches a road near Park Cottage. The route continues on this road to Sheriffmuir, the site of the inconclusive Battle of Sheriffmuir, which was part of the Jacobite rising of 1715. Part of the British comedy film *Monty Python and the Holy Grail* was filmed here. The route passes what was the Sheriffmuir Inn – this whitewashed drovers' inn dates back to the late seventeenth century but has recently been converted into a private house. The route follows a single-track road on the left towards Dunblane; it is downhill all the way.

Just before Dunblane, which is a worthwhile detour to see the cathedral, the route joins Sustrans National Route 765 through the fantastic wild woodland of Kippenrait Glen, a Site of Special

due to Stirling's location at the lowest bridging point on the River Forth. Several mill towns, including Menstrie, Alva and Tillicoultry, expanded in the early Industrial Revolution to tap the water power of the Ochils. You can still visit some of the mills today as they are museums. Nowadays, since the local industries have all but vanished, these towns have transitioned into commuter towns.

The route leaves Sustrans National Route 768 and

A ZIGZAG GRAVEL TRAIL NEAR MENSTRIE THAT ONCE PROVIDED ACCESS TO MINE WORKINGS.

Scientific Interest and one of the most unique parts of this ride.

It is thought that Kippenrait Glen, where the Wharry Burn cuts a narrow channel through the valley, and the adjoining, more level riverbanks of the Allan Water have been continuously wooded since the last ice age. This means that the area has an amazingly rich and varied biodiversity, including many species of beetles, birds, mosses, trees and fungi, and some rare and beautiful woodland plants. The woodland is delightful to cycle through any time of the year: early spring is a highlight, when carpets of fragrant wild garlic and delicate white wood anemones can be seen, along with later in the spring, when bluebells flower. The former road through the glen is a cycle and walking path now; its tarmac is crumbling in places.

The route continues on Sustrans National Route 765 into Bridge of Allan, a former spa town, with many grand and impressive nineteenth-century villas built on wide roads. Notably, Robert Louis Stevenson visited the town every year during his youth. The route passes the edge of Mine Wood on a tarmac road; the wood is home to a great network of mountain bike trails. The gravel path on the left is a welcome alternative if you prefer off-road riding.

The route continues through town past some impressive houses and meets Old Sheriffmuir Road, where the grounds of the University of Stirling start. The Meadowpark Bar and Kitchen provides a good opportunity for refreshments, before the route takes a path on the edge of Hermitage Wood alongside a wall towards Logie Old Kirk, one of the oldest Christian sites in Scotland. This wide path is mostly fun to ride, but be aware that some sections can be muddy. You know you've arrived at Logie Old Kirk when you see the arched gateway in the kirkyard wall. The uphill section on the road from the kirk is an iconic hill climb; it is used for the Scottish Cycling National Hill Climb Championship, which Walter won in 2015.

The newer Logie Kirk stands a few hundred

DISTANCE **29km/18 miles** 〉 ASCENT **555m/1,821 ft** 〉 GRADE **Straightforward** 〉 START/FINISH **Corrieri's Cafe, Stirling** 〉 START/FINISH GRID REF **NS 806956** 〉 BIKE-FRIENDLY PUBLIC TRANSPORT **Stirling railway station (3km from the route)** 〉 HIGHEST POINT **442m/1,450 ft** 〉 TERRAIN **Hilly; at times very exposed** 〉 RECOMMENDED TYRES **Schwalbe G-One Allround**

BEST TIME TO RIDE

JAN	FEB	MAR	APR	MAY	JUN	JUL	AUG	SEP	OCT	NOV	DEC

PATH **35%**   CYCLE PATH **15%**   ROAD **50%**

metres down the road and dates from 1805, although it has been remodelled several times. Shortly after the church, the route joins the B998, which skirts the boundary of the University of Stirling, one of the most beautiful campuses in Britain. There are several paths across the campus, which provide an alternative to the busy road if preferred.

The B998 passes the main car park for the Wallace Monument, from where you can divert to see a series of woodcarvings which line the main path up to the monument. This is very steep in places, but can be cycled. The Wallace Monument hosts exhibitions on the various floors that lead to the top, including the Hall of Heroes on the second floor, which tells the story of eminent Scots who have contributed to the history of the country. Right at the top of the 246-step spiral staircase, inside the monument's crown, there is a viewing gallery, from where visitors can enjoy extensive views of the Forth Valley and the Ochil Hills. From here the route follows Logie Road back to the start.

OTHER ROUTES NEARBY
> Explore Your Boundaries Clackmannanshire
> Mine Wood mountain bike trails
> Sustrans National Route 76
> Sustrans National Route 765
> Sustrans National Route 768

WHERE TO EAT
> Corrieri's Cafe, Stirling
> The Forge Coffee Shop and Gallery, Menstrie
> Meadowpark Bar and Kitchen, Bridge of Allan

BIKE SHOPS
> Stirling Cycles, Stirling (T 01786 451 559)
> Stirling Active Travel Hub, Stirling (T 01786 474 160)
> Velow Bikeworks, Portobello, Edinburgh
  (T 07814 112 151)

WHERE TO STOP
> Menstrie Castle, NS 849969
> River Devon Bridge, NS 851959
> Sheriffmuir, NN 827021
> Wharry Bridge, NS 800996
> Kippenrait Glen, NS 797997
> Logie Old Kirk, NS 815970
> Wallace Monument, NS 809956

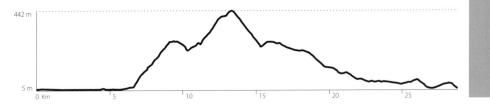

EAST LOTHIAN

08 EXPLORE YOUR BOUNDARIES: EAST LOTHIAN

169KM   MARK BEAUMONT

This route offers a multi-day gravel adventure that combines the remote Lammermuir Hills with the stunning East Lothian coastline, with beautiful beaches and plenty of places to stop and enjoy.

ABOUT MARK

Gravel riding for Mark in three words
adventure; memories; fun

'If I was to summarise gravel riding in a sentence, it would be: creating memories. I never come back from my gravel rides and define it by how far I went. I define it very much by moments in time. Gravel riding for me has been about redefining why I ride a bike.'

No other name is so closely connected with the Guinness World Record for fastest circumnavigation of the globe by bicycle as Mark Beaumont's. On 14 February 2008 the Scot completed his first lap in 194 days and 17 hours, and so began a decade of record attempts by other riders. His record was broken multiple times before Mark regained it by rolling through the Arc de Triomphe on the Champs-Élysées on 18 September 2017, having completed his second lap in 78 days, 14 hours and 40 minutes.

'Gravel riding in Scotland I think is particularly spicy in the fact that it is not North American gravel where you are doing fire trails. You are often on very wet and very technical routes where you need to use all your agility as a bike rider in terms of keeping grip and handling quite technical sections. I love that challenge.'

For a man whose life until his second record-breaking cycle around the world had really been defined by numbers, Mark's motivation for getting into gravel was a way of focusing on the map instead of average speed. Since most of his cycling thus far had been on tarmac, he was

interested in pushing himself in a different way as a bike rider.

'I feel that gravel bikes have really connected me with those trails and allowed me to still move really efficiently, but to do almost everything. I feel that my bike handling has gotten a lot better just with that variety of terrain.'

Growing up on a farm in rural Perthshire, Mark had some of the best gravel riding in Scotland on his doorstep, even if the term wasn't commonplace back then. Aged only 15, Beaumont embarked on his first solo adventure by bike from John o' Groats to Land's End, supported by his parents. His fascination with this classic British end-to-end-journey hasn't diminished. In 2021 he had a go at the route three times over the summer: first as a relay, then on a tandem, both times with his GCN partner-in-crime James Lowsley-Williams.

A ROAD LEADING TO SEACLIFF BEACH WITH THE MIGHTY BASS ROCK IN THE BACKGROUND.

SUNRISE IN DUNBAR.

But it was the third attempt on a gravel bike that was the most memorable. And it ultimately helped him to achieve the aim that got Mark into gravel riding in the first place – becoming a better bike rider. Joining 45 other starters on the 2,000-kilometre GB Divide route in August 2021, Mark cycled away from GBDURO21, his maiden gravel bikepacking race, as the winner.

ABOUT MARK'S ROUTE

Mark's route of choice is part of a joint project which we started in December 2020, just before the second Covid-19 lockdown was announced. With 'Explore Your Boundaries' Mark and I jointly turned a limitation – having to start any exercise within or close to the boundary of our local council area of Edinburgh – into an opportunity, by using the boundaries to map 24 different gravel routes throughout Scotland. During the course of 2021 we cycled six of them in all weather conditions we could imagine. Edinburgh in ice and snow, Midlothian in perfect crisp and cold early spring conditions, Clackmannanshire in gusty winds, East Lothian in perfect sunshine, Falkirk in overcast conditions and finally Glasgow in, at times, pouring rain. Out of the six, East Lothian presented the biggest surprises to Mark, and became one of his favourite gravel routes close to home.

ROUTE DESCRIPTION

The ride starts at Fisherrow Harbour in Musselburgh, where there is a small cafe and a fuel station providing provisions if needed. There has been fishing in the Musselburgh and Fisherrow area since Roman times.

The current Fisherrow Harbour dates from the seventeenth century and is very close to the site of the Roman harbour. The Roman harbour was at the mouth of the River Esk and served the Inveresk Roman Fort, which was situated on high ground to the east of the river. The harbour, once home to a large fishing fleet, is now mainly used by leisure craft.

The route follows quiet residential streets first and then joins Sustrans National Route 1 along the banks of the River Esk. This is also the first section of the Capital Trail, another popular bikepacking journey, which was developed in 2015 as the first of many Bikepacking Scotland routes. Our route continues on a small track at the edge of a field past Whitecraig to connect with Sustrans National Route 1 again. If this path is too overgrown, simply follow the signs for

The Lammermuir Hills, clearly visible all the way from the start, is one of the best areas close to Edinburgh, Scotland's capital city, for gravel riding. The hills are not particularly high – the highest points are Meikle Says Law at 535 metres and Lammer Law at 529 metres – but the steep gradients and the strong exposure to the elements make them a challenging but rewarding place for cycling. Seeing fellow cyclists or hillwalkers, even in the busy summer season, is the exception rather than the norm.

After another short section on a tarmac road the route follows a good gravel track through a farm and climbs steeply towards a wind farm. Depending on gear range and fitness, this might be the first place where you have to push your bike. The views from the top will make up for the hard work on this steep climb. After passing a gate, extra care is needed at certain times of the year, as large herds of cattle graze the land here. The route follows gravel roads through a wind farm as the route undulates over the Lammermuir Hills. Steep climbs are followed by fast downhills through open moorland. From midsummer into early autumn, when the heather is in full bloom, this route provides an amazingly scenic ride. The route shortly overlaps with the Capital Trail again, which takes a different route south after Waddelscairn Moor. As for any adventure in exposed places, it proves worthwhile checking the wind direction and weather before setting off on this ride. This section on the top in particular can be very challenging in high winds and offers no shelter at all. What it provides is a succession of American-style 'gravel highways' through remote territory, comparable to top gravel destinations like the Flint Hills in Kansas. A rockier descent towards the Faseny Water is followed by some tarmac so you can relax for a while. This is part of a classic road cycling route from Gifford to Duns; it comes in handy as an escape route if necessary.

After about 3 kilometres the route ventures back off-road and climbs steeply towards Priestlaw Hill. The hard work is rewarded with a fantastic descent and views over Whiteadder Reservoir, which was constructed in the 1960s and is one of the main fresh water supplies for East Lothian. In the summer, multiple water sports can be enjoyed here. The route

Sustrans National Route 1 through Whitecraig for an alternative. Shortly afterwards, the route proceeds on another popular route in East Lothian, Sustrans National Route 196, which leads to the Pencaitland Railway Walk, a former railway line that served local collieries and an iron works. Before Ormiston, Scotland's first planned village, the route follows a small path over a river and then joins a wider track onwards. After the next section on roads of varying degrees in size, a gravel track is followed, which offers great views northbound towards the Lomond Hills. From Costerton, quiet roads lead to the first proper opportunity to stop for refreshments at Humbie Hub, a community-run village shop, post office and cafe. This is also the last food supply point until Dunbar, about 80 kilometres away. Be aware that natural water sources along the route are sparse and filtering is needed.

From Humbie the riding gets much more strenuous and remote. Mostly on gravel tracks, the route climbs into the Lammermuir Hills, which form a natural border between East Lothian and the Scottish Borders. As for all the Explore Your Boundaries routes, this itinerary offers a mixture of well-known paths and attractions paired with new finds off the beaten track, to explore a lesser-known part of Scotland.

THE LAMMERMUIR HILLS ARE A PARADISE FOR GRAVEL RIDING.

crosses Whiteadder Reservoir on a road and follows a gravel track on the edge of a small woodland, before it climbs on to open moorland again. The climb passes the ruins of Gamelshiel Castle on the south side of the Hall Burn. All that remains of this sixteenth-century tower house is part of the east and west walls. After crossing a burn, the route follows a faint track, where pushing might be required at times. Shortly afterwards, a good gravel road provides fantastic gravel riding across the Crystal Rig Wind Farm, the second largest in the United Kingdom.

The route more-or-less follows the boundary between East Lothian and the Scottish Borders here, but the ride can be shortened at kilometre 69, if necessary, by cutting straight across the valley. At the wind farm there are also several other alternative tracks to either shorten or extend the ride. Please watch out for possible closures or diversions, as there is a lot of construction still ongoing. After a more technical descent through a woodland, the route rejoins a quiet tarmac road for a while. After another gravel section a road leads to Oldhamstocks, the first human settlement for a while, which also marks the end of the Lammermuir Hills. After following a mixture of roads, doubletrack and singletrack, you'll reach Dunglass Collegiate Church. This scheduled monument sits within landscaped parkland and is cared for by Historic Environment Scotland; it is one of the top attractions in East Lothian. Shortly afterwards the route joins Sustrans National Route 76.

An eyesore for most, but fascinating for others, Torness Nuclear Power Station is hard to ignore when emerging from the hills into the flatter coastal landscape. At Thorntonloch, the route leaves Sustrans National Route 76 and joins the John Muir Link. This is a coastal path which runs between Dunbar (linking to the John Muir Way) and Cockburnspath (linking with the Berwickshire Coastal Path and the Southern Upland Way). The next section of the route follows the John Muir Link northbound. There is a succession of great beaches all the way to Dunbar, but picturesque Skateraw Harbour is definitely one of the highlights of the route. With the beauty of the coast comes some more technical riding at times, with short sections that require pushing. (Continuing on Sustrans National Route 76 provides a less technical and faster alternative for this coastal section to Dunbar.)

The route passes Barns Ness Lighthouse, which was constructed at the turn of the twentieth century by brothers David Alan Stevenson and Charles Alexander Stevenson, cousins of the novelist Robert Louis Stevenson. The stone of the lighthouse proved to be very resilient during World War II, when the lighthouse was machine-gunned but didn't sustain any damage. The lighthouse was decommissioned in 2005; the keepers' cottage is now holiday accommodation. The route continues along the coast, bypassing a golf course, before joining East Links Road into Dunbar. Routes and descriptions for shorter gravel cycling rides from here, including the Barns Ness Gravel Adventure, a great loop combining the John Muir Link with Sustrans National Route 76, are available on the Visit East Lothian website.

Alongside Musselburgh, at the start of the route, and North Berwick, about three quarters of the way through the ride, and Prestonpans, close to the finish, Dunbar is one of four towns on this ride. Due to its strategic location, Dunbar has a rich history. The remains of Dunbar Castle are visible next to the harbour. The castle was commanded to be destroyed by an order of the Parliament of Scotland in 1567; shortly afterwards the harbour was built. Nowadays the harbour is home to a fleet of fishing boats and the second-oldest RNLI station in Scotland. The town is well connected by rail to Edinburgh and London and is the birthplace of one of the most influential Scottish immigrants – John Muir. An explorer, naturalist and conservationist, he is known as 'father of the national parks' for his role in the establishment of national parks in the USA. John Muir's Birthplace in the High Street is now a museum and well worth visiting. A statue beside the town clock also commemorates Muir, as well as the latest sculpture by Andy Scott, an artist who created the well-known *Kelpies* in Falkirk. *The DunBear*, on the outskirts of town, is only a small detour from the route and worth visiting. Dunbar offers a wide range of accommodation. The recently refurbished Dolphin Inn, an independent hostel, is a great choice for cyclists, with bright, airy rooms, some nice retro features and secure bike storage.

From Dunbar the route follows the John Muir Way for a time, along stunning red sandstone cliffs. The rock formations you can see are the result of a unique combination of volcanic activity, continental drift and erosion from the sea. Arriving at Belhaven Bay, you'll pass Belhaven Bridge, which is known as the 'Bridge to Nowhere'. At low tide the bridge crosses a stream to reach Belhaven Bay beach. However, at high tide the water covers the surrounding land and completely isolates the bridge – the bridge literally leads to nowhere.

THE FORD ACROSS SALTERS' BURN.

Nearby East Links Family Park is a popular weekend destination, while surfers can often be seen at the beaches. From Belhaven Bay the route overlaps with the Go East Lothian Trail, another Bikepacking Scotland route. The trails here can be sandy at times, and the route crosses a bridge, which requires lifting the bike on a set of steps at either side. After passing East Links Family Park, the route follows a succession of singletrack trails along the mouth of the River Tyne, also known as Hedderwick Sands. Anti-tank blocks can be seen at several places along the East Lothian coast, but the best examples are right next to the trail here, and later on at Longniddry Bents. These coastal defences were created along the Firth of Forth at the beginning of World War II to provide protection in case of invasion from the sea, in particular from landing craft with tanks and artillery.

The route soon rejoins the road and passes through Tyninghame, where Tyninghame Smithy is a popular stop for cyclists. After a small tarmac road to a car park, the route continues on fine gravel tracks along the coast, passing Ravensheugh Sands and Seacliff Beach, which are among the finest beaches in East Lothian. Looking north across the Firth of Forth, Bass Rock dominates the view. An island in the outer part of the estuary, this steep-sided volcanic rock, measuring 107 metres at its highest point, is home to the world's largest colony of northern gannets. Boat trips to Bass Rock are offered regularly in the

THE JOHN MUIR WAY NEAR DUNBAR.

summer, departing from the Scottish Seabird Centre in North Berwick. Extra attention is needed on the small road from Seacliff Beach, which can get very busy in summer. Shortly afterwards, Tantallon Castle, another East Lothian landmark, comes into sight. The route follows the main road, and a stop just after the houses at Auldhame offers the opportunity to admire and photograph both Bass Rock and Tantallon Castle together. The road passes Canty Bay, with Drift, another popular cafe, on the right. At Tantallon Caravan Park, the route leaves the road again and crosses the golf course, and then follows a succession of roads through the seaside town of North Berwick.

There is no shortage of places to eat, stay or to play golf in North Berwick, with views in all directions dominated by the North Berwick Law, an extinct volcano. Robert Louis Stevenson spent many holidays in the town during his childhood and as a young man, and the island of Fidra, visible from the beaches from here onwards, is believed to be the original inspiration for *Treasure Island*. Much of Stevenson's later novel, *Catriona* (which is the sequel

to *Kidnapped*) is set locally.

Just after leaving Abbotsford Road, the route crosses a large field. After being freshly ploughed this can be a rather bumpy track, which gets smoother as the year progresses. The route then follows a succession of singletrack trails, passing Yellowcraig Beach and several more beaches along the route. At times pushing might be required. An alternative to this part of the route is to follow the John Muir Way from Yellow Craig Plantation to Dirleton, then continuing to rejoin the main route at Gullane.

From Gullane the route follows the John Muir Way once again, with a great gravel path circumnavigating the golf course, before passing Aberlady Bay Nature Reserve on roads and continuing into the small village of Aberlady. The Ducks Inn is a popular stop for cyclists and offers food and accommodation. A nice singletrack trail through the forest provides excellent riding after Aberlady. Sadly, Gosford House doesn't allow bikes in its grounds, but for a small entrance fee the Curling House with its flanking rustic walls, as well as Gosford House itself, are worth

DISTANCE **169km/105 miles** 〉 ASCENT **1,760m/5,774 ft** 〉 GRADE **Expert** 〉 START/FINISH **Fisherrow Harbour, Musselburgh** 〉 START/FINISH GRID REF **NT 334731** 〉 BIKE-FRIENDLY PUBLIC TRANSPORT **Musselburgh railway station (2km from the route)** 〉 HIGHEST POINT **467m/1,532 ft** 〉 TERRAIN **Open moorland, urban areas and coastal paths; at times very remote** 〉 RECOMMENDED TYRES **Schwalbe G-One R or G-One Allround**

BEST TIME TO RIDE

| JAN | FEB | MAR | APR | MAY | JUN | JUL | AUG | SEP | OCT | NOV | DEC |

SINGLETRACK **10%**   PATH **30%**   CYCLE PATH **10%**   ROAD **50%**

a look. Gosford Bothy Farm Shop & Butchery acts as a ticket office and offers refreshments as well – it is signposted from the route. Shortly afterwards, another set of anti-tank barriers can be seen in the woodland, before the route rejoins the road past Longniddry and into Seton Sands.

You continue to follow the coast on a mixture of cycling paths and walking paths. At the edge of Prestonpans, the route follows a low-tide diversion off the John Muir Way. Extra care is needed here, as the concrete path is covered in algae on some sections and can be slippery. A very short section over sand is almost impossible to ride. However, the murals and views across the sea make this a nicer route than the alternative on the road through the town (at high tide it's necessary to follow the route through the town). The Battle of Prestonpans took place near the town in 1745. Prestonpans was established in the eleventh century and has some interesting examples of important historical architecture, including a dovecote, Preston Tower and the market cross, which is the only monument of this type in Scotland which is in its original location. Prestonpans is also known as Scotland's 'Mural Town'; many of the murals depict local history. The industrial history of the town can be explored at Prestongrange Museum, an open-air museum on the site of a former colliery, which is only a very short detour from the route at Morrison's Haven.

The last section along the coast not only offers a fantastic gravel path to complete the Explore Your Boundaries experience, but it is also a haven for birdwatchers. The track along the sea wall from Morrison's Haven to Goose Green Crescent is excellent to observe seabirds and ducks, and the existing ash lagoons are used as high-tide roosts by waders, gulls and terns. The ride finishes at Fisherrow Harbour in Musselburgh.

OTHER ROUTES NEARBY

> Berwickshire Coastal Path
> Capital Trail
> Go East Lothian Trail
> Gravel routes on the Visit East Lothian website
> John Muir Link
> John Muir Way
> John Muir Way Bikepacking Route – see **www.bikepackingscotland.com/johnmuirway**
> Southern Upland Way
> Sustrans National Route 1
> Sustrans National Route 76
> Sustrans National Route 196

WHERE TO EAT

> Humbie Hub, Humbie
> Hector's Artisan Pizzeria, Dunbar
> Tyninghame Smithy, Tyninghame
> Drift, Canty Bay, North Berwick
> Steampunk Coffee Roasters, North Berwick

BIKE SHOPS

> Belhaven Bikes, Dunbar (**T** 01368 860 300)
> Law Cycles, North Berwick (**T** 01620 890 643)

WHERE TO STOP

> Ruins of Gamelshiel Castle, NT 650648
> Dunglass Collegiate Church, NT 767719
> Skateraw Harbour, NT 737756
> Barns Ness Lighthouse, NT 723772
> *The DunBear*, NT 684774
> John Muir's Birthplace, NT 679790
> Belhaven Bridge, NT 662789
> World War II barriers, NT 636787
> Ravensheugh Sands, NT 626816
> Seacliff Beach, NT 605845
> Tantallon Castle, NT 596850
> Scottish Seabird Centre, NT 554856
> Yellowcraig Beach, NT 519858
> Gosford House, NT 456791
> Prestongrange Museum, NT 371736

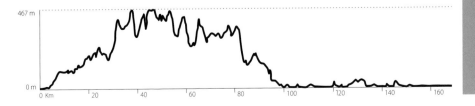

09 MÒR TWEED VALLEY GRAVEL

29KM   ANEELA MCKENNA

With an abundance of tracks, the Tweed Valley is one of Scotland's hottest gravel destinations. This route offers a great mix of off-road riding through woodland and open moorland.

ABOUT ANEELA

Gravel riding for Aneela in three words
old-school mountain biking

'Since the tragedy of the death of George Floyd, since Black Lives Matter, I think the outdoors and cycling community and the industry has really woken up to the fact that we're not very diverse.'

One aspect that follows Aneela McKenna's impressive career in cycling, whether as mountain bike guide and partner of Go-Where Scotland, co-chair of British Cycling's Diversity and Inclusion Advisory Group, or founder of Mòr Diversity, is to increase opportunities for everyone to ride bikes. Having recently left her 'other' career as a public servant, she is now fully concentrating her efforts by working with brands and organisations to help change the face of the outdoors – to make them more inclusive.

'To me, gravel cycling is like old-school mountain biking. I absolutely love it.'

While she appreciates the technical riding that mountain biking offers her, Aneela also loves the new opportunities that picking up a gravel bike offers. Gravel biking comes with the freedom to enjoy all the routes that used to be the access trails for getting to the mountain bike descents, of which the Tweed Valley has plenty.

'My culture didn't really tell me about the outdoors and my husband, who was my partner back then, asked me to go for a ride as a date. And I have not looked back since.'

Living in Glasgow in the late 1990s, where she met her husband Andy, Aneela loved the nearby Tweed Valley so much that she moved there in 2005. Aneela wasn't lucky enough to ride a bike as a child, and many of her friends didn't either – she only started cycling in her twenties when she met Andy. Starting cycling gave her access to the outdoors and it was Andy, who was into BMX and mountain biking, who introduced Aneela to off-road cycling. Many of Aneela's adventures have been joint adventures with Andy, even though Andy was diagnosed with multiple sclerosis in 2007 and lives with the condition.

'We should all work together to try and change the face of cycling and to make it a space where everyone can feel that they belong.'

Cycling grew into Aneela's big passion; she made it her job and became a professional mountain bike guide, taking groups all over Scotland. More recently, she developed into a full-time

DESCENDING INTO GLEN.

Innerleithen

B709

B709

Tweed

Leithen Water

A72

B7062

Lee Pen

Lee Burn Head

Chester

Cardrona

Cardrona Forest

Wallace's Hill

Beards Hill

Castle Hill

Tweed

A72

Kailzie Hill

Kirkhope Law

B7062

Tor Hill

Craig Head

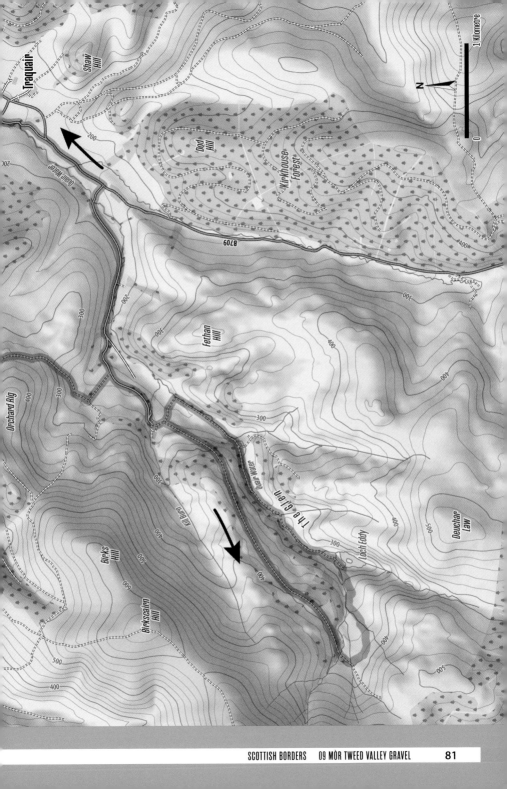

Traquair

Shaw Hill

Dod Hill

Kirkhouse Forest

Quair Water

B709

Fethan Hill

Orchard Rig

Quair Water

The Glen

Loch Eddy

Deuchan Law

Birks Hill

Kirn Law

Birkscairn Hill

N

1 Kilometre

0

NEAR CASTLE KNOWE.

diversity and inclusion consultant. Her work is about welcoming people from all backgrounds to be able to participate in cycling, whether it's businesses, communities, clubs or individuals.

'What's so special about being a guide? I think, for me, it's just seeing the impact it has on people when you get a group of people together and you can take them to places.'

The impact guiding has on people is what Aneela loves most about it. The effect it has, not just in terms of the journey or the ride itself, but also the social interaction and being connected to the environment. She has the ability to show people places they've never been, and enjoys how confident and happy cycling makes them. And does she plan to run any guided gravel experiences? Not yet, but possibly in the future.

ABOUT ANEELA'S ROUTE

The Tweed Valley has been Aneela's home for more than 15 years now, and offers many possibilities for cycling, whether on- or off-road.

There are so many options that parts of this route were new to Aneela, even after spending such a long time riding here. This route gives you a great taste of what this part of Scotland has to offer, with splendid views, extensive forest trails, Scotland's oldest inhabited house and a town that has embraced cycling like no other.

ROUTE DESCRIPTION

Over the last decade the Tweed Valley has become one of the hottest regions for mountain biking in Britain, if not even

BRIDGE OVER THE TWEED ON THE TRAFFIC-FREE TWEED VALLEY RAILWAY PATH.

worldwide. TweedLove has attracted thousands of bike enthusiasts into the region for its annual festival events that run from April to September, including Gritopia, a gravel sportive. The Enduro World Series welcomes the world's enduro elite to Innerleithen, and the two 7Stanes hubs in Glentress and Innerleithen provide some of the best man-made trails in Britain for mountain bikers.

Sandwiched between the two mountain bike hubs of Innerleithen and Glentress lies Cardrona Forest and Glen, a residential community and farm. Glen House was built in the nineteenth century; there are over 30 other residential buildings in the estate. The landscaped parkland and surrounding heather moorland provide a stunning backdrop to this gravel adventure.

Starting at No1 Peebles Road, a friendly cafe in the heart of Innerleithen, the route is served by one of the only bike-friendly bus services in Scotland. The X62 connects Edinburgh with the towns of the Scottish Borders, with most services offering two or four bike spaces per bus. If you'd like to experience Scotland's industrial heritage first-hand, Robert Smail's Printing Works is a fully functional Victorian-era letterpress printing works, now preserved by the National Trust for Scotland as a museum. Located only a short distance from the start on the High Street, it shows visitors the operation of a local printer at the turn of the twentieth century; they run regular workshops if you fancy having a go.

The route follows Traquair Road, and then turns right on to the Tweed Valley Railway Path, an old

GLENSHIEL BANKS ON THE CAPITAL TRAIL.

railway line along the River Tweed. The River Tweed lends its name to the world-famous tweed cloth and is one of the most important salmon rivers of Britain. This traffic-free route takes you on tarmac all the way into Cardrona, crossing a very scenic bridge and passing a small pump track at the edge of the village.

The route leaves the cycle trail at a roundabout and continues on a small road out of Cardrona to meet the B7062 at the next junction. It follows this road to the parking and picnic area at the edge of Cardrona Forest at Kirkburn. This is where the fabulous Tweed Valley gravel starts. For those with more time on their hands, Cardrona Forest offers many peaceful walks, gentle gravel tracks and some

great horse riding to explore further. You can spot red squirrels and a wide variety of birdlife; Cardrona Tower, now a ruin but still home to a colony of bats, and the site of an Iron Age fort at Castle Knowe are also worth a visit.

The route follows a track into the forest, which meets a forest road that climbs steadily towards Orchard Rig. The riding here is superb for gravel bikes. The route reaches its highest point at the intersection with another forest road, and then descends on a 4x4 track out of the forest and on to open moorland. The views from the track are superb on a good day, and make up for a few more rutted sections to follow on this track. After a sheepfold, the route follows the

DISTANCE **29km/18 miles** 〉 ASCENT **483m/1,585 ft** 〉 GRADE **Straightforward** 〉 START/FINISH **No1 Peebles Road, Innerleithen**
START/FINISH GRID REF **NT 330366** 〉 BIKE-FRIENDLY PUBLIC TRANSPORT **At the start** 〉 HIGHEST POINT **407m/1,335 ft** 〉 TERRAIN **Fast-flowing riding with some technical sections through open moorland and forested areas** 〉 RECOMMENDED TYRES **Schwalbe G-One Bite**

BEST TIME TO RIDE

| JAN | FEB | MAR | APR | MAY | JUN | JUL | AUG | SEP | OCT | NOV | DEC |

SINGLETRACK **10%**   PATH **40%**   CYCLE PATH **15%**   ROAD **35%**

Cross Borders Drove Road for a short while, and then a short section of tarmac into Glen.

The next section of the loop follows the Capital Trail, a popular bikepacking route through the Scottish Borders and East Lothian, passing Glen House and climbing gradually towards the end of this extensive valley. Glen House is a stunning Scots baronial house, built in the nineteenth century by the Scottish industrialist and MP Charles Tennant. Described as the Bill Gates of his time, Tennant was only 29 years old when he bought Glen. The route passes various woodlands on the way to Glenshiel Banks, from where our route leaves the Capital Trail to follow a track across the heather and shortly afterwards descends on a quite rugged and technical path to Loch Eddy. A man-made loch developed in the 1880s, it's no surprise that this tranquil spot has charmed many visitors. Its name is said to derive from the war poet Edward Tennant, grandson of Charles Tennant of Glen House, who was killed at the Battle of the Somme during World War I.

From the loch, a well-surfaced track takes you back to Glen House, from where a small road continues through Glen, following the route of the Cross Borders Drove Road again. From Kirkhouse, the route follows the B709 for a short section then turns on to a minor road through Traquair Mill. The route then joins the B7062 for a short distance, before joining a private road to Traquair, which is Scotland's oldest inhabited house, dating back to 1107. Traquair, which has been home to the Stuart family since 1491, has been visited by an impressive 27 Scottish kings and queens over the years. The house is worth a visit, and the Garden Cafe offers a great incentive to stop. Shortly after crossing the Quair Water, the route follows a newly built gravel path, which meets the main road near the River Tweed, and takes you back to the start in Innerleithen.

OTHER ROUTES NEARBY

> Bike Valley Trails (download fee)
> Capital Trail
> Cross Borders Drove Road
> Southern Upland Way
> Sustrans National Route 1
> Tweed Valley Railway Path
> 7Stanes Glentress and Innerleithen

WHERE TO EAT

> No1 Peebles Road, Innerleithen
> Loulabelles, Innerleithen
> Nashy's Coffee House, Cardrona
> Garden Cafe, Traquair

BIKE SHOPS AND TOURS

> The Bike Shop, Innerleithen (T 07770 974 201)
> Tweed Valley Bikes, Innerleithen (T 01896 831 429)
> i-Cycles, Innerleithen (T 01896 829 680)
> Go-Where Scotland (guided rides), Clovenfords, www.go-where.co.uk

WHERE TO STOP

> Robert Smail's Printing Works, NT 332367
> Tweed Valley Railway Path bridge, NT 308380
> Glen House (not open to public), NT 298331
> Loch Eddy, NT 281309
> Traquair, NT 331355

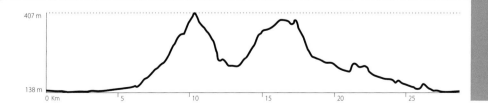

10 RAIDERS GRAVEL

82KM ESTHER TACKE AND WARREN SAUNDERS

Galloway Forest, the largest forest in Britain and its first ever Dark Sky Park, is a fantastic gravel paradise. This route offers a long day in the saddle or the opportunity to enjoy the starlit skies on an overnighter.

ABOUT ESTHER AND WARREN

Gravel riding for Esther in three words
fun; space; headspace

Gravel riding for Warren in three words
linking interesting places

'Galloway Forest is 300 square miles of unintentional gravel paradise.'
Shortly after Esther Tacke and Warren Saunders came back from a round-the-world trip a few years ago, they visited Dumfries and Galloway, and instantly fell in love with the area. Looking for a new home, they moved close to Kirkcudbright and bought a business offering guided cycle tours. They then started incorporating gravel cycling holidays into their offering, alongside classic road cycling holidays.

'We were actually coming from the road cycling scene, and during wintertime it was just not very nice to be out on the roads. We absolutely loved gravel cycling! We could actually go out in wintertime and just ride.'
As Warren was watching what was happening in the bike sphere, both Esther and Warren thought it would be interesting to pick up some gravel bikes, mainly because of the forestry paths and tracks in the surrounding area that could provide for an alternative riding in winter. For them, gravel bikes were the opportunity to cycle in all seasons – and they both got hooked.

'Just because it's not known, it doesn't mean it's not good.'
Because of their own experience with gravel cycling, Warren and Esther were looking into how they could promote Dumfries and Galloway for cycling. They knew it was brilliant but, in their eyes, others didn't. When Golazo, a big events promoter, was looking for an area for potential gravel cycling events for an article, they jumped on the chance

straight away. Warren picked up the telephone, and the idea of Raiders Gravel was born.

'It is such an amazing place to take out the bike, and just experience this gravel. The vision is that people from all over the world enjoy this place as a gravel playground.'
Organising the Raiders Gravel event is not a one-off for them, but part of a wider strategy to grow Dumfries and Galloway into a centre that is of world-class quality, with the community at the heart of the idea. The Galloway Forest Park and the biosphere community offer the perfect backdrop for all sorts of cycling, but it is the gravel riding that has the most potential for Esther. Growing Raiders Gravel organically, she hopes that in 5 years' time more than 1,000 teams

GLENCAP FOREST.

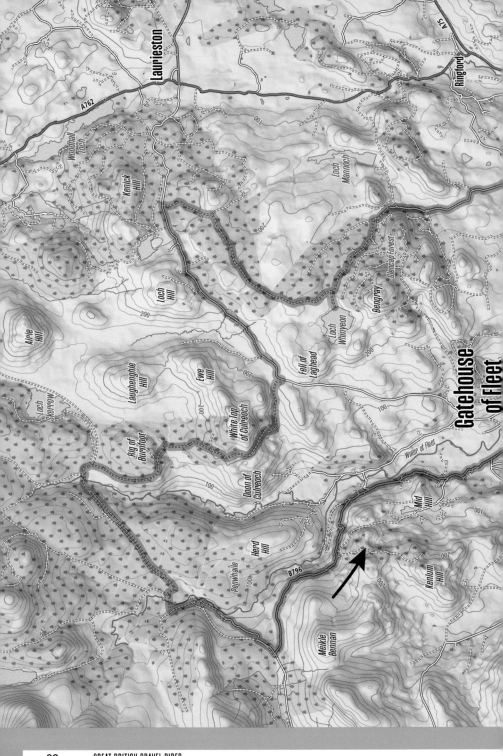

Laurieston

Ringford

A75

A762

Woodhall Loch

Kenick Hill

Loch Mannoch

Glenlap Forest

Bengray

Loch Hill

Loch Whinyeon

Fell of Laghead

Airie Hill

Loch Skerrow

Laughenghie Hill

Ewe Hill

White Top of Culreoch

Rig of Burnfoot

Doon of Culreoch

Water of Fleet

Gatehouse of Fleet

Mid Hill

Kenlum Hill

Herd Hill

Penwhaile

B796

Meikle Bennan

100

200

200

200

200

200

200

100

100

100

100

100

200

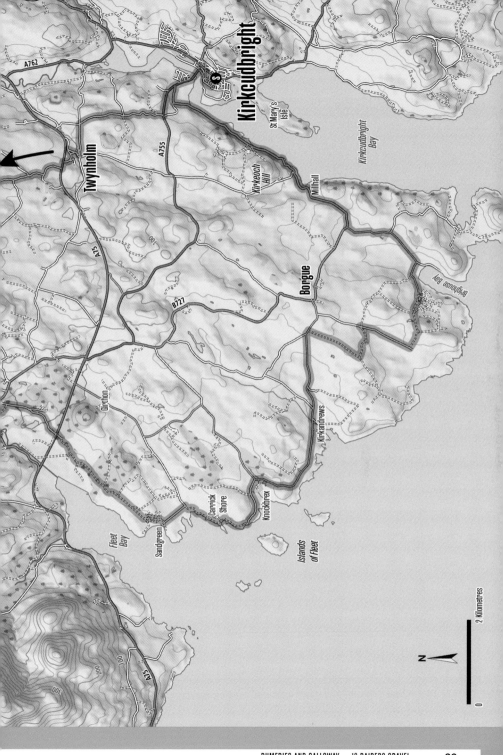

Kirkcudbright

St Mary's Isle

Kirkcudbright Bay

Twynholm

A762

A755

Kirkeoch Hill

Millhall

Borgue

Brighouse Bay

A75

B727

Kirkandrews

Girthon

Kirkardrews

Knockbrex

Carrick Shore

Sandgreen

Fleet Bay

Islands of Fleet

A75

N

0

2 Kilometres

BIG WATER OF FLEET VIADUCT.

will flock to the area and see what a great playground Esther and Warren can enjoy daily.

'I just think women should have fun, and can have fun. For women, it's a really easy way to get into cycling as well.'

The magic thing about gravel cycling for Esther is that it can be enjoyed, even for someone at the beginning of the cycling journey. And as a woman she is happy to 'hold the flag' and inspire not just other women into the sport, but also anybody else. Gravel cycling is all encompassing; no one is left out.

ABOUT ESTHER AND WARREN'S ROUTE

Mountains, moorland, trees, rivers, streams, and the sea – this description from Warren fits perfectly. This is a long day in the saddle, but there is amazing scenery and beautiful sandy beaches to admire, along with some of the world's best ice cream to keep you going. Most of the gravel in this route is smooth and not very technical, so it's a great route to help you make the transition from shorter into longer gravel rides. Esther and Warren also run guided tours on this route, and part of this loop is featured in their event, Raiders Gravel.

ROUTE DESCRIPTION

Kirkcudbright, a small town in Dumfries and Galloway, has long been a centre for artists and is now known as the 'Artists' Town'. The roadside signs when entering the town include colourful dots on a painter's pallet, and there are artists' studios across the town.

The route starts at the Selkirk Arms in the centre of town. After following the High Street, it continues for a short while on Sustrans National Route 7 across the River Dee. Sustrans National Route 7 forms the southern part of the Lochs and Glens Way cycling route from Glasgow to Inverness.

The route continues on the A755 and then follows a small road on the right towards Sourhill, and passes a few houses and areas of woodland along the way. Still on tarmac, it continues through Twynholm, the birthplace of David Coulthard, a former Formula One racing driver. A small museum dedicated to Coulthard in the premises of the Cocoabean Company, a family-run chocolate factory, had to close in 2018, but for those who are after a sweet treat, the factory is just a short detour off the route on the A75, which the route joins for a brief section shortly after the village.

The route follows another small road north to Glengap, from where the first proper gravel section starts. The route passes a few houses first, and then follows a smooth gravel track through Glencap Forest. The route climbs gradually out of the forest and turns off to Loch Whinyeon, a small reservoir on the edge of the forest. Constructed in the eighteenth century, the water from the reservoir was once used to power cotton mills in Gatehouse of Fleet. Nowadays the reservoir is used for water storage and is also a trout fishing lake.

Returning the same way from the loch, the wide gravel track is joined again, which climbs to the highest point of the route at 241 metres, with great views across the surrounding countryside. The route enters a woodland again shortly afterwards and descends through Laurieston Forest towards a quiet road. The road climbs gradually at first, parallel to the Kenick Burn, and then descends through a dense woodland. The woodland gives way to open moorland for the next part of the route, with Corbie Craig and the Fell of Laghead dominating the views ahead.

Underneath Corbie Craig, a gravel road to the right is followed, which descends towards the Castramont Burn first and then climbs out of the valley and into a woodland. From where the route enters the woodland, a descent follows all the way down to the Little Water of Fleet. From here, the line of the former Portpatrick Railway is followed, which once connected Castle Douglas and Portpatrick and was intended to revive a transport link to the north of Ireland via sea from Portpatrick. Due to its connection to Ireland, the line became known as the Paddy.

The route follows a smooth gravel track along the former railway line, then leaves its path to connect with Sustrans National Route 7 just before the Big Water of Fleet. Still on very good gravel tracks, it passes under the impressive Big Water of Fleet Viaduct, a disused 275-metre-long single-track viaduct with 20 arches, standing at a height of 21 metres. The viaduct piers are encased in red brick,

GALLOWAY SCENERY.

giving it an unusual appearance.

After another short section of gravel, the route follows the Big Water of Fleet and climbs gradually on a tarmac road on Sustrans National Route 7 to New Rusko, the halfway point of the route. From here the riding gets easier, as there is much less climbing in the second half of the route. It is almost all downhill to Gatehouse of Fleet on the road, still following the Sustrans route. The road switches between open countryside with great views and stunning sections of woodland, before the route descends into the town.

The imposing Cardoness Castle, a well-preserved fifteenth-century tower house, is a short detour away to the south-west. Gatehouse of Fleet has the look of an eighteenth-century cotton mill town; it was reputedly used by Sir Walter Scott as a model for the fictional Kippletringan in his novel *Guy Mannering*. The town is located near the mouth of the Water of Fleet, which then empties into Fleet Bay and on into Wigtown Bay. The town is on the site of a 'gait house' (toll booth) on the stagecoach route from Dumfries to Stranraer (the modern day A75), which, along with the name of the river, led to the town's name. Gatehouse of Fleet was a haven along this eighteenth-century stagecoach route: there were numerous highwaymen and bandits active along the road, so travellers would frequently choose to stop in the relative safely of the town, rather than venturing further and travelling at night.

The Mill on the Fleet, a great example of a former working mill, is very close to the route. It was built in 1788 as a cotton spinning mill and restored as a visitor and exhibition centre by Dumfries and Galloway Council in the 1980s; it also houses a tourist information centre. Gatehouse of Fleet is the start and finish of the Raiders Gravel multi-day gravel cycling event, held at the end of August. With great places to eat and stock up in town, Gatehouse of Fleet would also provide a great alternative starting point for this route.

The route continues on Sustrans National Route 7 through the Arkland Plantation along Cally Avenue to Cally Palace, which was previously known as Cally House; this eighteenth-century country house is now a hotel and golf resort. The riding through the woodland is fabulous. Shortly after the hotel, the route leaves Sustrans National Route 7 and continues on a gravel track through Laundry Wood and Cally Mains Wood, and through a holiday park to Sandgreen. The views from the track over open countryside and across Fleet Bay are stunning.

If you are into swimming or want to cool down on a hot summer's day, the beaches on the next stretch of the route are very clean. Fleet Bay is very shallow, so there is a large area of beach at low tide. In sunny weather, the sea comes back in over the heated sand, which then warms the sea up nicely. At low tide, a walk out to the offshore islands is another great idea, but please carefully check tide times to avoid getting stranded.

A short section on a road follows. The nearby Cream o' Galloway Ice Cream Parlour is spectacular,

and just a short detour from the route. To get there, continue on tarmac where the route branches off to the right.

Shortly after turning right, the route follows another gravel track past the Shorefield Scout Campsite. The gravel track continues to Carrick Shore, another fine sandy bay backed by chalets, with a rather stony bay on each side of it. At Isle Mouth, the route continues on a road to rejoin Sustrans National Route 7, and then passing Knockbrex Castle, now a holiday rental property.

Continuing along the coast, the route passes Coo Palace. This listed building was constructed in the early twentieth century by James Brown, co-founder of a Manchester department store, to house his prized Belted Galloway cows (you'll probably spot this breed of cows along the route). Following Brown's death in 1920, Coo Palace deteriorated, but

DISTANCE **82km/51 miles** › ASCENT **679m/2,228 ft** › GRADE **Expert** › START/FINISH **Selkirk Arms, Kirkcudbright** › START/FINISH GRID REF **NX 683508** › BIKE-FRIENDLY PUBLIC TRANSPORT **Dumfries railway station (45km from the route)** › HIGHEST POINT **241m/791 ft** › TERRAIN **Wide gravel roads through forests mixed with roads along beaches and open moorland; mostly sheltered** › RECOMMENDED TYRES **Schwalbe G-One Allround**

BEST TIME TO RIDE

| JAN | FEB | MAR | APR | MAY | JUN | JUL | AUG | SEP | OCT | NOV | DEC |

PATH **30%**   ROAD **70%**

GREEN, ROLLING HILLS ON THE ROAD TO GATEHOUSE OF FLEET.

has since been refurbished and turned into luxury holiday apartments.

At Chapelton Row, the route leaves Sustrans National Route 7 again for another excursion to the coast on gravel tracks and tarmac lanes. Passing a few houses, the route reaches the Graplin Plantation and passes Brighouse Bay. Set in a quiet, secluded peninsula, the bay boasts magnificent views and a great array of outdoor activities. From the bay, the route follows a road north to meet up with Sustrans National Route 7 once again. From Nun Mill Bay the route sweeps along Kirkcudbright Bay and the mouth of the River Dee, all on road. There are great views from here towards St Mary's Isle, a narrow peninsula that separates Manxman's Lake to the east from Goat Well Bay to the west, and on to Kirkcudbright. The route crosses the River Dee and then follows quiet roads through town back to the Selkirk Arms.

OTHER ROUTES NEARBY
> Lochs and Glens Way (Sustrans National Route 7)

WHERE TO EAT
> Selkirk Arms, Kirkcudbright
> The Crafty Crow, Gatehouse of Fleet
> Cream o' Galloway Ice Cream Parlour, Rainton

BIKE SHOPS
> Galloway Cycling Holidays, Castle Douglas, **www.gallowaygravelholidays.com**
> WM Law (bike hire), Kirkcudbright

WHERE TO STOP
> Loch Whinyeon, NX 629609
> Big Water of Fleet Viaduct, NX 558643
> Cardoness Castle, NX 590553
> Mill on the Fleet, NX 599564
> Airds Bay, NX 577521
> Coo Palace, NX 591485
> Brighouse Bay, NX 636459
> MacLellan's Castle, NX 682511

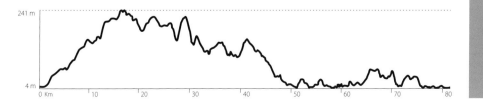

NORTHERN ENGLAND

11 TYNE AND WEAR GRAVEL

94KM OLLY TOWNSEND AND FRANCIS KING

This urban adventure mixes industrial heritage, modern and Victorian architecture and old railway lines with the charm and beauty of the County Durham coastline.

ABOUT OLLY AND FRANCIS

Gravel riding for Olly in three words
fun; flexible; local

Gravel riding for Francis in three words
traffic-free; fun; explore

'We are fortunate in the North East that we have an amazing industrial heritage: all the old waggonways and railway lines are perfect for gravel riding, with bridleways and other trails mixed in as well.'

Olly Townsend and Francis King are friends and call Newcastle upon Tyne their home. They love riding the local gravel trails. Both also have a professional connection with gravel cycling: Olly as the editor of *Gravel Union*, one of the leading websites in the UK that covers all things gravel, from bikes and people to events, and Francis as a bike guide who works across the UK and further afield with Saddle Skedaddle.

'It just gave that sense of wow factor, even if it was trails that were on your doorstep. It just makes fairly tame trails feel fun.'

Both are enthusiastic about the wide variety of different types of riding that there is in the Newcastle and Sunderland area – a region that has a high population density. Particularly during the Covid-19 lockdowns, a gravel bike was the perfect tool for them to ride, as they could cycle straight from their front doors. They couldn't, and didn't have to, drive anywhere first. There was no need to ride anything super gnarly. A gravel bike offered them all the fun they needed.

'My crystal ball: gravel riding will probably differentiate itself in the same way that mountain biking has.'

For Olly, gravel cycling will possibly head into the same direction as mountain biking did over the last couple of decades. At one end of the spectrum there'll be the more road-based gravel riding, which attracts

riders who make the transition from road bikes, or beginners. At the other end of the spectrum there will be the 'slightly more hardcore', Grinduro-style type of riding, which really pushes the technical skills of a rider. And in between there is the riding from your front door, exploring the local urban trails. Different bikes for different niches, instead of one that fits all.

For Francis the rise of gravel bikes has given hybrid bikes a new lease of life. This is what he experiences when guiding people. But putting gravel bikes in the same box as hybrid bikes doesn't work either, as gravel bikes are much lighter and much more fun to ride.

'We are riding similar trails but with way better technology.'

So, for two people that have

PREVIOUS PAGE VALLEY BETWEEN LONSCALE FELL AND BLEASE FELL (ROUTE 12).
OPPOSITE MILLENNIUM BRIDGE AND THE BALTIC CENTRE FOR CONTEMPORARY ART.

NEWCASTLE AND SUNDERLAND   11 TYNE AND WEAR GRAVEL   **97**

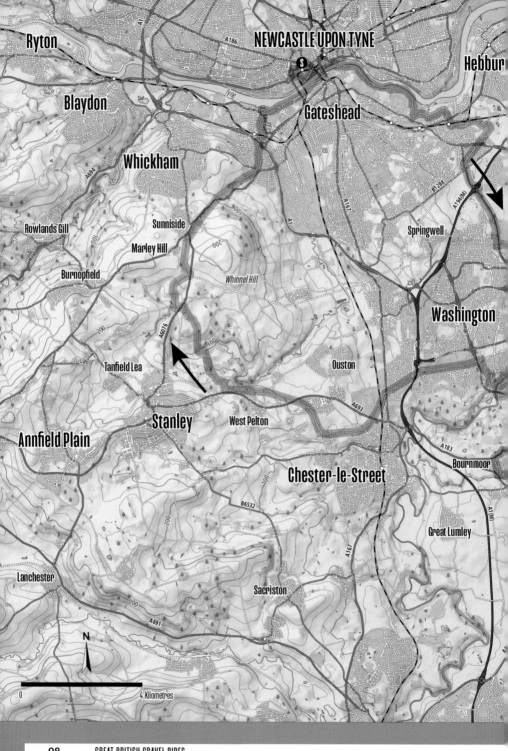

North
Sea

Jarrow

tunnels

Cleadon

Whitburn

West Boldon

A184

A1290

A1231

Wear

SUNDERLAND

A183

100

A1018

Penshaw

A690

A19

100

Houghton-le-Spring

Seaham

Windmill Hill

Murton

B1285

Hetton-le-Hole

Batter Law
Hill

A19

Pittington Hill

A182

RIVER WEAR NEAR COX GREEN.

extensive experience with gravel bikes, the question 'are we going around in circles with gravel bikes?' seems a fitting one.

Are gravel bikes not much more than 1990s mountain bikes, just with a different price tag? The clear answer from them both is 'no'. Gravel bikes are much more confident. The geometry is better, and the equipment on them is way better: disc brakes, gears that work and tubeless tyres. While the trails to enjoy them haven't changed much, the bikes have.

ABOUT OLLY AND FRANCIS' ROUTE

This route has the ingredients of a classic doorstep ride. Both Olly and Francis have ridden this route many times, but rediscovered it recently during the Covid-19 lockdowns. Looking at the various types of riders Olly describes, this ride suits the urban, trail-exploring rider. The riding isn't always picturesque; at times it is grubby and industrial. Newcastle and the wider Tyne and Wear area have a long industrial past, and this is reflected in this route. But there are immensely beautiful places along the route as well, like the coastline at Seaham and the many bridges

that have shaped Newcastle's appearance over the years.

ROUTE DESCRIPTION

Newcastle upon Tyne, often simply called Newcastle, is the largest city and metropolitan borough in North East England, situated in one of the most populous urban areas in the United Kingdom. The city, situated on the River Tyne's northern bank, is famous for the seven bridges, within a 2-kilometre stretch of river, across to Gateshead, on the southern bank of the river. The Millennium Bridge, opened in

ON A LANE NEAR SEAHAM.

2001, is the youngest of the seven. This elegant foot and cycle bridge is notable as it tilts to allow ships to pass under it. Swing Bridge, crossed at the end of this urban gravel adventure, opened in 1876; at the time of construction, it was the largest swing bridge ever built. The city is also the home of Greggs, a British bakery chain most famous for its sausage rolls and, more recently, vegan sausage rolls.

The route starts right in the centre of Newcastle upon Tyne at the railway station. It follows a number of roads to the river, joining Sustrans National Route 72, better known as Hadrian's Cycleway, for a while. This long-distance cycling route traces the line of the Roman frontier from Ravenglass in Cumbria to South Shields in Tyne and Wear. Impressive architecture can be admired as the route passes the Queen Elizabeth II Bridge first, then the High Level Bridge, Swing Bridge

and Tyne Bridge, before it crosses the river at Millennium Bridge.

On the southern side of the river, you'll see the BALTIC Centre for Contemporary Art. Since it opened its doors in July 2002, over 226 exhibitions of work have been presented by 476 artists of 64 nationalities and over 8 million people have visited. The futuristic Sage Gateshead, a concert venue and centre for musical education, dominates the view towards the west, while the route continues eastbound on Sustrans National Route 14 after passing BALTIC. The route follows South Shore Road and then continues on a cycle path. It briefly ventures off Sustrans National Route 14 at Friars Goose and shortcuts along a bridleway. This section isn't the most scenic riding, but it is necessary to get the better parts. At Gosforth Terrace the route leaves Sustrans National Route 14

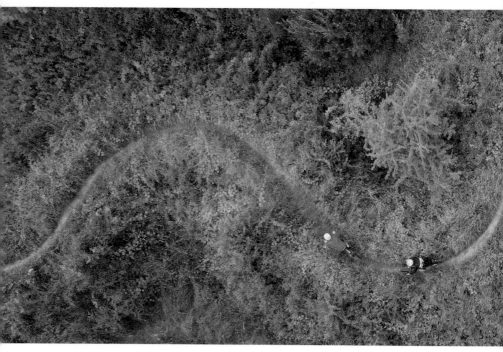

THE LAMBTON WORM SECTION OF SINGLETRACK.

and continues on a number of roads to Pelaw, and shortly afterwards another cycle path is followed parallel to the railway line. The route leaves the tracks behind and joins the Bowes Railway Path.

At Lingey Lane the route follows a cycle path next to the road and continues on this to Follingsby Interchange. Right after Sunderland College the route crosses the A195 (Northumberland Way) and continues on quiet residential streets through Sulgrave. The route passes through a big industrial area, across Sunderland Highway and eventually ends up on Sustrans National Route 7. This section is also part of the UK's most popular challenge cycle route, C2C, short for 'Sea to Sea'. This route travels between the Irish Sea and the North Sea from Cumbria to Tyneside. At Cox Green the route leaves Sustrans National Route 7 and crosses the Wear on a footbridge. The route passes a pub, and then follows a quiet road to meet a multi-purpose gravel path at Coxgreen Gill. The path ends at New Penshaw, where roads are followed through the town.

Penshaw Monument is clearly visible from here. This memorial, which sits on Penshaw Hill, is in the style of an ancient Greek temple; it has been owned by the National Trust since 1939 and commemorates John Lambton, the first Earl of Durham. The route doesn't go directly

past the monument, but it is worth a short detour on foot. The route crosses Chester Road and continues on a wide gravel path through Herrington Country Park and on another path into Middle Herrington. A number of roads follow, before the route joins Sustrans National Route 70, which forms the principal part of Walney to Wear, another coast-to-coast route, from Walney Island to the River Wear in Sunderland. Near Burdon the route continues on quiet country lanes and on a great path to join the North Sea Cycle Route (EuroVelo 12 – on this section it follows Sustrans National Route 1) just outside Seaham. There are a couple of

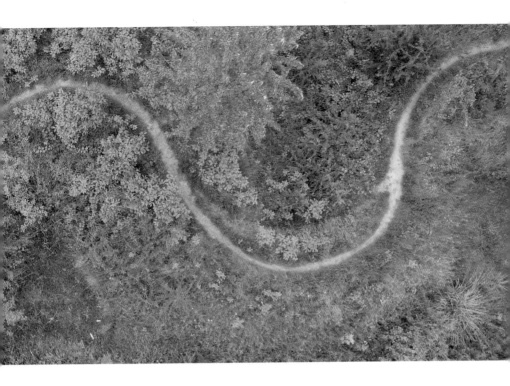

shortcuts where our route deviates from this slightly, but we follow the North Sea Cycle Route most of the way into Seaham, a seaside town located on the Durham Coast. As a result of investments in its coal mines and harbour, the town grew from the late nineteenth century onwards.

The most memorable feature on the Seaham seafront is *1101*, locally known as *Tommy*, a larger-than-life-size statue by artist Ray Lonsdale of a World War I soldier with a rusty red patina. Wearing his uniform of a greatcoat and tin hat and holding his grounded rifle, the soldier rests on an ammunition box while enjoying the first minute of peace as the armistice came into force at 11.00 a.m. on 11 November 1918. Seaham Chippy is not far away from the shore, and there are a number of places to eat in the Seaham Harbour Marina. Flamingo Bar and Cafe is recommended for its food and location, as you'll get great views on to Featherbed Rocks and the small, sandy beach in front.

The route now follows a bridleway to Nose's Point, a Site of Special Scientific Interest both for its geology and ecology. The views from here on to the dramatic and rugged coastline with its cliffs and sea stacks carved out by the action of the waves are second to none. The route travels on a cycle path away from the coast to rejoin Sustrans National Route 1 for a short while, and then continues on to reach East Murton; you'll have done more than half of the route by now. Follow some singletrack and another cycle path into Hetton Lyons Country Park. This picturesque park on the site of a former colliery, just on the outskirts of Hetton-le-Hole, features a small sporting lake. You'll join Sustrans National Route 70 again here; the riding in the park is great, following smooth gravel paths all the way.

Nothing remains of the mining industry of Hetton-le-Hole, where coal was mined from Roman times into the 1950s. Shortly after the town the route leaves Sustrans National Route 70 and follows

THERE IS NO SHORTAGE OF BRIDGES IN NEWCASTLE.

a trail to East Rainton, and further on through Rainton Meadows Nature Reserve to Chilton Moor. Rainton Meadows was created by the restoration of the Rye Hill opencast coal mine in 1996. The route joins tarmac roads from Chilton Moor to Lambton, crosses a woodland and continues on roads through Bournmoor.

The route follows the Weardale Way through Lambton Park alongside the A182, and then crosses the Wear at Worm Hill. The Lambton Worm is a fable that involved John Lambton and his battle with a giant worm (or dragon) that had been terrorising the local villages. As with most myths, details of the story change with each telling. The legend inspired a short, and nowadays quite overgrown, section of singletrack, north of Chester-le-Street, which we pass once our route has joined Sustrans National Route 7 again on the Consett and Sunderland Railway Path.

This former railway route is followed all the way to Beamish, famous for its open-air museum; Beamish is a living museum showcasing urban and rural life in North East England in the early twentieth century.

Following the Beamish Loop for a while, the route continues on a road past the golf course, and with a stiff climb on Coppy Lane through the tranquil Coppy Wood to Causey New Row. From here a final climb on a gravel track leads to Marley Hill, where shortly afterwards the highest point of the route is reached at 176 metres. It's all downhill from here to Sunniside, where a cycle path is joined that leads all the way back to the banks of the Tyne. At Dunston Staiths the route rejoins Sustrans National Route 14.

The wooden coal staiths, which first opened in 1893 as a structure for loading coal from the Durham coalfield on to ships, are reputed to be the largest wooden structure in Europe. Along with the decline

DISTANCE **94km/58 miles** ⟩ ASCENT **786m/2,579 ft** ⟩ GRADE **Expert** ⟩ START/FINISH **Newcastle upon Tyne railway station** ⟩ START/FINISH GRID REF **NZ 246639** ⟩ BIKE-FRIENDLY PUBLIC TRANSPORT **At the start** ⟩ HIGHEST POINT **176m/577 ft** ⟩ TERRAIN **Urban gravel riding without remote sections. Section near and along the coast can be very windy** ⟩ RECOMMENDED TYRES **Schwalbe G-One Allround**

BEST TIME TO RIDE

| JAN | FEB | MAR | APR | MAY | JUN | JUL | AUG | SEP | OCT | NOV | DEC |

SINGLETRACK **10%**   PATH **20%**   CYCLE PATH **45%**   ROAD **25%**

in the coal industry, the staiths' output also declined; they were closed and partially dismantled in 1980. In 2003, a section of the staiths was destroyed by fire. It is not possible to access the staiths themselves; they can be viewed from a riverside walkway, constructed as part of the Staiths South Bank development. Alternatively, you can also marvel at this stunning piece of architecture with a coffee and cake in The Staiths Cafe.

The route follows the riverside walkway and a short section of road to Swing Bridge. Since its completion in 1876, it is estimated that the bridge has swung around 300,000 times to allow approximately 500,000 boats to pass through, although since November 2019 it has technically been unused. Cross the bridge and follow The Close and Hanover Street to return to the start.

OTHER ROUTES NEARBY
> Beamish Loop
> C2C (Sea to Sea)
> Consett and Sunderland Railway Path
> Hadrian's Cycleway (Sustrans National Route 72)
> North Sea Cycle Route (Sustrans National Route 1)
> Sustrans National Route 7
> Sustrans National Route 14
> Walney to Wear (Sustrans National Route 70)

WHERE TO EAT
> Coffee on the Quayside, Newcastle upon Tyne
> The Cycle Hub, Newcastle upon Tyne
> Greggs, Peel Retail Park, Washington
> Flamingo Bar and Cafe, Seaham
> Seaham Chippy, Seaham
> Kings Delicatessen, Hetton-le-Hole
> Stables Bar and Restaurant, Beamish
> The Staiths Cafe, Gateshead

BIKE SHOPS
> The Cycle Hub, Newcastle upon Tyne (**T** 01912 767 250)
> Backyard Bike Shop, Gateshead (**T** 07519 098 963)

WHERE TO STOP
> Millennium Bridge, NZ 257640
> BALTIC Centre for Contemporary Art, NZ 258639
> Penshaw Monument, NZ 334544
> *1101* (*Tommy*), NZ 430496
> Nose's Point, NZ 437479
> Lambton Worm, NZ 298544
> Beamish, NZ 220539
> Dunston Staiths, NZ 234626
> Swing Bridge, NZ 252637

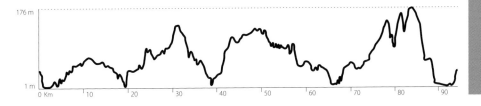

CHALLENGING

LAKE DISTRICT

12 LAKES GRAVEL

40KM   JAIMI WILSON

*A rugged gravel route away from the busier parts of the
Lake District, with challenging climbs and beautiful descents.*

ABOUT JAIMI

Gravel riding for Jaimi in three words
fun; freedom; more fun

*'Had I performed in exactly the same way
but came last, I would have still had exactly
the same experiences and learned the
same lessons. The only difference would
have been the result, so it's quite important not to get caught up in external
measures of success.'*

Jaimi Wilson stunned the bikepacking world with a third-place finish
at GBDURO in 2021, posting the fastest women's time when she arrived
at the John o' Groats signpost, which marks the end of one of Britain's
most challenging gravel races. While her voice sounded happy, there
was a small hint of disappointment, as second place had been in sight
for Jaimi. But as GBDURO was only her second ultra-race, and Jaimi didn't
have any idea of how she would measure up against others, this was not
only an excellent result, but an amazing experience for the round-the-
world cyclist.

The race was an interesting one. Jaimi was one of two round-the-
world cyclists taking part, who had not yet properly dipped their toes into
the breezy ocean of endurance bikepacking races, but had a wealth of
experience otherwise. She lined up at Land's End, Britain's most southerly
start for any bike adventure, with Mark Beaumont and a field of 45 other
starters. Just before the end, a mechanical problem took the leader out,
and Mark Beaumont's time of 5 days, 15 hours and 24 minutes became
the winning time. While Mark had been a comfortable second all along,
the race for third and fourth between Ollie Hayward and Jaimi was much
tighter. Riding more slowly than Ollie during stage 1, Jaimi gained a
massive 10-hour lead on stage 2, the most technical of the stages. It was
Ollie who made another big gain on stage 3, and he also managed to ride

2 hours faster than Jaimi on stage
4, which in the end secured him
the second place and Jaimi the
third fastest time overall.

*'In some ways I was naive, but
I was excited about the massive
challenge, eager to learn and pretty
confident in my ability to give it a
good go. I had a rough idea of the
route I wanted to take but you have
to be flexible and willing to adapt
as you go.'*

Jaimi's love for gravel bikes
and her confidence on tricky and
challenging terrain doesn't really
come as a surprise, as her home
trails are just that – challenging.
She just recently made the switch
to gravel riding, but is no stranger
to cycling, after spending over
3 years cycling around the world
on her own. She doesn't wait long
to tackle a new challenge, and
riding GBDURO was just that.
Her round-the-world trip took her
from her home in Penrith across
Europe and Asia, then across

THE TRAIL TOWARDS SKIDDAW HOUSE.

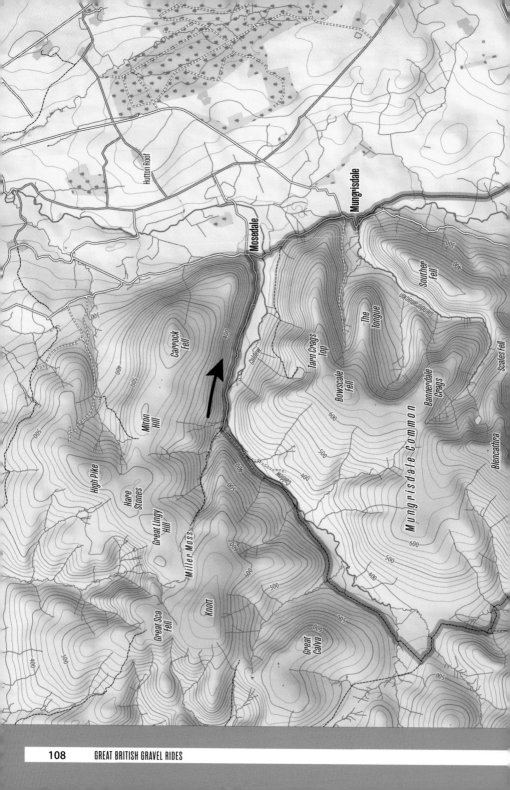

Hutton Roof

Mungrisdale

Mosedale

Souther Fell

Carrock Fell

The Tongue

Tarn Crags Top

Bowscale Fell

Bannerdale Crags

Scales Fell

Milton Hill

Caldew

Mungrisdale Common

Blencathra

High Pike

Hare Stones

Great Lingy Hill

Grainsgill

Miller Moss

Knott

Great Sea Fell

Great Calva

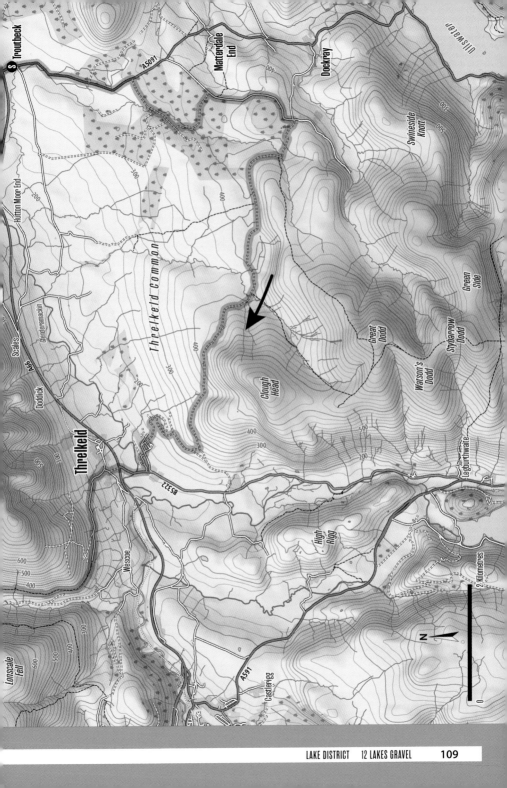

ROAD FROM SWINESIDE TO MOSEDALE.

Australia, where she spent some time working. From there she cycled across South America and the US, and finally back home to the Lakes. The whole trip was planned in a 3-month period, and upon leaving Jaimi had never been on a fully loaded touring bike, wild camped, used a camping stove, repaired a puncture or been to a non-English-speaking country alone.

'I've been around the world on my bike, and some of the gravel sections were the most memorable, because they were the most remote.'

So how did her first gravel race compare to the 3 years she spent cycling around the world? The sleep deprivation was the worst bit, but riding around the world was harder. When cycling in remote areas, her bike weighed around 60 kilograms fully loaded. Her gravel bike was the exact opposite, weighing in at a sixth of that weight, or a fourth if fully loaded. So, what did she think about her first gravel race? She loved it.

'It's a little bit less intimidating than mountain biking. I love how easily accessible it is. You can link up little pieces of road, and I think it is definitely a lot more approachable. If I am going to hurt myself, I'll be the one to hurt myself.'

For Jaimi, gravel riding is much more chilled; she has more time to enjoy it. It's a bit like riding around the world: it offers her the chance to explore new terrain and provides a different routine from most of her rides on the road, which are often out of the saddle, in the saddle. On her road bike she can be very focussed on keeping the speed up, so doesn't take in as much in around her. After a year of gravel riding, she'd rather just get out on the trails instead these days, escaping the heavy traffic

that can often be found on the roads in the Lakes.

'The thing about the Lake District is that there is not a lot of smooth, easy gravel. You've got to look around and link up certain sections, and I really like doing that.'

For Jaimi, the Northern Lake District is the ideal place to ride bikes, as it is a lot quieter than the southern part of the region. It requires looking a bit harder but, for Jaimi, her home trails are a hidden gem. Quiet trails, and just as good, if not better, riding as in the popular bits. Just without all the people.

ABOUT JAIMI'S ROUTE

As you'd expect from someone who has ridden around the world and seriously challenged much more experienced riders at GBDURO, Jaimi's route offers a real gravel riding challenge to those up for it. There are a number of technical uphill and downhill sections in here, but always paired with those amazing views that make you forget the 'type 2 fun'. Throw in some fantastic stops for coffee and this route is almost as memorable as a round-the-world trip.

ROUTE DESCRIPTION

The small hamlet of Troutbeck, about 15 kilometres west of Penrith, sits within a picturesque, but quiet, part of the Lake District. Great Mell Fell, situated immediately to the south-east of Troutbeck, is on open-access land which belongs to the National Trust, and is a popular hillwalking destination. The route begins and finishes at the Troutbeck Inn, which was a railway hotel serving the line between Keswick and Penrith. The A66, which connects Troutbeck to Penrith and Keswick, follows the course of an old Roman road; two forts and three temporary marching camps lie just north of it. In 1974, when the road was widened, the course of the road was changed to avoid the Roman ruins and to preserve any remaining archaeology.

HEADING TOWARDS SKIDDAW HOUSE.

The route follows a short section of the A5091 first, which can be busy. Shortly after the Rookin House activity centre, it follows a wide gravel path towards Pencil Crag, pursuing the course of the Thornsgill Beck through a commercially planted woodland. This is the first stretch of superb off-road riding on this route, with great views on to the Cumbrian fells. Ullswater, the second largest lake in the Lake District, can be seen in the distance, while you enjoy cycling on a track with a smooth surface.

The route joins Sustrans National Route 71 at the road and continues on tarmac around the eastern edge of Cockley Moor. At High Row, the route continues on the Old Coach Road, which crosses the flanks of Clough Head and Matterdale Common at the northern end of the Helvellyn range. This old track is not only part of Sustrans National Route 71, but also the Lakeland 200, a bikepacking route which is suitable for mountain bikes and devised by Alan Goldsmith. The riding here is a combination of moderately technically challenging stretches, paired with some fantastic descents on chunkier gravel. The views on a clear day are stunning, but this is pretty remote cycling, so come equipped for all weathers.

The Old Coach Road has no access restrictions, so be prepared to meet anyone from walkers to 4x4 enthusiasts.

This has been a working landscape for centuries. There are quarries all over the area, which have now been abandoned and left for nature to take over. After Clough Fold, the next part of the route passes the Threlkeld Quarry and Mining Museum. Riding through here is a journey back in time, with historic machinery in various stages of demise lining the path. The museum offers a tour of an underground mine and a railway; several locomotives are in regular use with the remainder on display.

After the museum the route joins the B5322 and crosses the A66, before following a cycle path into Threlkeld. The area around the village has seen human activity for at least 2,700 years; there was an Iron Age settlement near Threlkeld, just below Threlkeld Knotts. This was a substantial community with around 40 hut circles along with some enclosures above the quarry. The name Threlkeld derives from the Norse meaning 'the well of the thrall' (a *thrall* is a medieval term for a man who is bound in service to his lord). The cafe in Threlkeld has an excellent outdoor area and fabulous coffee and cakes.

ON THE CUMBRIA WAY.

As the steepest and toughest climb of the route is yet to come, this is a great place to stop.

The next section of the route follows the Lakeland 200 trail again. From Threlkeld, the route climbs steeply on tarmac, passing a number of farms along the way. The hard work is rewarded with fantastic views towards Low Rigg and High Rigg and across the valley. From the car park at Blencathra Field Centre, the route climbs on a wide gravel track into the valley between Blease Fell and Lonscale Fell. The track gets steeper and narrower towards the top. The last section, from where the route joins the Cumbria Way, is either very demanding technical riding on a gravel bike for some, or a hike-a-bike section for most. The views are once again stunning, and the riding gets easier once Skiddaw House, Britain's highest hostel, is reached. There is no mains electricity, phone signal, TV or internet to distract from the wilderness here – this is a truly remote place and only accessible by bike or on foot.

The Cumbria Way is a 117-kilometre walking route through the heart of the Lake District National Park, linking the two notable Cumbrian towns of Carlisle and Ulverston. Continuing on the Cumbria Way, the route descends on a long 4x4 track across the hillside below the peaks of Coomb Height, Great Calva, Bowscale Fell and Mungrisdale Common, following the course of the River Caldew. This is best ridden

DISTANCE **40km/25 miles** › ASCENT **737m/2,418 ft** › GRADE **Challenging** › START/FINISH **Troutbeck Inn** › START/FINISH GRID REF **NY 389271**
BIKE-FRIENDLY PUBLIC TRANSPORT **Penrith railway station (15km from the route)** › HIGHEST POINT **466m/1,529 ft** › TERRAIN **Exposed open moorland with at times technical and rocky trails** › RECOMMENDED TYRES **Schwalbe G-One Ultrabite on front; Schwalbe G-One Allround on rear**

BEST TIME TO RIDE

| JAN | FEB | MAR | APR | MAY | JUN | JUL | AUG | SEP | OCT | NOV | DEC |

SINGLETRACK **5%**   PATH **40%**   CYCLE PATH **10%**   ROAD **45%**

OLD COACH ROAD.

in the drier months, as this section of the route can get pretty boggy and wet. Near Swineside, the route rejoins a tarmac road and follows the Lakes & Dales Loop, a cycle route that follows the quieter lanes of Cumbria, from Mosedale to Undercrag.

From Undercrag, the route continues through Mungrisdale and joins Sustrans National Route 71, descending gently on tarmac in a southerly direction to meet the A66 at Lisco Farm. A cycle lane along this busy main road is followed by another climb on the old road, passing Roman camps and forts. After crossing the A66, the Troutbeck Inn provides a great place to enjoy some food and drink after this technical, yet rewarding, ride in the Lakes.

OTHER ROUTES NEARBY
> GB Divide
> Lakeland 200
> Lakes & Dales Loop
> Sustrans National Route 71

WHERE TO EAT
> Troutbeck Inn, Troutbeck
> Threlkeld Coffee Shop, Threlkeld
> Simple Goodness, Penrith

BIKE SHOPS
> Arragon's Cycle Centre, Penrith (T 01768 890 344)

WHERE TO STOP
> Threlkeld Quarry and Mining Museum, NY 326246
> Skiddaw House, NY 287291

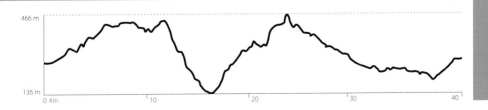

13 BUZZARD LOOP

67KM   GUY KESTEVEN

This loop combines the outstanding beauty of Brimham Rocks, the charm of Knaresborough and some more technical riding to make an unforgettable tour of North Yorkshire.

ABOUT GUY

Gravel riding for Guy in three words
just enjoy it

'Bikes have always been in my life. And I've been lucky enough to make a profession out of it.'

Guy Kesteven has been a professional bike and kit tester for over two decades. He holds an archaeology degree from the University of Exeter, then spent a few years digging up medieval cattle markets and working in bike shops and warehouses, before he started writing and testing for bike magazines in 1996. He is the author of *Being Gary Fisher and The Bicycle Revolution* and *1001 Bicycles to Dream of Riding,* and his love for archaeology is reflected in his recent guidebook, *King Alfred's Way,* for Cycling UK. Guy's love for bikes started when he was tiny enough to sit in the grocery box on his mum's bike. For him, cycling has always been a way of getting around exploring, finding limits, and sometimes exceeding those limits too.

'When we started it was rough stuffing. I went out with the CTC when I was 10.'

It wasn't called gravel cycling back in the days when Guy grew up, but knowing that he could miss out a bit of road by joining up the farm tracks always appealed to him. He has photographs of the time, at the age of 14 or 15, when he took a racing bike up Rudland Rigg to ride across the Yorkshire Moors in true Rough-Stuff-Fellowship style.

'My sister said the handlebars would get in the way of the dustman coming up the back entry.'

He tried to convince his mum to get him a mountain bike when the early Ridgebacks appeared on the market, but it never happened. The bars were too wide, so he had to come up with an alternative. He took the studs out of his football boots to make them look like proper cycling shoes. But as he couldn't get his feet out of the toe clips, crashing

'horribly' was part of Guy's early cycling routine.

'It's exploring, however you want to phrase that. Whether it's exploring what you can do, exploring what your bike can do, or just exploring the locality.'

For Guy, gravel riding is a sort of 'teleport' – he can join everything together in a way that's still enjoyable. Either combining a mountain bike route with a road bike route, or joining two road rides together, or two mountain bike rides. And the good thing is that nothing is either too boring or too scary; gravel riding for Guy is a happy medium. And unlike other forms of cycling, in order to find a great gravel route, all he has to do is leave his back door.

'If you ride a gravel bike, there's no pressure.'

Unlike in mountain biking, there is less 'rad' stuff in gravel riding. In Guy's opinion, it reduces the barriers for people new

BRIMHAM ROCKS.

A SMOOTH GRAVEL TRACK NEAR BIRCHFIELD FARM.

to this form of cycling. And there is no pressure to progress through various scales of difficulties; a ride to the pub can be just as exciting and rewarding as something further afield.

'There's just so many reasons why people are valid, and so many reasons why different bikes are valid, and different approaches. It's good; it's just very modern in that sense.'

Gravel riding is attracting a variety of people to cycling, and especially people whose skills are not necessarily just in cycling. Diversity is what is at the heart of gravel riding, and what makes it attractive. He compares gravel riding to superhero movies, where everybody's got their own skill set. There's someone who is really good at route planning, someone who is really good at fixing bikes and bleeding brakes in the middle of nowhere, someone who knows the best bivvy spots and someone who knows about this really nice bakery. Gravel riding combines all of those different skill sets in a way neither mountain biking nor road cycling normally do.

ABOUT GUY'S ROUTE

Guy's idea for this route was to take me on one of his favourite local rides that he enjoyed during recent Covid-19 lockdowns and to showcase how much variety there is in his patch of Yorkshire. Guy has ridden more bikes than most of us can dream of, and this route reflects his attitude to gravel cycling. It's a route to explore the local area as much as exploring what you are capable of as a rider and what your gravel bike is capable of.

In addition to the many great places that serve the famous Yorkshire Tea, there is loads of off-road riding close to Harrogate. Unlike other routes and trail centres, which are more difficult to get to, this route starts on a nice section of cycle path. There are plenty of opportunities along the way to make this route easier if needed, as some sections do require good bike-handling skills.

ROUTE DESCRIPTION

Most people visit Harrogate for its spa waters and the Royal Horticultural Society's garden at Harlow Carr, but the North Yorkshire town has been voted the happiest place to live in Britain several times and offers great cycling too. Harrogate is the birthplace of Mike Hall, a British ultra-cycling icon, who was tragically killed in a race in

KNARESBOROUGH VIADUCT.

Australia in 2017. In 2014 the Tour de France's early stages, known as the Grand Départ, were held in Yorkshire, with the first of the two stages starting in Leeds and finishing in Harrogate.

The route starts at the eastern entrance of Harrogate railway station. It follows Sustrans National Route 67 northbound, parallel to the railway line, on a number of roads through the town. From the Dragon Road car park, it follows the Nidderdale Greenway, a short, traffic-free path (also part of Sustrans National Route 67) tracing the course of the former railway line between Harrogate and Pateley Bridge. This passes through peaceful woodland, beautiful wild-flower meadows and golden wheat fields, before crossing the River Nidd on the Nidd Gorge Viaduct. Standing 32 metres above the river, this Grade-II-listed, seven-arch viaduct was built in 1848. The views from the top into the steep-sided Nidd Gorge are impressive.

The route continues on the Nidderdale Greenway into Ripley. Shortly before Ripley, the Tour de France monument remembers the 2014 Grand Départ and provides a fabulous photo opportunity. Ripley has many listed buildings and a fifteenth-century castle, which has been the home of the Ingilby family for 700 years. The route passes the very picturesque cascade waterfall on Hollybank Lane, which also provides a great view towards the castle.

From Ripley, the route continues on Sustrans National Route 67, a well-paved cycle path with nice sections though woodland mixed up with views over the countryside. The cycle path becomes a small lane just before it climbs gently towards Clint; shortly afterwards, the route leaves the Sustrans trail and continues on a busier road to Birstwith, a village situated on the River Nidd. The route follows Nidd Lane out of the village, which eventually becomes a path at the edge of a woodland and leads to an impressive bridge over the River Nidd. The bridge, which dates from 1822, is located on the packhorse track from Ripon to Otley. Shortly afterwards, the route joins a tarmac road through Wilson's Plantation then, just before Darley, follows Nidd Lane and crosses the river again to reach White Oak. After a short section of singletrack, the route climbs on a wide and smooth gravel track passing Birchfield Farm to reach the B6165.

The route crosses the B6165 and continues on a track to another farm on Hartwith Hill, and then climbs on a grassy track through a field to Hartwith. After a short section on tarmac, the route turns left

to follow a singletrack section on New York Lane. The views from here to the Yorkshire Dales in the west are fabulous. The climb is rewarded with a fast descent on a windy section of singletrack to Summerbridge. The track meets a road into the village and heads towards the River Nidd. On the riverbank, a singletrack trail leads to New York, where the route joins the B6165 for a while to reach Low Laithe. From here, a gravel path leads to Smelthouses, where the route follows a very short section of the Way of the Roses on Brimham Rocks Road. The Way of the Roses is a coast-to-coast cycle route which passes through the white rose county of Yorkshire and the red rose county of Lancashire.

A stiff climb on a fairly technical track follows from Low Wood House to Maud's Farm. This section can be bypassed by following the Way of the Roses route on Brimham Rocks Road to Maud's Farm. After another short section on the road, the route takes a left to Brimham Rocks, where the route reaches its highest point of 287 metres at the visitor centre and cafe.

The outcrop of Brimham Rocks is set on Brimham Moor and is part of the Nidderdale Area of Outstanding Natural Beauty. The rocks at Brimham were formed over 325 million years ago and are renowned for their remarkable water- and weather-eroded forms. There is also a birch woodland and a large area of heathland. The cafe here is a great place to get a Yorkshire Tea, leave the bike and have a walk around the impressive rock formations.

The route returns the same way, following the Way of the Roses in the opposite direction and then continuing on another road to Burtree Hill. From here, the route follows a track alongside the course of the medieval Monk Wall for about 1 kilometre until it reaches a short section of road at Beck Side Farm, and then continues on a track to High Gill Moor. This is another point where the route connects with the Way

of the Roses. The route continues to Gill Moor Farm on a paved track, and on a mixture of gravel paths, concrete paths and singletrack to Cut Throat Lane, where it rejoins Sustrans National Route 67 through Bishop Thornton. After the village, the route leaves Sustrans National Route 67 to follow a bridleway to High Cayton through a stunning woodland, and continues on a small road to South Stainley.

From South Stainley the route follows the Ripon Rowel Walk and Rakes Lane to Robert Beck, and from there another great gravel track follows into Farnham. The route continues on tarmac through the valley, and follows residential roads into Knaresborough, a picturesque market and spa town.

St Robert's Cave, a very rare surviving example of a medieval hermitage, is the next landmark on the route, right at the start of Sustrans National Route 636. The trail follows Abbey Road along the banks of the river through the picturesque Nidd Gorge. It passes the early-fifteenth-century Chapel of Our Lady of the Crag, which sits in an old sandstone quarry in the gorge. The chapel is reached via a narrow path and steps from Abbey Road. The route continues on Waterside into the centre of Knaresborough, with plenty of opportunities for eating and drinking,

DISTANCE **67km/42 miles** 〉 ASCENT **830m/2,723 ft** 〉 GRADE **Expert** 〉 START/FINISH **Harrogate railway station** 〉 START/FINISH GRID REF **SE 305553** 〉 BIKE-FRIENDLY PUBLIC TRANSPORT **At the start** 〉 HIGHEST POINT **287m/942 ft** 〉 TERRAIN **A mixture of remote moorland with technical sections and gentle riding on cycle paths** 〉 RECOMMENDED TYRES **Schwalbe G-One Ultrabite**

BEST TIME TO RIDE

| JAN | FEB | MAR | APR | MAY | JUN | JUL | AUG | SEP | OCT | NOV | DEC |

SINGLETRACK **10%**   PATH **15%**   CYCLE PATH **20%**   ROAD **55%**

BRIDGE ON THE PACKHORSE TRACK FROM RIPON TO OTLEY.

and a chance to visit the remains of the castle.

The castle provides the best vantage point to marvel at the impressive Knaresborough Viaduct, which spans the River Nidd, carrying the Harrogate line. The viaduct was due to open in 1848, but it collapsed into the river when it was almost finished; a new viaduct had to be built which delayed the opening of the railway through Knaresborough by 3 years.

Shortly after going under the viaduct, the route crosses the river on a road bridge and continues on a cycle path, better known as the Beryl Burton Cycleway (which is part of Sustrans National Route 636). Beryl Burton, OBE, was an English racing cyclist; she rose to the top of women's cycle racing in the UK having won over 90 domestic championships along with seven world titles and setting numerous national records. She died in 1996; the first section of the Beryl Burton Cycleway was opened the following year.

Only a short section of the Beryl Burton Cycleway is followed to Pig Wood, from where the route continues south on a mixture of roads to Stonefall Cemetery. It then reconnects with Sustrans National Route 67, which leads all the way back to Harrogate railway station.

OTHER ROUTES NEARBY

> Beryl Burton Cycleway (Sustrans National Route 636)
> Nidderdale Greenway
> Sustrans National Route 67
> Way of the Roses
> Yorkshire Dales 200
> Yorkshire Dales 300
> Yorkshire Dales Cycleway

WHERE TO EAT

> Prologue Performance Cycling Cafe, Harrogate
> Birchfield Ice Cream Parlour, Birchfield Farm, Summerbridge
> Brimham Rocks Cafe, Summerbridge
> The Ugly Duckling, Knaresborough

BIKE SHOPS

> Prologue Performance Cycling, Harrogate (T 01423 503 000)
> Stif Mountain Bikes North, Summerbridge (T 01423 802 208)
> Pedalheads Cycles, Knaresborough (T 01423 866 163)

WHERE TO STOP

> Nidd Gorge Viaduct, SE 307583
> Tour de France monument, SE 286600
> Cascade waterfall near Ripley Castle, SE 282604
> River Nidd packhorse bridge, SE 236603
> Brimham Rocks, SE 207650
> St Robert's Cave, SE 361561
> Chapel of Our Lady of the Crag, SE 351564
> Knaresborough Viaduct, SE 348571

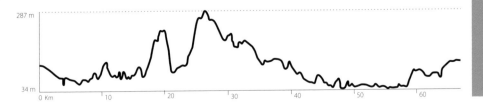

UPPER CALDER VALLEY

14 PACKHORSE GRAVEL

32KM   EMMA OSENTON

Offering gravel of a larger size than normal, with challenging climbs, super scenic views and long, flowing descents, this loop follows old packhorse trails in the South Pennines.

ABOUT EMMA

Gravel riding for Emma in three words
fun; adventure; dirt

'Something just made me want one. It was a little bit like a drug that got slightly more addictive.'

Living in the town of Hebden Bridge in West Yorkshire, Emma Osenton describes herself as a gravel cyclist and occasional mountain biker. She is also a big fan of bikepacking rides, especially in Germany. In 2018 she took on the Grenzsteintrophy, which follows the line of the former Iron Curtain. It was a bike that got her into gravel riding – the Kinesis Tripster. She is a sponsored rider and had seen 'sneaky' images long before the bike was officially released. Brought out in the early 2010s, it was one of the first gravel bikes to hit Britain.

'There are definitely more women riding. I remember when I started cycling a long time ago, you had one token woman in the club, maybe two. I think the lack of being in a hurry makes gravel (riding) more appealing.'

Emma has regularly organised new events, including City Cross and Aggregate100, and enjoys her role as a guide. After we had completed her loop around Hebden Bridge, she had arranged for a number of people on all kinds of bikes – mountain bikes, handcycles and gravel bikes – to meet up, and took us all out for a great and chilled ride around the town. The club she regularly rides with has an equal representation of women and men, and she sees more and more events where there are lots of women turning up. Gravel riding for Emma also means more personal freedom and less hurry when riding with mates. For her, it is often connected with being out on an adventure, in whatever time this requires. There is a lot of crossover to the audax world. For Emma, audax means going on an adventure without feeling like the clock is pushing her along. And gravel riding is much closer to this than any other type of cycling.

'It's certainly not finished work and there's definitely room for improvement. I think with gravel being a little bit more accepting, and that quite often you build your gravel bike to your own shape, it means that women get a better deal on the bikes.'

For Emma, gravel bikes share more similarities with classic touring bikes, but they have proper brakes, much more sensible gears and are much comfier. And with new innovations like carbon pannier racks, some elements from her bygone touring days have their advantages, especially when it comes to smaller frames that often can't fit the larger bikepacking bags.

'I think we'll end up on rigid mountain bikes with funny shaped bars.'

Emma jokes about her lack of off-road skills, but the places she takes her drop handlebars on the Tripster ATR would leave most

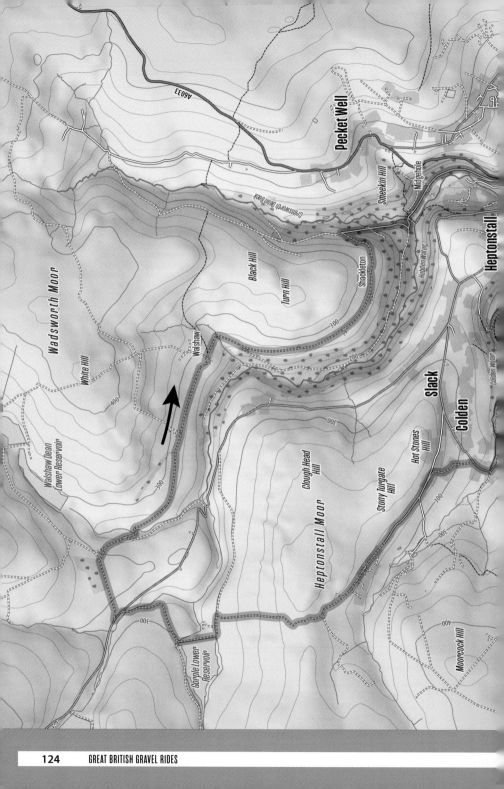

Pecket Well

Heptonstall

Slack

Colden

Midgehole

Smeekin Hill

Shackleton

Black Hill

Turn Hill

Crimsworth Dean Beck

Hebden Water

A6033

Wadsworth Moor

White Hill

Walshaw

Walshaw Dean
Lower Reservoir

Heptonstall Moor

Clough Head
Hill

Stony Turngate
Hill

Hot Stones
Hill

Colden Water

Gorple Lower
Reservoir

Moorcock Hill

400

300

200

100

300

400

300

300

300

300

Hebden Bridge

Mytholmroyd

A646

Cragg Vale

B6138

Eppingden Moor

Law Hill

Withens Clough Reservoir

Edge End Moor

Lodge Hill

Stoodley Pike

Charlestown

Rochdale Canal

Pry Hill

Upper Eastwood

Mankinholes

Heeley Hill

Blackshaw Head

Lumbutts

Todmorden

A646

N

1 Kilometre

0

LUMB MILLS CHIMNEY.

people walking. Emma believes that gravel cycling will progress, and the result will be somewhere more towards mountain biking: bigger tyres with drop bars, making the most of the technology that comes from mountain biking.

'I'd like to see more utility cycling exist, because you can do everything on a gravel bike if you want to. But it certainly opens it up for getting people to reach beyond their normal little routines.'

For Emma, gravel bikes are an invitation to explore. They can be perfect commuter bikes, but they are also very capable when ridden off-road. She doesn't have to worry about having different bikes – a gravel bike takes her anywhere she wants.

ABOUT EMMA'S ROUTE

The trails around Hebden Bridge are possibly the furthest away from the metalled dirt road type of gravel you can find in the US. Or, as Emma nicely puts it: *'Hebden Bridge gravel can be slightly larger than normal gravel'.*

There is a lot of gritstone around the Upper Calder Valley, so the route conditions can be very varied depending on the weather – anything from bone dry and sandy to very muddy. Emma's favourite loop is a perfect route for bikes with chunkier tyres, exploring the old packhorse tracks that once connected Hebden Bridge with the outside world before roads, canals and railways existed. The route's steep ups and downs, mixed with the chunky gravel and all sorts of different textures, are as colourful as Hebden Bridge itself is.

ROUTE DESCRIPTION

Calderdale, in the county of West Yorkshire, is the southernmost of the Yorkshire Dales. It is also part of the South Pennines, an area renowned for its beautiful moorland, hill country and river valleys. This route circles around Hebden Bridge in the Upper Calder Valley; Hebden Bridge was once known as 'Trouser Town', due to the amount of clothing manufacturing which took place in the town. Steep hills with fast-flowing streams and good access to major wool markets meant that Hebden Bridge was ideally placed for water-powered weaving mills; as a result, the town underwent a pivotal period of development during the nineteenth and twentieth centuries. Before the Industrial Revolution, marshland covered much of the Upper Calder Valley; this was drained in order to construct a road through the valley. Before this road was built, the only way through the area was by ancient packhorse routes which ran along the hilltops and dropped into the valleys where needed.

During the 1970s and 1980s many artists, musicians, writers and photographers set up home in Hebden Bridge. This led to the town, and the wider Calder Valley, becoming a tourist destination. In the following decades Hebden Bridge became a commuter town, with local residents travelling to work in the nearby cities of Bradford, Leeds and Manchester.

The Upper Calder Valley has a firm place in Britain's cycling landscape as well. *Singletrack* magazine has its base in nearby Todmorden, and the Cragg Vale hill climb – which is claimed to be the longest continuous ascent in England – has featured in the 2014 Tour de France and the Tour de Yorkshire.

The route starts at Hebden Bridge railway station and follows Sustrans National Route 66 eastbound along the River Calder towards Mytholmroyd. The route leaves the cycle path at Hawks Clough and follows a road to the right over the railway line. This is where the first steep climb starts, beginning on tarmac and, once on Spencer Lane, on cobbles. As the road climbs out of the valley, you'll get spectacular views across this part of Yorkshire. At Old Chamber the route passes a great campsite and the Honesty Box, a great wee shop. Make sure you bring some change with you on this ride, as cards are not accepted in the Honesty Box. Here the paved road becomes a gravel path. The route continues to climb, but much more gradually from here, following a number of different lanes, lined by stone walls. Above Kershaw Farm the route meets the Pennine Bridleway. This 330-kilometre National Trail, which was designed especially for cyclists and horse riders, traces drove roads and ancient packhorse routes through the Pennines, with some newly created bridleways thrown in.

Stoodley Pike Monument is clearly visible from here. Standing at a height of 37 metres on a hill of the same name, the structure dominates the moorland of the rugged and steep-sided Upper Calder Valley. The first monument on this hill was erected in 1814 to commemorate the end of the Napoleonic Wars. It collapsed in 1854; the current structure dates from

THE SINGLETRACK GANG ON THEIR RIDE NEAR STANDING STONE HILL.

2 years after this. The bridleway does not go up to the monument, but you can reach it on foot.

The next section on the so-called London Road, a former packhorse track, offers fantastic gravel cycling, although at times the trail can be a bit rougher. The track climbs until it crosses the Pennine Way; it then descends, with fantastic views over the Upper Calder Valley. At times you might have some friendly cows as spectators, and a couple of gates will slow you down too. At Mankinholes, a hamlet with a youth hostel, the route follows the road on the right. The hamlet has a magnificent drinking trough and a lovely range of seventeenth-century cottages and farms, which are signs of its historic importance on this packhorse route. Take the next right here, following Sisley Lane and leaving the Pennine Bridleway. You can ride over some interesting, washed-out sections of sandstone here. At the edge of a small woodland the route follows Lee Bottom Road on the right, which eventually becomes a track. It continues on Stoodley Lane, crosses the Rochdale Canal and then joins the cycle path along the canal, Sustrans National Route 66. The Rochdale Canal is one of three canals to cross the Pennines; it is a popular route for leisure boaters today. At the height of the Industrial Revolution, it was used to transport a wide variety of goods and general merchandise, including coal, limestone,

AMAZING VIEWS OVER THE CALDER VALLEY FROM THE PENNINE BRIDLEWAY.

wool, cotton, salt and timber. As it is a broad canal, it was more successful than the nearby Huddersfield Narrow Canal, and became the main canal in use across the Pennines.

The next section on compacted gravel along the canal is mainly flat, as the route heads north-east back towards Hebden Bridge. At Stubbing Wharf, the route leaves the cycle path and crosses the canal, continuing along King Street on the other side. The Stubbing Wharf is an eighteenth-century inn located between the Rochdale Canal and the River Calder, in which the English poet, children's writer and translator Ted Hughes set his poem, *Stubbing Wharfe*. Hughes was born in neighbouring Mytholmroyd. The route takes a left along Church Lane, passing Saint James the Great church. A gravel track leaves the road and follows the Colden Water uphill, through a beautiful native woodland.

You can spot the distinctive chimney of Lumb Mills from quite a distance away. Higher Lumb Mill closed in the late nineteenth century, but Lower Lumb Mill ran until the early twentieth century. Nearby is Lumb Bank, an eighteenth-century mill owner's house, which once belonged to Ted Hughes. It is now run as a creative writing centre by the Arvon Foundation, a charitable organisation. Both are just a short detour away from the route, which continues down to the river and joins a singletrack trail through the forest.

The route climbs steeply up the singletrack, but soon after the gradient becomes more gentle as the route leaves the woodland. The views from this more open section across the river valley are once again spectacular. The route passes through Riverdene, and then climbs on Fold Lane to Colden. At this convenient point, around halfway round the route,

DISTANCE **32km/20 miles** ⟩ ASCENT **629m/2,064 ft** ⟩ GRADE **Challenging** ⟩ START/FINISH **Hebden Bridge railway station** ⟩ START/FINISH GRID REF **SD 995268** ⟩ BIKE-FRIENDLY PUBLIC TRANSPORT **At the start** ⟩ HIGHEST POINT **378m/1,240 ft** ⟩ TERRAIN **A mixture of remote moorlands and gentle urban riding with steep climbing sections** ⟩ RECOMMENDED TYRES **Schwalbe G-One Bite**

BEST TIME TO RIDE

| JAN | FEB | MAR | APR | MAY | JUN | JUL | AUG | SEP | OCT | NOV | DEC |

SINGLETRACK **20%**   PATH **35%**   CYCLE PATH **15%**   ROAD **30%**

you'll find May's Aladdin's Cave, just a small detour to the right down Edge Lane. It is an absolute must-do and stocks everything imaginable from whisky to aniseed balls, and serves home-baked pastries and coffee with a picnic bench outside to enjoy your treats. The route now continues on the Pennine Bridleway to Heptonstall Moor. The road becomes a wide gravel track, which reaches its highest point at Reaps Bottom. Nearby Standing Stone Hill has, as you might guess, a standing stone at its top, although not a very tall one.

The route descends across the wide open moorland, still following the Pennine Bridleway, to Gorple Lower Reservoir. From the reservoir the route continues on a service road, joins a larger road and Sustrans National Route 68 for a very short section and then continues on the Calder/Aire Link to Holme Ends. From here the route continues on gravel across New Laithe Moor to New Laithe Farm, where it leaves the Calder/Aire Link. Following the Hebden Water, the route continues on a gravel path to Shackleton. It's downhill from here through a woodland, on a gravel path first, then on a road to New Bridge. Nearby Hardcastle Crags is a spectacular wooded valley which contains the nineteenth-century Gibson Mill, one of the first powered mills built at the start of the Industrial Revolution. The mill was powered by water and has been renovated to showcase renewable energy sources. It is surrounded by unspoilt woodland and crossed by an extensive network of footpaths.

The route continues on Midgehole Road, with the last gradual climb, which is followed by a descent into Hebden Bridge. The route meets Sustrans National Route 68 then crosses the Rochdale Canal and the River Calder to return to Hebden Bridge railway station.

THE COBBLES OF SPENCER LANE.

OTHER ROUTES NEARBY
> Calder Valley Greenway
> GB Divide
> Pennine Bridleway
> Pennine Cycleway
> Sustrans National Route 66
> Sustrans National Route 68

WHERE TO EAT
> Vocation & Co., Hebden Bridge
> Honesty Box, Old Chamber Farm & Camping, Hebden Bridge
> May's Aladdin's Cave, Highgate Farm, Colden
> Cafe Solo, Hebden Bridge

BIKE SHOPS
> Blazing Saddles, Hebden Bridge (T 01422 844 435)

WHERE TO STOP
> Stoodley Pike Monument, SD 973242
> Lumb Mills chimney, SD 976282
> Hardcastle Crags, SD 989292

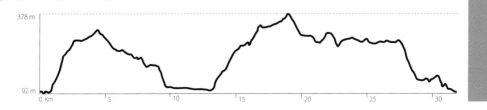

PEAK DISTRICT

15 PANNIER GRAVEL
55KM   STEFAN AMATO

This linear route takes you on a mixture of gravel tracks, singletrack and roads through the heart of the Hope Valley in the Peak District into Sheffield – the Outdoor City.

ABOUT STEFAN
Gravel riding for Stefan in three words
escape; challenge; bridleways

The first time I bumped into Stefan Amato from Pannier was at the Silk Road Mountain Race. We weren't cycling at the 'Pannier pace' of 15 kilometres per hour – this was a race, and we didn't have much time to chat.

'The way I got into riding bikes many moons ago was escaping Sheffield really.'

This had all changed by the time I met up with Stef properly, in his new home in the heart of the Peak District, from where he also runs Peak Bunkhouse, a six-bed bunkhouse for groups. For around a decade he has been the mastermind behind **Pannier.cc**, and he has recently edited his first book, *Bikepacking: Exploring the Roads Less Cycled*. Originally based in London, he now lives close to where riding bikes for him started, as an architecture student in Sheffield.

'A lot of people use these trips and other events to get into slightly more off-road riding. The route planning becomes a different beast. If someone has ridden a route before, you can trust it.'

Pannier started back in 2012 as a cycle touring blog. Stef got into this way of life and work through realising what a great way of seeing places and travelling riding bikes was. On the road at first, he slowly headed more and more off the beaten track. And so everything slowly morphed into planning his own guided trips, sharing inspirational content and getting out taking people on cool trips.

Joining group rides is a great way of experiencing the gravel cycling world, and Stef's trips attract a real mixture of people: those who have never ridden bikes before, experienced outdoor enthusiasts who are looking to try something new, or people that are experienced bikepackers, but enjoy the social side of the group trips. Stef loves the mix of his clients, and all his trips are undertaken at a leisurely pace, hence he called Pannier the '15 kilometres per hour club'.

'You can get that wild, remote feeling, especially riding the gravel stuff, but it's got a vibe to it.'

The Peak District has a very good road network, and mountain biking is also pretty established here. And, as in a lot of other places in the UK, the definition of gravel varies wildly. There are routes where a mountain bike is more beneficial; on others a road bike will get you to your destination more quickly. But for Stef there is enough stuff here which is rideable on a gravel bike.

There is another thing that is special about Stefan's riding: he always carries a small stove for brews, and a homemade Bakewell tart is never too far away. This English dessert, consisting of a shortcrust pastry base topped with layers of jam and frangipane then finished with flaked almonds,

QUIET LANES ABOVE SHEFFIELD.

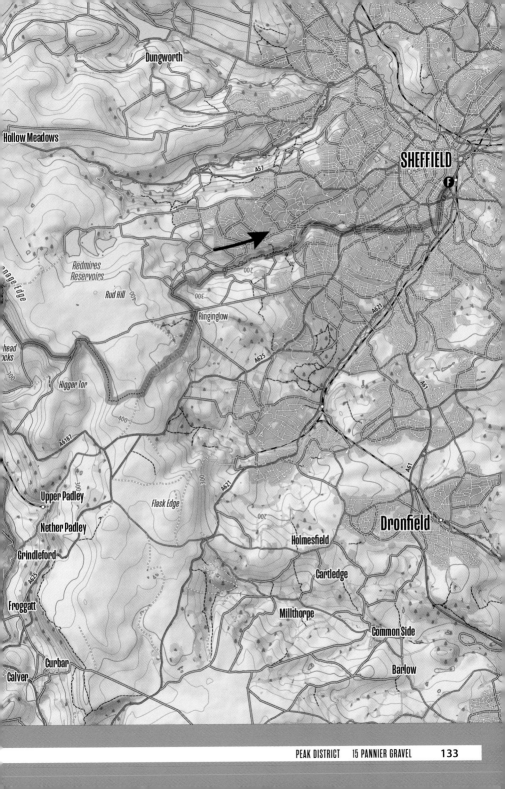

is not only closely associated with the town of Bakewell in the Peak District, but also with Stef's rides. As a trained architect, he hasn't lost his love for drawing. The slower speed of Pannier rides not only provides the perfect opportunity for a brew and cake, but also to create one of his many beautiful sketches that illustrate the paths less travelled.

ABOUT STEFAN'S ROUTE

This route took a few years to stitch together, but the result is stunning. On Stefan's linear route through the Hope Valley on his favourite gravel tracks, you can find accessible adventures quite close to a lot of towns and villages. Although it feels remote, you are never too far from supplies or places to stock up.

For Stef, the UK is a particularly good cycling destination, not just because of the variation of terrain, surfaces, villages and countryside. Hospitality is a big part of it as well. Heading off the beaten track and still having that welcome in a pub is a great thing, all best enjoyed at 15 kilometres per hour.

ROUTE DESCRIPTION

Access to the countryside in England and Wales is very closely connected to one event in the Peak District: the Kinder mass trespass of 1932. This was a landmark in the campaign for open access to moorland in England and Wales; it eventually led to the formation of the national parks. The Peak District National Park, the first in the UK, was established in 1951; around 20 million people live within an hour's car journey from the Peak, including the populations of the nearby cities of Manchester, Sheffield, Derby and Stoke-on-Trent. Millions of people visit the park every year. Tourism in the Peak District first became popular with the arrival of the railways; visitors came to enjoy the spa towns and Castleton's show caves, along with the beautiful landscape. Today, walking, road cycling, mountain biking, rock climbing and caving are popular, and the area is also a growing destination for gravel riders. This route is a great one-way journey from the heart of the Hope Valley in the Dark Peak to Sheffield, one of England's largest cities, with an abundance of woodlands and parks.

The route starts at Hope railway station, on the outskirts of the village of Hope. This picturesque settlement is situated where the River Noe and Peakshole Water meet, and has a range of hills to explore to the north, including Win Hill and Lose Hill. The village has a selection of cafes and pubs; Cafe Adventure is a great first stop for a coffee or breakfast. Just a short detour away, the remains of the Roman Fort of Navio can be found in the village of Brough. The route follows Station Road into Hope and then follows Pindale Road south of Peakshole Water to Castleton. The imposing ruins of Peveril Castle, one of England's earliest Norman fortresses built by Henry II in 1176, stand high above the pretty village.

Mam Tor dominates the view from Castleton – it lies around 2 kilometres north-west of the village, between the White Peak and the Dark Peak. From Castleton, which also offers nice places to stop, the route follows the Mam Tor Road. The A625 Manchester to Sheffield road, which went via Mam Tor, was constructed by the Sheffield Turnpike Company in 1819, using spoil from the nearby Odin Mine. However, as Mam Tor is prone to landslips, the road needed repairing many times over the next 160 years. In 1977 the road was restricted to single-lane traffic,

SHATTON LANE WITH AMAZING VIEWS OVER THE PEAK DISTRICT.

before being permanently closed to motor traffic in 1979. It is interesting to see the road today and view the effects of landslide movement and repeated road reconstruction; it is also a great alternative to the nearby Winnats Pass for gravel and mountain bikes. The route starts climbing gradually on tarmac first. Where you cross the landslide it offers some more technical gravel riding, and fantastic views over the valley. Blue John Cavern is just a short detour from the route, with a cafe and the chance to see eight of the fourteen known varieties of Blue John stone, an attractive fluor-spar. The mineral has been mined in the area for centuries and continues to be today, although on a smaller scale.

After the landslide area the route follows tarmac again to Eldon Hill, where a fantastic gravel path scrapes the edge of Eldon Hill Quarry. A large proportion of the 470-metre Eldon Hill, the highest limestone hill north of the River Wye, has been lost to quarrying. The hill is of significant interest for its geology, along with its historic and industrial heritage. It sits on the northern edge of the Peak District's carboniferous limestone; further north it blends into the Dark Peak's millstone grit. Vast quantities of limestone, mainly for road building, were excavated from Eldon Hill from the 1950s. The quarry closed in 1999; since then there have been some attempts at natural restoration. Cavers can now explore some of the narrow caves exposed by the work, including Sidetrack Cave, which was discovered in 2002.

The views from the track into the quarry are impressive, and they get even better once the route reaches its highest point at 452 metres. The beautiful white limestone track turns into grassy singletrack and then again into a gravel highway. The route crosses the Limestone Way, a waymarked long-distance footpath which runs

A MANDATORY COFFEE STOP ON STANAGE EDGE.

for 74 kilometres through the White Peak (cycling is allowed on some sections only). At Dirtlow Rake, the route joins a tarmac road and descends all the way into the small hamlet of Little Hucklow. Still on tarmac, the route climbs gradually again and, after crossing another road, continues on a byway to Great Hucklow. The route passes the small village and climbs on roads to the Camphill Gliding Field, a great place to stop on a nice day and watch various gliders taking off and landing. A fast descent with great views follows on the road to Abney.

From here, the route climbs gradually out of the small village on tarmac first, and then joins another paved track towards the top of Abney Moor. It joins Shatton Lane, which provides fantastic views north across the Hope Valley. A cracking descent follows once the transmitter mast is reached, and the last section of the downhill into Shatton is on a mixture of road and gravel. The route turns right on to the A6187, passing the Hope Valley Garden Centre,

which has a great cafe and a bike shop, before cutting across towards Bamford railway station on a cycle path across the River Derwent and a minor road. From here, the route heads left on to Station Road (A6013), passing Bamford railway station, then gradually climbs through Bamford, which hosts Derbyshire's first community-owned pub (and post office and cafe), the Anglers Rest.

A number of lanes, both paved and unpaved, follow, before the route joins Sustrans National Route 6 for a brief section on Bole Hill. Instead of following the Sustrans route on a road, we follow the Long Causeway, a medieval packhorse route which ran between Sheffield and Hathersage, passing Stanage Edge. Stanage Edge, or simply Stanage (from 'Stone Edge'), is a gritstone crag which is very popular for climbing. The Long Causeway was once thought to be part of a Roman road crossing Hallam Moor and passing Stanedge Pole, a historic waymarker on the route to Sheffield, although this had been disputed

DISTANCE **55km/34 miles** 〉 ASCENT **1,135m/3,724 ft** 〉 GRADE **Expert** 〉 START **Hope railway station** 〉 FINISH **Sheffield railway station**
START GRID REF **SK 181833** 〉 FINISH GRID REF **SK 358869** 〉 BIKE-FRIENDLY PUBLIC TRANSPORT **At the start and finish** 〉 HIGHEST POINT **452m/1,483 ft**
TERRAIN **Open moorland riding, at times technical, combined with some great sheltered lanes** 〉 RECOMMENDED TYRES **Schwalbe G-One Bite**

BEST TIME TO RIDE

| JAN | FEB | MAR | APR | MAY | JUN | JUL | AUG | SEP | OCT | NOV | DEC |

SINGLETRACK **20%**   PATH **15%**   CYCLE PATH **5%**   ROAD **60%**

STANAGE EDGE.

in recent years.

What is indisputable are the amazing views from here. This is a perfect place to take a picnic to and enjoy the views. Don't let the sign at the bottom of the track put you off: this 'rough track' is perfectly fine on a gravel bike. The route continues through Stanage Plantation and rejoins Sustrans National Route 6 on the road. Further on, the route takes a gravel path at Upper Burbage Bridge and continues on a permissive bridleway past Burbage Rocks, an extension of Stanage Edge.

The last climb of the route follows on a gravel track across Burbage Moor, before the route starts descending on the same track to Lady Canning's Plantation. Shortly afterwards, at Ringinglow the route first follows Sustrans National Route 6 (occasionally deviating on to alternative quiet roads) into Sheffield, and then continues on a mixture of quieter and busier roads to Sheffield railway station.

OTHER ROUTES NEARBY
> Limestone Way
> Sustrans National Route 6
> Tour de Peak District

WHERE TO EAT
> Cafe Adventure, Hope
> The Wild Kettle Cafe, Hope Valley Garden Centre, Bamford
> Anglers Rest, Bamford
> Birdhouse Tea Bar & Kitchen, Sheffield
> Hagglers Corner, Sheffield

BIKE SHOPS
> 18 Bikes, Hope (T 01433 621 111)
> Bike Garage, Hope Valley Garden Centre, Bamford (T 01433 659 345)
> A Different Gear, Sheffield (T 01142 507 717)

WHERE TO STOP
> Peveril Castle, SK 149826
> Blue John Cavern, SK 132832
> Eldon Hill Quarry, SK 116816
> Camphill Gliding Field, SK 181783
> Stanage Edge, SK 240844
> Burbage Rocks, SK 268822

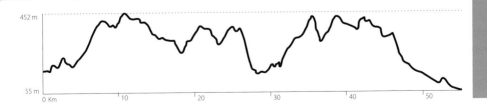

SOUTHERN ENGLAND

EXPERT

EAST ANGLIA

16 FURTHER EAST

605KM   JOSH IBBETT AND GAIL BROWN

This multi-day route is a surprising mix of old and new landscapes, travelling along Roman roads, rivers, dykes and quiet roads, and back in time through millennia.

ABOUT JOSH AND GAIL

Gravel riding for Josh in three words
lots of fun

Gravel riding for Gail in three words
exploring the in-between

'I am trying to ride my bike as much as I can, but real life gets in the way sometimes.'

Josh Ibbett's first quote describes him pretty well as a rider. One of the most accomplished racers on the ultra-endurance circuit, he has packed in many of the most excruciating races out there. He also went on his very own definition of a round-the-world trip. This is when Josh came up with the idea for a new kind of gravel bike. It's safe to say that not many riders in this book have helped to develop a bike for their own adventures. The idea of Mason's InSearchOf – a gravel bike with fatter tyres that takes people further – was developed when Josh was in his bivvy bag way out in the desert. (**02 In search of gravel on the Monega Pass** (pages 13–19) is a route which suits this bike well.)

'That's the thing about it. Gravel bikes are a bit of a do-it-all bike. It's not really specific to anything, but it's able to take in a lot of surfaces. On some bits today you would have definitely been faster on a mountain bike. There's a lot of road, so you would definitely be faster on a road bike. But the beauty of the gravel bike is that it does everything pretty well. Around here, there is a lot of variety, so it kind of makes sense.'

So it doesn't come as much of a surprise that Josh used the 18 months of various Covid-19 lockdowns and restrictions to venture further from his front door in Cambridgeshire on a gravel bike than he ever had before. The difference to endurance racing is that he came back each night to a bed instead of a bivvy bag. He mapped each local trail he could find and the idea for Further East was born. And when GBDURO changed its race format in 2020 and riders had to complete

the 2,000-kilometre route from Land's End to John o' Groats while carrying all their food provisions and staying outside, Josh won the race on the InSearchOf in 7 days, 17 hours and 44 minutes, one of only five finishers.

'All the different types of terrain that I was missing when I was younger, in a way I have never cycled before.'

Gail Brown, also born and bred in Cambridgeshire, had her breakthrough on to the bikepacking circuit by finishing GBDURO20 as the fastest women in 9 days, 15 hours and 45 minutes. The physiotherapist, now based in Bristol, describes herself as an enthusiastic cyclist, and Further East gave her a whole new insight into the area that she thought she knew so well from her childhood.

'I am not clear in my mind what gravel cycling is. I don't have a

PREVIOUS PAGE THE SOUTH DOWNS (ROUTE 21).   OPPOSITE EARLY MORNING LIGHT AT HARLESTONE HEATH.

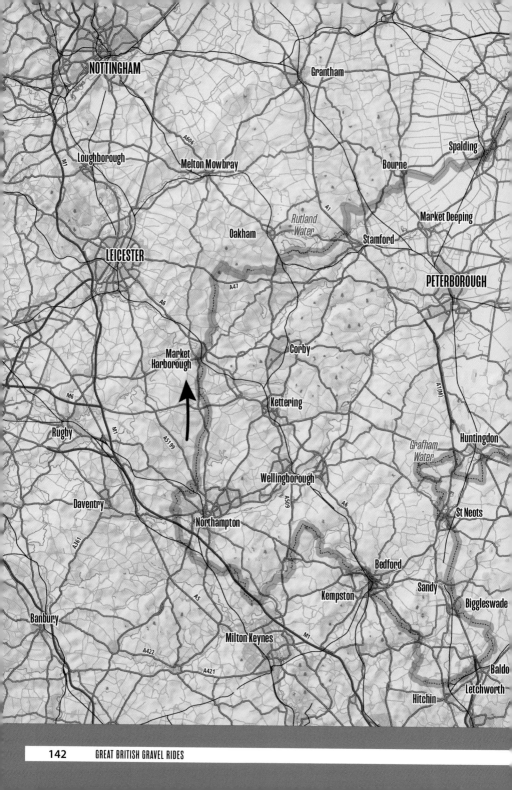

QUIET COUNTRY ROAD NEAR RUTLAND WATER.

gravel bike, but I guess I have been doing what are classed as gravel races. Gravel bikes are broadening the spectrum of people that are engaging with cycling.'

In many ways Gail is the opposite to Josh when it comes to bike choice. For riding Further East, she wasn't prepared for the extra work she'd have to put in on a mountain bike, so just put some sturdier tyres on a road bike and went for it. Sometimes gravel riding can be as simple as that.

ABOUT JOSH AND GAIL'S ROUTE

Further East is the longest route in this book. It can be ridden in around 3 days, or more quickly if you prefer. Neil Phillips won the inaugural race in 27 hours and 56 minutes – this time was set on a slightly longer route than the one described here. For those with less speed in their legs or less time on their hands, Further East can also be broken up into various different stages. The route overlaps with another route in the book, **17 Windmill gravel** (pages 151–157).

Further East was originally the brainchild of Camille McMillan, an artist and photographer. He spends a large amount of his time exploring and documenting the Pyrenees, but also calls the East of England his home. To him, his home is a sadly maligned area of the UK. 'Unloved, from Luton to Southend, Norfolk to Bedfordshire. It is the region of Essex lads and Alan Partridge. The East of England is not taken seriously, culturally or crucially, to a bicycle rider.'

Josh Ibbett and Gail Brown took this as inspiration to create

Sepulchre, one of only four Norman round churches which are still in use in England. The church was built in the twelfth century and its rectangular chancel was added in the fifteenth century.

After more roads the route joins a cycle path parallel to the longest guided busway in the world, locally known as The Busway, which connects Cambridge, St Ives and Huntingdon. The Busway crosses Fen Drayton Lakes Nature Reserve, a flooded former sand and gravel quarry which is situated next to riverside meadows. There is a wide variety of wildlife to see in the nature reserve, including dragonflies, swans, ducks, geese and otters. In St Ives the route leaves The Busway and continues on roads to Godmanchester Nature Reserve, and on to Godmanchester.

Godmanchester is on the site of the Roman town of Durovigutum; the town had a *mansio* (inn) and is also on the Roman road network. There is also archaeological evidence of Celtic and earlier habitation in the area, indicating that the area has most likely been continuously occupied for more than 2,000 years.

From Godmanchester, the route follows a mixture of roads and paths through Offord Cluny and Buckden, and travels around Grafham Water, England's third largest reservoir; the reservoir was designated as a Site of Special Scientific Interest in the 1980s. This area is home to reed beds, ancient woodlands and valuable populations of numerous species of amphibians and birds – it also offers fantastic gravel riding.

a route that is a serious bike ride. It is not just its sheer length that makes it one of the more serious routes in this book. Although mostly flat, the route traverses a multitude of different types of terrain, and requires cyclists to pedal most of the time. But you'll be surprised how much the route has to offer. It definitely shows that East Anglia deserves to be taken seriously – at whatever speed you wish.

ROUTE DESCRIPTION

While the race route starts outside of the world-famous university town, this variation of the route starts and finishes at Cambridge railway station. Passing the Cambridge University Botanic Garden, it follows roads through the centre of town past a few colleges and well-known attractions like the Round Church, officially known as the Church of the Holy

The route crosses St Neots, a busy market town, and Biggleswade, another market town. In between, the route passes large fields; this part of England is a major agricultural area. After Pirton, Further East joins the Chilterns Cycleway, a 274-kilometre cycle route through the Chilterns Area of Outstanding Natural Beauty. The route passes several picturesque villages with small pubs, which all make welcome stops if you have time. After Bedford, a large market town with a population of around 100,000 people, the route follows a section of the Ouse Valley Way, which accompanies the River Great Ouse for a while and then crosses it at Harrold. The River Great Ouse is the fifth longest river in the United Kingdom. The route

PEDDARS WAY.

continues through more beautiful countryside and crosses the river again at Olney and Gayhurst. Around Olney, the route briefly overlaps with a section of **17 Windmill gravel**. More small villages with lovely pubs follow, while the riding is comprised of a mixture of rural roads, paths on the edges of fields and singletrack. At times, as the route travels north past Northampton, the grassy field paths mean that progress is slow.

With a population of over 200,000, Northampton is one of the largest towns in England (like Milton Keynes it has not received city status). North of the town, which Further East bypasses on its western edge, the route joins Sustrans National Route 6. This section is a joy to ride on a gravel bike. It follows the Brampton Valley Way, a cycling route on part of the former railway line from Northampton to Market Harborough; it is also part of the Midshires Way. You'll pass Pitsford and Brampton railway station, which has been revitalised as the headquarters of the heritage railway, the Northampton and Lamport Railway, which runs parallel to the Sustrans route for a while.

The Brampton Valley Way continues on a great gravel cycling path into the smaller town of Market Harborough – this is a great place to eat and stock up on supplies. From here, the route follows Sustrans National

Route 64 until Cranoe then joins Sustrans National Route 63 at Tugby to travel north. From Oxey Cross Roads, Further East changes direction and heads east for a time.

The route follows a variety of quiet roads and gravel paths to Manton at the edge of Rutland Water. When measured by surface area, it is the largest reservoir in England – however, Kielder Water in Northumberland has a larger capacity. The reservoir is a popular water sports hub: along its perimeter runs a 40-kilometre track, which is great for walking and cycling. The route continues on this gravel path to Howells Inlet. From here, the route follows a road then a bridleway to Great Casterton, where it crosses the A1, also known as the Great North Road.

Spalding is the next sizeable town along the route. This market town is situated on the River Welland and is part of the South Holland district of Lincolnshire. The region is known as an important producer of tulips and this, together with the nature of the landscape, are a nod to the cultural links between the Fens and South Holland. Until 2013, this link was celebrated by the annual Spalding Flower Parade.

As in the 'real' Holland, much of the district is low-lying and is kept free from inundation by land drainage. On the way out of Spalding, the route passes several marshes that lie only just above sea level, before it joins Sustrans National Route 1 for a short section and then follows the River Welland on dykes. This part of the route can feel very surreal. It provides a real challenge too, as it is very exposed. The route passes the tranquil water of Moulton Marsh – this man-made nature reserve features salt marsh, creeks, lagoons, and woodland – before it reaches The Wash. The route doesn't pass directly on the shores of this rectangular bay, but it can be seen from the route. The Wash is fed by the rivers Great Ouse, Nene, Welland and Witham, and is one of Britain's broadest estuaries. This beautiful and challenging section of the route ends in Sutton Bridge, from where a cycling route connects the village with the town of King's Lynn. In 2006, King's Lynn joined The Hanse (*Die Hanse*). This is a network of towns and cities across Europe which historically belonged to the Hanseatic League, which was a significant medieval trading association that connected merchant towns around the Baltic Sea and the North Sea. Boston and Kingston upon Hull are the only other UK members of *Die Hanse*.

From here the route follows Sustrans National Route 1 again, which is also part of the North Norfolk Coast Cycleway, passing Sandringham House, one of the two homes owned by Queen Elizabeth II in a private capacity rather than as head of state. In stark contrast to the exposed paths along waterways, this is a sheltered part of the route, travelling through extensive woodland. The route leaves Sustrans National Route 1 at Snettisham and reaches its northernmost point at Hunstanton. As the seaside

THETFORD FOREST.

resort faces west across The Wash, it is one of the few places on the east coast of Great Britain where the sun sets over the sea. It's worthwhile stocking up on supplies here, as the next section of the route doesn't offer many possibilities. Great Birchham's windmill is worth a stop, as the route travels on a mixture of paths and roads to Great Massingham and picks up the Peddars Way just south of the village.

The Peddars Way is a 74-kilometre walking route (most of it is also suitable for cyclists), which follows the course of a Roman road. The name is reputed to be derived from the Latin *pedester* ('on foot'). The name first appeared on a map in the sixteenth century. Mostly off-road, it provides for fantastic gravel riding; however, it can be overgrown at times, leaving just narrow singletrack to enjoy.

Castle Acre, which showcases the best of Norman town planning, is the next place for supplies on the Peddars Way. The Spar store at the northern end of the village is fantastic to stock up and a great stop

THREE SHIRES WAY NEAR OLNEY.

for a coffee as well. The village is best known for the ruins of Castle Acre Castle (to the east of the village) and Castle Acre Priory (to the west of the village), however, the village itself was once fortified. The route passes through the Bailey Gate, which was part of these fortifications, before heading south out of the village.

Further East passes Stanford Training Area, a massive military training site, established in 1942. The military takeover of the area involved the compulsory evacuation of several villages, including Tottington,

West Tofts, Langford and Stanford. The route follows the eastern and southern boundary of the training area, before it continues into the trail labyrinth of Thetford Forest. The forest, which contains a vast network of singletrack, is comprised of an assortment of pine trees, broadleaved trees and heathland – it is the largest man-made lowland forest in the UK. While this section is fun to ride, extra time is needed here, as progress through the area, some of it on sandy trails, can be slow.

The route follows a section of the Icknield Way

DISTANCE **605km/376 miles** ⟩ ASCENT **2,861m/9,386 ft** ⟩ GRADE **Expert** ⟩ START/FINISH **Cambridge railway station** ⟩ START/FINISH GRID REF **TL 461572** ⟩ BIKE-FRIENDLY PUBLIC TRANSPORT **At the start** ⟩ HIGHEST POINT **180m/591 ft** ⟩ TERRAIN **A mix of open farmland and other cultivated landscapes and urban areas. Some sections are remote and have little shelter** ⟩ RECOMMENDED TYRES **Schwalbe G-One Bite**

BEST TIME TO RIDE

| JAN | FEB | MAR | APR | MAY | JUN | JUL | AUG | SEP | OCT | NOV | DEC |

SINGLETRACK **20%**   PATH **15%**   CYCLE PATH **10%**   ROAD **55%**

OTHER ROUTES NEARBY

> Brampton Valley Way (Sustrans National Route 6)
> Chilterns Cycleway
> Icknield Way Trail
> Midshires Way
> North Norfolk Coast Cycleway (Sustrans National Route 1)
> Peddars Way
> Rutland Water off-road circular route
> Sustrans National Route 64

WHERE TO EAT

> Old Bicycle Shop, Cambridge
> The Robin Hood, Clifton Reynes, Olney
> Spar, Castle Acre
> Wilde & Greene, Tuddenham

BIKE SHOPS

> PRIMO Cycles, Cambridge (T 01223 500 502)
> Townsends Light Blue, Cambridge (T 01223 315 845)
> Rutland Cycling, Cambridge (T 01223 352 728)
> Rutland Cycling, Grafham Water (T 01480 812 500)
> Richardsons Cycles, King's Lynn (T 01553 767 014)

Trail, which runs along an ancient chalk ridge and links the Peddars Way with The Ridgeway. Travelling over open heathlands, this is one of the most scenic parts of the route, but it also feels very remote. Further East follows the Icknield Way Trail until Cheveley, where it takes a shortcut and rejoins the trail near Brinkley. Shortly after Balsham, the route follows an old Roman road. This is a fitting end to a great gravel loop, which provides fast and flowing off-road riding, before the route follows a road into Cambridge and back to the start at the railway station.

WHERE TO STOP

> Round Church, TL 449588
> Fen Drayton Lakes Nature Reserve, TL 339696
> Pitsford and Brampton railway station, SP 735667
> Rutland Water, SK 927056
> The Wash, TF 381356
> Sandringham House, TF 694290
> Hunstanton, TF 671407
> Castle Acre Castle, TF 819152
> Castle Acre Priory, TF 814149
> Thetford Forest, TL 811849
> Roman road, TL 574492

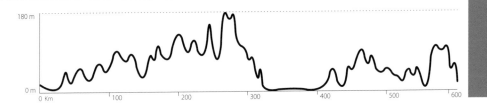

CHALLENGING

17 WINDMILL GRAVEL

58KM   GRANT WILDMAN

Towpaths, fast-flowing tracks, beautiful small towns and a Dutch-style windmill offer a great gravel adventure on the northern edge of Milton Keynes.

ABOUT GRANT

Gravel riding for Grant in three words
exploration; individuality; fun

'It doesn't matter what bike you're on. Today I was on a mountain bike; sometimes I ride my drop-bar bike; sometimes I ride a single-speed bike. I think gravel is an expression of just being out exploring.'

Grant Wildman works as representative for Schwalbe Tyres UK. His role takes him across Britain but, having been born and bred in Milton Keynes, it's here where his favourite riding is. He is a trial and street rider, loves single-speed bikes but also owns a mountain bike. No matter which bike he chooses, his riding is predominantly off-road these days. The nice thing about gravel riding for Grant is that it makes it easy to link trails together and traverse between sections – from tarmac to bridleways, along field edges and through woodlands. It's tough to find any definition of gravel. For Grant it's just exploration, defined only by the fact that it enables riding on multiple surfaces.

'People are less tolerant on the roads, both cyclists and motorists. Gravel riding is a good way of exploring and getting out doing big miles, if that's what people want to do, without the danger of being on the roads.'

That Grant is thinking about the dangers of riding on the road isn't surprising, as Milton Keynes itself and the surrounding areas are heavily populated. The cycling infrastructure in the town is above average, as Milton Keynes hasn't got the restraints other historic towns in Britain have. In the town it's almost impossible to get away from motor traffic, but the surrounding countryside offers quiet spots for getting away from the noise. While we were out riding, I asked if the noise of the motorway that runs nearby disturbs Grant? It doesn't – over the years Grant has mastered the ability of tuning it out.

Not being able to travel much during the long months when restrictions were brought in to control the Covid-19 pandemic, Grant rediscovered his local area. In his opinion, this is exactly why gravel riding has picked up so rapidly. It enabled people, especially in areas with high population density, to break out of the town and explore the nature around them, in a much safer manner than on the road.

'The gravel bike is a nice extension. People can do everything on one bike; I think that's kind of where some of the ethos originally came from.'

Grant not only has access to a wide variety of Schwalbe tyres; but he also owns an impressive selection of vinyl records and multiple bikes. But what if he only had space for one bike? For him, a gravel bike is quite nice, because it can do most things pretty well. And with its popularity growing,

BEAUTIFUL SHADES OF GREEN ON THE OUTSKIRTS OF MILTON KEYNES.

THE REMAINS OF ST PETER'S CHURCH.

he is hopeful that networks and infrastructure for cycling will continue to improve throughout the country.

'Essentially they're fast-rolling mountain bike tyres.'

At the end of our chat, we inevitably spend some time talking about tyres. So where is the gravel tyre different from a mountain bike tyre? For our ride Grant was using a mountain bike tyre, which would also make a great gravel tyre. Gravel tyres usually have a lower tread pattern, are slightly less aggressive and faster rolling. At the same time, gravel tyres are evolving too; Schwalbe now has five different types in its range, with more to come. And as wider tyres are becoming more popular now, this also means that they will probably end up as mountain bike tyres too.

'I think gravel gives you that sense of vastness when you're out and about.'

As a former DJ, I am interested in Grant's opinion of what gravel riding would sound like on a record? While he struggles to pin it down, it would probably sound like the work of Jon Hopkins – a bit moody and sounding quite vast. Something not everyone likes, but a tune you can really immerse yourself in. Gravel is like a good record; it offers great escapism.

ABOUT GRANT'S ROUTE

The countryside around Milton Keynes doesn't really undulate much – it is pretty flat. The style of riding is very similar to that in **16 Further East** (pages 141–149), although this route is much shorter. At times, riding the route feels a bit like riding in Holland, amplified by the Redways, brick houses and a windmill. At other times the route offers exactly the vastness and escapism needed to forget the city, at least for a short while. Grant spent a lot of time re-exploring his local area during the winter of 2020/2021, and this route is his favourite loop. Perfect to simply go out and crunch some miles, regardless of if you are on a mountain bike or a drop-bar bike.

ROUTE DESCRIPTION

Wolverton, at the start of this ride, is situated on Milton Keynes' northern edge, beside the Grand Union Canal and the River Great Ouse. Wolverton is one of the towns in historic Buckinghamshire that was formally incorporated into the new town of Milton Keynes in the 1960s.

Although describing Milton Keynes as a cyclist's paradise goes a step too far, the town has a lot in common with Dutch cities, as it has an extensive network of shared-use paths, known as Redways. These traffic-free paths cover most parts of the city, with some connecting to the older towns around the edges.

The route starts at Wolverton railway station. After a mini-roundabout the route follows a cycle path on the right and connects with Sustrans National Route 6 alongside Grafton Street and through New Bradwell Park. Shortly afterwards, the route turns on to a path on the left to follow the northern side of the Grand Union Canal. This canal, which links London to Birmingham and passes through beautiful countryside, quiet villages and industrial towns, is the 'trunk route' of the English canal system and England's longest canal.

The riding on a grassy path alongside the canal is easy and fast rolling, through a mixture of wood and wetlands. The route follows the banks of the canal through Stanton Low Park. Although it is one of the newer parks in Milton Keynes, Stanton Low is rich in heritage. The route leaves the canal and joins the Hanslope Circular Ride heading towards the north-west corner of the park, where the remains of the former Stantonbury Manor lie below the ground. Next to the site of the manor are the above-ground remains of St Peter's Church. It is believed that a church has stood on this site for more than 1,000 years, while parts of old church walls visible today date back to the twelfth century.

The route passes the lake, reed beds, wet woodland and several small meadows of the Linford Lakes Nature Reserve on a paved path, and then crosses the River Great Ouse near Hill Farm, still following the Hanslope Circular Ride. After a brief section on the road the route follows grassy paths along field edges to Little Linford Wood, a small nature reserve. This section of the route follows the Midshires Way, a 360-kilometre multi-use trail across the Shires of England, linking the Ridgeway National Trail with the Trans Pennine Trail. The path through the woodland provides a welcome change before more grassy paths take you to Hanslope Park, which hosts the Foreign and Commonwealth Office's archives.

The route continues on a road and a paved path to Tathall End, crossing under the M1 on an underpass and continuing on grassy field edge paths

BRADWELL WINDMILL.

to a four-way junction. This section of the route is also part of **16 Further East**. The route takes a left following the Swan's Way, a long-distance multi-use route which runs between Goring-on-Thames in the south and Salcey Forest in the north. The route continues on gravel paths on the eastern edge of Salcey Forest. If you feel peckish, there is a nice cafe with a large outside eating area in the forest, which adds a detour of a few kilometres. The best way to get to the cafe is to follow the Midshires Way, which meets the route again at the northern end of the forest. From the forest the route follows a cycle path to Piddington; it then continues on a bridleway and a section of the B526 to Horton.

The route continues on a road to Manor Farm, and carries on along a gravel track through Barnstaple Wood and Great Wood. It then traverses a number of farm tracks past Hanger's Spinney, with great views across the surrounding countryside. Where the route meets a single-track road, a small detour takes you in the opposite direction to Cowper's Alcove, or just The Alcove. This delightful folly is one of the places where William Cowper, an English poet and hymn writer, was inspired to write his poetry. The folly was built by the owners of Weston House in around 1753, and it is

a great place to stop and gaze across the open fields towards the distant town of Olney.

The route follows the road to Weston Underwood and continues on a road to Olney. This town on the River Great Ouse offers various places to eat and drink and a bike shop; it is best known for the Olney Pancake Race, a tradition celebrated since 1445, and the *Olney Hymns* by William Cowper and John Newton. One of those hymns is the world-famous *Amazing Grace*. The Cowper and Newton Museum celebrates the work and lives of these two famous local residents. The route passes near the museum and continues on Bridge Street across the river, before it follows the Ouse Valley Way on a cycle path into Emberton Country Park.

Transformed by Milton Keynes council from a gravel works, Emberton Country Park became England's first country park in 1965; it boasts meadows and wooded glades with paths and trails winding their way around five different lakes. The

route follows the cycle track to the south-west corner of the park. Grounds Cafe, a good place to get some additional caffeine, is just a short detour to the left. Once again overlapping with **16 Further East** for a short while, the route continues on a gravel path, still following the Ouse Valley Way, to Rectory Farm and on past Ash Spinney woodland. At the southern edge of this woodland you need to push your bike for about 200 metres to a small triangular wood, from where a gravel path takes you southbound to meet the Ouse Valley Way near End Farm, and continues on this into the village of Sherington.

The route follows roads through the village to the sports ground, from where a number of paths are followed into Chicheley. The route continues on the busy Newport Road (A422) for a short while, and then follows lanes through Longclose Spinney and Newfield Spinney. It meets the North Crawley Road which takes you past an industrial estate into Newport Pagnell, once home to the luxury car maker Aston Martin. After a short section on London Road the route follows a cycle path along the River Ouzel, crosses the river and continues through town on Tongwell Lane, on which the motorway is crossed once again. This route is defined by the stark contrast of the really quiet countryside mixed with the noise and business of the greater Milton Keynes urban area.

The route continues on a mix of quiet roads and cycle paths through the town, passing through Great Linford Manor Park, a unique site with a history stretching back to at least the Saxon times. Several features of the park, including the Wilderness Garden and nearby Water Gardens, date back to the seventeenth and eighteenth centuries, when the park was landscaped to complement the now privately owned manor house.

You pass the house shortly after the route meets Sustrans National Route 6 in the park, on which the

DISTANCE **58km/36 miles** 〉 ASCENT **347m/1,138 ft** 〉 GRADE **Challenging** 〉 START/FINISH **Wolverton railway station** 〉 START/FINISH GRID REF **SP 821415** 〉 BIKE-FRIENDLY PUBLIC TRANSPORT **At the start** 〉 HIGHEST POINT **118m/387 ft** 〉 TERRAIN **A mix of open farmland and other cultivated landscapes and urban areas. Some sections can be muddy** 〉 RECOMMENDED TYRES **Schwalbe G-One Allround**

BEST TIME TO RIDE

JAN	FEB	MAR	APR	MAY	JUN	JUL	AUG	SEP	OCT	NOV	DEC

SINGLETRACK **30%**   PATH **30%**   CYCLE PATH **10%**   ROAD **30%**

GRAND UNION CANAL.

route continues for a short while. The house was a famous recording studio, hosting artists including PJ Harvey and Biffy Clyro. Jamiroquai recorded their album *Travelling Without Moving* here. With over 8 million copies sold, it holds the world record for the best-selling funk album of all time.

The next section of the route offers two options: either follow Sustrans National Route 6 on a cycle path (also marked as the Railway Walk on some maps) or, as in the GPX file, follow the Swan's Way and Midshires Way, which runs parallel to the cycle path on a grassy track. Either way is fine and legal to ride; the cycle path will be the quicker option, as it is an old railway line.

Just before V6 Grafton Street the route follows Nightingale Crescent then detours on a small path to Bradwell Windmill – one of Milton Keynes' most distinctive historic features. The route then follows a cycle path parallel to V6 Grafton Street back to Wolverton railway station.

OTHER ROUTES NEARBY
> Hanslope Circular Ride
> Midshires Way
> Sustrans National Route 6
> Swan's Way
> Woburn Bike Trails

WHERE TO EAT
> Grounds Cafe, Salcey Forest
> The Spread Eagle, Piddington
> Grounds Cafe, Emberton Country Park
> Brewery Tap House MK, Milton Keynes

BIKE SHOPS
> Corley Cycles, Milton Keynes (T 01908 311 424)
> 2Pedalz, Olney (T 01234 240 716)

WHERE TO STOP
> Ruins of St Peter's Church, SP 836427
> Cowper's Alcove/The Alcove, SP 861514
> Cowper and Newton Museum, SP 890513
> Emberton Country Park, SP 885507
> Great Linford Manor Park, SP 851424
> Bradwell Windmill, SP 831411

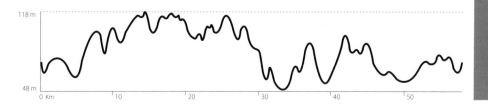

BATH AND THE COTSWOLDS
18 COTSWOLD GRAVEL
51KM   EMMA KINGSTON

A short but demanding ride, which packs in some exciting singletrack, Britain's longest cycling tunnel, the idyllic villages of the Cotswolds and the beautiful architecture of Bath.

ABOUT EMMA
Gravel riding for Emma in three words
exploration; dirt; fun

'It's just such a beautiful place to go riding.'

I met Emma Kingston virtually for the first time when I interviewed her about her first book, *Bikepacking England,* which is full of inspirational routes to enjoy south of the Scottish Border. That I hadn't come across her name beforehand wasn't too much of a surprise. Emma isn't a former pro-cyclist, influencer or journalist, but a full-time primary school teacher who really enjoys reading, mountain biking and spending long evenings looking at maps. The routes featured in her book make great weekend bikepacking trips. They are demanding, but not extreme.

Emma didn't own a gravel bike when we rode one of her favourite loops around the Cotswolds, which added another angle to this book as well. I was not only interested in people on the forefront of the gravel scene in Britain, but also in people, like Emma, who are simply adventurous cyclists. Most of the routes in *Bikepacking England* can be ridden on a gravel bike, but could also be enjoyed on other bikes too. Emma's knowledge of the area around Bristol and Bath is astonishing, so after a few email exchanges we met in Bristol and enjoyed a fun day cycling.

'If you throw in an odd tea room, or a waterfall, or an old railway, it just adds the focus for a ride that I enjoy.'

Emma's wealth of knowledge about the South West of Britain stems from the fact that she has lived most of her life here. She grew up in the western side of Bristol and has recently moved to its eastern side, so riding out to Bath from her home was an obvious choice.

Sharing her knowledge is a crucial part of why she started writing a book in the first instance. A lot of people asked her over the years how she rides and where she rides so, from Emma's point of view, the lack of route knowledge was a barrier to those people. And while there has been a huge surge in different route-planning apps, they can't replace the wealth of knowledge of somebody who is familiar with the area and has ridden the trails themselves, and can guide people towards a route or a bikepacking experience they are going to love. And as literature is one of her hobbies too, making the connection between literature and flowy singletrack was an obvious leap to make.

'I really like trails that have really good flow. They take me to places that I wouldn't get to see if I stayed on the road.'

While she owns a road bike too, it simply doesn't interest her as much as her mountain bike. Gravel trails and singletrack is

BRIDLEWAY NEAR UPPER WESTON WITH THE CITY OF BATH IN THE BACKGROUND.

Monkton
Farleigh

A363

100

Bathford

Batheaston

Bathampton

A36

River Avon and Kennet Avon Canal

Bathampton
Warren

BATH

Little Solsbury
Hill

Upper
Swainswick

100

Tam Brook

200

Cold Ashton

Henley
Hill

A46

100

200

Langridge

Lansdown

200

200

100

100

Freezing Hill

Hanging
Hill

200

200

Penn Hill

100

200

North Stoke

Kelston
Round Hill

200

100

100

A431

A4

Wick

Newton
St Loe

THE CIRCUS IN BATH.

what rocks Emma's boat; nothing too technical. But this doesn't mean that she doesn't like trying routes that are quite different, another aspect well reflected in her book. It's the places those trails take her to which are ultimately more important than just the riding itself.

'I probably never viewed myself as a role model outside my teaching career, but it has definitely been a really nice thing for women to get in touch and say that they have really enjoyed reading the routes that I put together. A lot of them have started going out and riding them too.'

With bikepacking still being a male-dominated domain, Emma's book is a refreshing exception at a time where women's interest and participation in cycling is growing. Beyond her book, she is keen to share her wealth of experience at events run by organisations like Sisters in the Wild, a community where women can feel empowered to expand their comfort zones in a safe and supportive environment. Her book has been a great first step for women who would like to try more adventurous cycling and bikepacking themselves. But being able to meet and talk to other women, especially those who are new to off-road or have never bikepacked before, has been one of the most rewarding outcomes of Emma's debut in the publishing world.

ABOUT EMMA'S ROUTE

Emma's route mixes great singletrack sections with relaxed cycling paths along canals and rivers, as well as a lot of architectural heritage. It's the perfect choice if you find the gentle riding on gravel paths along canals enjoyable, but want to spice it up with some steeper climbs and gain the rewards you'll get for them. Just like the routes she featured in *Bikepacking England*, this loop around the Cotswolds has much more to offer than just turning the pedals.

ROUTE DESCRIPTION

Designated as an Area of Outstanding Natural Beauty in 1966, the Cotswolds is the third largest protected landscape in England, ranking after the Lake District and Yorkshire Dales national parks. While the city of Bath, where the route starts and finishes, isn't part of the Cotswolds, it is a fantastic place to visit in itself. Attracting up to 1.3 million visitors every year, the city is named after its Roman-built baths. Bath became a UNESCO World Heritage Site in 1987 and was later added to the Great Spa Towns of Europe (a UNESCO collection) in 2021. It also hosts the headquarters of GCN – the Global Cycling Network. Most of the numerous eighteenth- and nineteenth-century buildings in Bath are made from the local, golden-coloured Bath stone.

The route starts right in the heart of the city, at Bath Spa railway station. It follows Manvers Street north, running parallel to the River Avon. A short, but very worthwhile, detour is to Pulteney Weir. This picturesque horseshoe-shaped weir sits under Pulteney Bridge and was initially built in the seventeenth century to prevent flooding in the town of Bath. The route follows Sustrans National Route 4 past Bath Abbey. The former Benedictine monastery was founded in the seventh century and rebuilt in the sixteenth century – it is one of the most impressive examples of Perpendicular Gothic architecture in the South West. The route continues on several roads through the city centre. As Bath has a multitude of one-way streets, it's highly recommended to follow the route in the described direction. It passes Queen Square, which was the first speculative development by instrumental Bath architect, John Wood, the Elder. Wood, who later lived in a house on the square, aimed to restore Bath to what he was convinced was its former ancient glory as one of the most significant cities in Britain.

Passing the Bath Cenotaph, the route follows Gay Street to The Circus, another superb example of Wood's grand Georgian architecture. Built between 1754 and 1768, The Circus is a ring of large, impressive townhouses, forming a circular shape with three entrances. More superb architecture follows as the route passes the Royal Crescent, 30 grand, terraced townhouses laid out in a sweeping semicircle, designed by Wood's son, the architect John Wood, the Younger, and built between 1767 and 1774.

DESCENDING TOWARDS ALDERMOOR WOOD.

The route crosses Royal Victoria Park and heads north-west towards Weston. The first proper lung-bursting climb of the route starts shortly after a roundabout, where the route follows Deanhill Lane and then a bridleway, which is also the route of the 164-kilometre Cotswold Way, which follows the Cotswold escarpment from Bath in the south to Chipping Campden in the north. As the name suggests, the route takes you right into the Cotswolds, with its outstanding natural beauty and charming settlements. The singletrack up to Kelston Round Hill is one of the many beautiful off-road sections of this route. A short walk to this ancient barrow is worth the detour (no bikes please). On a clear day, you might be able to see the Severn bridges from here. It is thought that the word Kelston translates as 'Hill of the Celts'.

The route continues round the hill, before it descends on another flowy section of singletrack with outstanding views towards North Stoke. From here, the track starts climbing steeply up another hill,

first on road, then on a permissive byway, towards Lansdown Golf Club. Stopping and looking back on the climb is highly recommended, as the views from the highest section of the route are great. You will pass Pipley Wood and the golf course and reach the route's highest point, where a few iron sculptures by David Michael Morse invite you to take a stop. The route follows a bridleway and a pretty busy road for a short while, and continues on another bridleway downhill. The descent which is to come is fantastic, passing the site of the 1643 Battle of Lansdown, the first English Civil War battle. The singletrack follows the open hillside into a small woodland, and then rejoins a tarmac road at Manor Farm. The route climbs gradually on tarmac into Upper Swainswick. For those who are thirsty, there's a small well in the village to fill up bladders or bottles. The route crosses the A46 on an underpass and then continues on roads to Batheaston, a village on the north bank of the River Avon. With the majority of tough climbing out of the way, this is a good place to stop for refreshments.

From Batheaston, the route becomes flatter for a while, initially following a cycle path on the southern bank of the river. The route continues on Mill Lane to Bathampton, where it joins Sustrans National Route 4 along the Kennet and Avon Canal. This makes for a welcome change from the steeper singletrack sections and provides flat and relaxed cycling on compacted gravel paths, with plenty of opportunities for refreshments along the canal. The impressive Dundas Aqueduct, which was completed in 1810 by John Rennie, carries the Kennet and

Avon Canal over both the River Avon and a railway line. In 1951, it became the first canal structure to be selected as a Scheduled Ancient Monument. The route continues on Sustrans National Route 4 on the banks of the canal. Take care along the canal sections, as they can get busy at times.

At Avoncliff, the route leaves the Sustrans route and climbs on a tarmac road out of the valley. The tiny village has a railway station as a bailout option if needed, but after an initially very steep climb, the riding gets much easier. The route continues on the road, then on a short section of bridleway, before it continues on tarmac into Freshford, an attractive village with a population of around 500. The views when the route climbs out of the village are yet again stunning, and there are

DISTANCE **51km/32 miles** ⟩ ASCENT **818m/2,684 ft** ⟩ GRADE **Challenging** ⟩ START/FINISH **Bath Spa railway station** ⟩ START/FINISH GRID REF **ST 753644** ⟩ BIKE-FRIENDLY PUBLIC TRANSPORT **At the start** ⟩ HIGHEST POINT **234m/768 ft** ⟩ TERRAIN **Urban riding with a rural touch, with some technical sections** ⟩ RECOMMENDED TYRES **Schwalbe G-One R**

BEST TIME TO RIDE

| JAN | FEB | MAR | APR | MAY | JUN | JUL | AUG | SEP | OCT | NOV | DEC |

SINGLETRACK **30%**   PATH **5%**   CYCLE PATH **25%**   ROAD **40%**

good places to refuel in the village as well. The route continues on smaller roads before it very briefly joins the busy A36 and continues to Hinton Charterhouse. From this picturesque Cotswold village it's downhill to Wellow, where the route joins Sustrans National Route 24, also known as the Colliers Way, to reach Midford.

The route follows the trackbed of the now-closed Somerset and Dorset Joint Railway between Midford and Bath Green Park. After crossing Tucking Mill Viaduct, its main feature is Combe Down Tunnel. Opened in 1874, this former railway tunnel was once the UK's longest tunnel without intermediate ventilation, and now forms part of the Two Tunnels Greenway (Sustrans National Route 244) walking and cycling path. At 1.6 kilometres, Combe Down is the UK's longest cycling and walking tunnel. Travelling through the tunnel for the first time is an incredible experience, heightened by *Passage,* an extraordinary audiovisual installation by United Visual Artists. Shortly afterwards, the route passes through Devonshire Tunnel; at 409 metres this is much shorter, but still provides another fabulous underground cycling experience. Although there are small LED lights in the tunnel, bringing good lights is highly recommended on this route.

The route passes through Lyncombe Vale into the Bath suburb of Oldfield Park and on to East Twerton. It crosses the River Avon and continues on the Bristol and Bath Railway Path into the city. The Bristol and Bath Railway Path itself is ideal for a day out, and this short section gives a good flavour of the route. Kelson's Field marks the end of the railway path; our route continues on a cycle path along the River Avon instead. Shortly after Riverside Parade, the route follows Ambury, Corn Street and Dorchester Street back to Bath Spa railway station.

A COTSWOLDS VILLAGE.

OTHER ROUTES NEARBY
> Bristol and Bath Railway Path
> Colliers Way (Sustrans National Route 24)
> GB Divide
> Sustrans National Route 4
> Two Tunnels Greenway (Sustrans National Route 244)
> West Country Way

WHERE TO EAT
> Bath Soft Cheese Cafe, Kelston
> Floating Baker, Kennet and Avon Canal (location dependent on mooring space)
> The Inn at Freshford, Freshford
> Society Cafe, Kingsmead Square, Bath

BIKE SHOPS
> Avon Valley Cyclery, Bath (T 01225 442 442)
> Cadence, Bath (T 01225 446 887)
> Bijou Bikeworks, Bath (T 01225 251 536)

WHERE TO STOP
> Pulteney Weir, ST 752649
> The Circus, ST 748653
> Royal Crescent, ST 745654
> Kelston Round Hill, ST 711675
> David Michael Morse iron sculptures near Lansdown, ST 718694
> Dundas Aqueduct, ST 785625
> Combe Down Tunnel, ST 763619

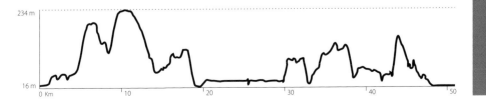

19 LONDON GRAVEL

67KM DALILA LECKY

A gravel adventure to discover the Big Smoke in a different light. A great route for Londoners to escape the city, or for visitors to discover the beautiful green spaces that surround it.

ABOUT DALILA

Gravel riding for Dalila in three words
fun; adventure; exploration

'I don't enjoy the really muddy stuff as much as I just enjoy smashing it along gravel trails. And I like climbs and things that are actually rideable.'

Dalila Lecky got into gravel cycling through cyclo-cross. Initially put off by the mud and the random barriers she'd need to jump across, she eventually gave it a go, and thought it was brilliant. Born and bred in London, cycling isn't her job, just a thing she really enjoys. She works as a building control officer, with the occasional modelling job thrown in. And like other riders I have met, she caught the cyclo-cross bug before she got into gravel.

Dalila used cyclo-cross to keep her motivated to ride over the winter months. But a lot of the riding she did with her friends to train was also very similar to gravel riding. And while she still loves cyclo-cross races, the thing she wasn't enjoying was the really muddy stuff and having to carry her bike too much. Eventually, she made the switch to gravel racing.

'I would say that gravel cycling has a very inclusive, very chilled out community. It doesn't feel as competitive as road cycling can and I've definitely seen loads of women getting into gravel cycling.'

While she likes other types of cycling, gravel riding has become Dalila's favourite. She has raced in the King's Cup, and came, unexpectedly for her, fifth in her category at Battle on the Beach in 2021. And while Dalila likes the competitive nature of events, she also loves the times when she can simply go out and let her curiosity run free. This other side of gravel riding is what she thinks appeals not only to her, but also to the many women who have taken up gravel cycling.

'There's something special in knowing that I can let my curiosity run free and explore the little paths and tracks just to see where they go, even if sometimes they go nowhere. Maybe one day our politicians will see how these open access restrictions disconnect the people from the land and make it harder for them to understand the impact we are having on the planet.'

Two of her trips took her to Scotland, to test ride the Raiders Gravel event, and to complete the Rapha Pennine Rally, which was her first multi-day gravel adventure. This is where she had a real taste of what open access means, not only for exploring by bike, but also to reconnect people to nature and let them understand the impact they have on the planet.

'There's nothing that sparks joy more than seeing a little sign saying: Not suitable for motor vehicles.'

ESHER COMMON.

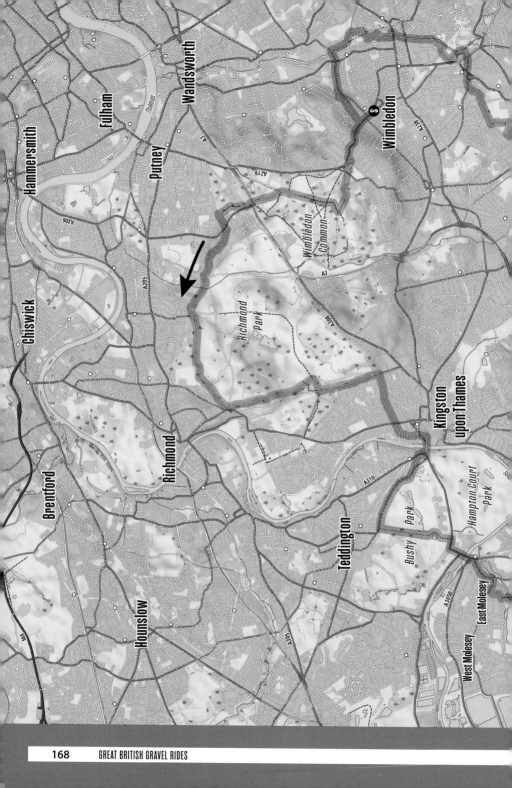

Hammersmith

Fulham

Wandsworth

Putney

Thames

A3

A219

Wimbledon

A238

Wimbledon Common

A3

A205

Chiswick

Richmond Park

A308

Brentford

Richmond

Kingston upon Thames

Hampton Court Park

A310

Bushy Park

Teddington

Hounslow

A305

M4

A3050

West Molesey

East Molesey

A BEAUTIFUL GRAVEL TRAIL AT ASHTEAD COMMON.

Gravel gives her the freedom to escape the city from time to time, while she doesn't have to worry about picking her line. It's the freedom that gravel offers which she likes the most. A gravel bike is the perfect bike to get into the countryside and then zip back in no time. And leave the cars behind, even if it's just for a brief moment.

ABOUT DALILA'S ROUTE

There is no shortage of gravel routes around Dalila's home town of London. Gravel riding differs hugely across the UK, and it's the fast riding that Dalila likes the most – luckily, there is a lot of this around London.

But Dalila's route isn't just one for riding fast: it also offers plenty of opportunities to stop and enjoy. London is a large and densely-populated city; at times, this route offers a real sense of getting away from it all. It's a great route for Londoners to escape the city, or for visitors to discover a different side of the Big Smoke, often far away from the crowds.

ROUTE DESCRIPTION

The route starts at Wimbledon railway station and follows Wimbledon Hill Road into Wimbledon Village. Leaving the main road, the route follows a cycle path and a cycle lane down a one-way street, and then continues on a bridleway on to Wimbledon Common. After a short off-road section, it continues on the road, joining London Cycle Network 73 for a short while, and then another bridleway, which turns into a cycle path at The Windmill.

The Windmill, which was built as a flour mill in 1817 by Charles March to benefit the local community, is a prominent feature of Wimbledon Common. As a hollow-post mill, it was more typical of the type of construction popular for Dutch mills at the time, rather than English mills; it is thought that March mirrored the design of a nearby mill at Southwark. Bizarrely, during this time The Windmill was also used as a vantage point for watching the frequent duels that took place on Wimbledon Common and

DEER IN BUSHY PARK.

Putney Heath. The mill had been operational for less than half a century when, in 1864, the mill was sold, and the machinery was removed; a few years later the mill was converted into residential accommodation. Although there is still no machinery in the mill, the sails have been fully restored and the building converted into an interesting museum, which houses interactive exhibits on local history and rural life. There is also a cafe nearby.

The route continues on the Windmill Ride (a paved cycle path), crosses Kingston Road and continues on a singletrack trail across Putney Heath, a quintessentially English green common land with open heath and wooded glades. The route joins London Cycle Network 71 on Roehampton High Street through Roehampton, then continues on Danebury Avenue through Roehampton Gate into Richmond Park.

Richmond Park, which was founded as a deer park by Charles I and is now the largest of London's Royal Parks, is vital for wildlife conservation, both nationally and internationally. You'll be able to spot the many deer roaming the park on this section of the route. Many famous artists have found inspiration among its landscapes, and it has served as a location for several films and TV series. Pedestrian gates into the park are open 24 hours per day, except during the deer culls (from November to early December and February to early March), when the gates are closed overnight.

The route follows the Tamsin Trail, a traffic-free gravel trail that forms a circuit of Richmond Park. The route passes East Sheen Gate, Bog Gate, Cambrian Gate and Bishop's Gate. From Richmond Gate it continues south on the Tamsin Trail and on a short section of Sustrans National Route 4 to Ham Gate, and continues on the Tamsin Trail to Kingston Gate. This stretch takes you far away from the hustle and bustle of London and provides for fantastic gravel riding on wide paths through stunning woodlands. Make sure to cycle at a reasonable pace, as all the paths are popular with other users too.

At Kingston Gate the route leaves Richmond Park on Kings Road towards the Thames. It joins London Cycle Network 75 for a short section and

SMOOTH GRAVEL ON WIMBLEDON COMMON.

THIS ROUTE IS FUN TO RIDE BY DAY OR NIGHT.

then connects again with Sustrans National Route 4 to cross the Thames on Kingston Bridge. Up until the early eighteenth century, Kingston Bridge was the only crossing of the Thames between London Bridge and Staines Bridge in Surrey; Putney Bridge, which is to the north-east of Kingston Bridge, provided an additional crossing point when it opened in 1729. Kingston upon Thames has a long history – Saxon kings were crowned in the ancient market town. Today, it is the administrative centre of the Royal Borough of Kingston upon Thames; it was also the setting for several cycling events during the 2012 Summer Olympics: the men's road time trial, women's road time trial, men's road race and the women's road race.

The route leaves Sustrans National Route 4 on the other side of the bridge and continues on Park Road into Bushy Park, the second largest of London's Royal Parks. The park is famed for its mix of waterways, gardens, and roaming herds of red and fallow deer; it is also where Parkrun began in October 2004. The route first follows a gravel path on the edge of the woodland and heads south through the park on Chestnut Avenue. Bushy Park is the location of Chestnut Sunday, when Londoners celebrate the blossoming of the trees along Chestnut Avenue. The tradition dates back to Victorian times; it stopped around the time of World War II, but the tradition has

been resurrected in recent decades.

The route passes the Diana Fountain, a seventeenth-century statue and water feature in honour of the Roman goddess, Diana. The statue hasn't always stood in its current location – it was initially produced for Somerset House in the 1630s, then remodelled a few decades later. It has been situated on Chestnut Avenue in Bushy Park since 1713. The route continues on Hampton Court Road and passes Hampton Court Palace, a royal palace and major tourist attraction. Along with the palace and gardens, other attractions include a huge grape vine, a hedge maze and the royal tennis court. The last monarch to reside in the palace was King George II.

The route crosses the Thames on Sustrans National Route 4 then continues on Bridge Road and a few smaller residential streets. It utilises a bridleway and crosses the River Ember, before continuing on roads to Esher railway station. Shortly afterwards, the route moves off-road again, crossing Littleworth Common, which makes for some fantastic riding. At one time, Littleworth Common was open heathland; most of it is now oak and birch woodland. The route continues on more roads to Esher Common. It follows a wide, smooth gravel path lined with conifer trees on the northern edge of the common, then heads south across the common, crosses the Cobham Bypass and continues in another section of woodland.

LUSH GREENERY AND SMOOTH TRACKS AT RICHMOND PARK.

Heading back, the route again crosses the bypass and continues through Arbrook Common and on Birchwood Lane to Birch Wood. The riding here is all off-road on well-graded gravel paths, but expect some muddy puddles at times.

The route continues through more forests, including Limekiln Wood, The Heckets and Prince's Coverts. This section of the route makes you forget that you are so close to one of the biggest urban centres in the world. Near Telegraph Hill, the route crosses Kingston Road and continues on a bridleway on the edge of Ashtead Common National Nature Reserve. There is the site of a Roman villa to explore, alongside ancient earthworks and beautiful grassy avenues. The route traverses Epsom Common, before the route crosses Christ Church Road and continues on a mixture of paths and cycle trails.

The route follows the Thames Down Link though Horton Country Park, a rustic landscape of ancient woodland, hedgerows, fields and wildlife-rich ponds.

After a short section on a road, the route follows a cycle path through Bonegate Open Space in Chessington, and then continues on a cycle path to the right along the Hogsmill River to Hogsmill Nature Reserve. This small strip of riverside space is a remnant of the farmland that once surrounded the Hogsmill River – today, various housing developments run fairly close to the river. The river was vital in the history of Ewell: it was used as the source of power for several mills, including a gunpowder mill, and as a location for famous artists, including Sir John Everett Millais.

The route crosses a railway line and then continues on roads into Ewell, passing the Bourne Hall Museum. A succession of residential roads and cycle paths follows, before the route enters Nonsuch Park, the last remaining part of the Little Park of Nonsuch, which was a deer hunting park centred on the former Nonsuch Palace and established by Henry VIII. The route passes the site of the former palace and continues on a cycle path through the

DISTANCE **67km/42 miles** ⟩ ASCENT **293m/961 ft** ⟩ GRADE **Challenging** ⟩ START/FINISH **Wimbledon railway station** ⟩ START/FINISH GRID REF **TQ 248706** ⟩ BIKE-FRIENDLY PUBLIC TRANSPORT **At the start** ⟩ HIGHEST POINT **76m/249 ft** ⟩ TERRAIN **Urban parks and cycle routes, with some sections in low-lying woodlands** ⟩ RECOMMENDED TYRES **Schwalbe G-One Allround**

BEST TIME TO RIDE

| JAN | FEB | MAR | APR | MAY | JUN | JUL | AUG | SEP | OCT | NOV | DEC |

SINGLETRACK **20%**   PATH **15%**   CYCLE PATH **30%**   ROAD **35%**

park, and on into Cheam Park. The park originally formed the grounds of the nineteenth-century Cheam Park House. The house and grounds were acquired by the local council in the 1930s and the house was used as a gas mask factory in the early part of World War II. However, the house was badly damaged during an air raid and was demolished shortly afterwards.

The route exits the park and descends gently up St Dunstan's Hill (A217) through Cheam, and then follows a cycle path to Mayflower Park. Turning right, it crosses a large cemetery and, after a few roads, into Morden Park. In Morden Park, the route joins Sustrans National Route 208 for a brief while and then continues on Links Avenue into Morden. The route continues through the National-Trust-owned Morden Hall Park, which sits on the banks of the River Wandle. The river splits into channels here, which is a legacy of the former mill leats. If the entrance to the park on Morden Hall Road is closed due to the time of day, the entrance further north on Morden Road is always open so you can reconnect with the route.

In the park, the route joins the Wandle Trail (Sustrans National Route 20), which provides another fun gravel section, before the route continues along the banks of the river. Briefly diverting from the Wandle Trail, the route passes Wandle Meadow Nature Park on a path and rejoins Sustrans National Route 20 where it crosses the River Graveney. At Plough Lane, where the Wandle is crossed again, the route leaves the Wandle Trail and continues on Gap Road. The route passes another cemetery and, after a railway crossing, the route joins London Cycle Network 29 to reach the end of the route at Wimbledon railway station. There is an excellent fish and chip shop, Vintage Fish, on Leopold Road, close to the end of the route, plus a number of other takeaways nearby, if you are ready for a proper meal.

OTHER ROUTES NEARBY
> London Cycle Network routes
> Sustrans National Route 4
> Sustrans National Route 208
> Tamsin Trail
> Wandle Trail (Sustrans National Route 20)

WHERE TO EAT
> Gail's Bakery, Wimbledon
> Windmill Tearooms, Wimbledon Common
> Colicci Roehampton Gate Cafe, Richmond Park
> Pembroke Lodge Kiosk, Richmond Park
> The Star, Leatherhead
> The Spring Tavern, Epsom
> Morden Brook, Morden
> Stableyard Cafe and Potting Shed Cafe, National Trust Morden Hall Park
> Vintage Fish, Wimbledon

BIKE SHOPS
> The London Cycle Workshop, East Sheen (T 02080 755 222)
> Richmond Cycles, East Twickenham (T 02088 924 372)
> Balfe's Bikes, Kingston upon Thames (T 02045 315 552)
> Sigma Sports, Hampton Wick (T 03330 068 833)
> London Cycles, Raynes Park (T 02085 424 076)
> Moose Cycles, Colliers Wood (T 02085 449 166)

WHERE TO STOP
> The Windmill, TQ 230725
> Roehampton Gate, TQ 212742
> Chestnut Avenue, TQ 160704
> Diana Fountain, TQ 158692
> Hampton Court Palace, TQ 156685
> Morden Hall Park, TQ 264687

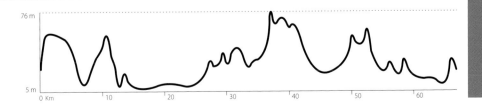

20 NOT THE SOUTH DOWNS WAY!

49KM RORY HITCHENS

With its open countryside, majestic woodlands, pubs, flint buildings and thatched roofs, there is a lot to explore on this loop around the South Downs.

ABOUT RORY

Gravel riding for Rory in three words
smiles and miles

'People are saying it's like old mountain biking, when we didn't have any suspension, and everything was a bit sketchy on the corners. And I think that's the appeal for me.'

Rory Hitchens is the Marketing and Senior Brand Manager for Upgrade Bikes. In 2012 Upgrade Bikes introduced one of the first gravel bikes to the UK: the Kinesis Tripster ATR. Rory has been a household name in mountain biking for a long time and is well known and respected in the bike industry as well. He started mountain biking in 1987, but this wasn't his first adventure into cycling.

'My connection with gravel bikes really harks back to those early touring days when bikes had dropped handlebars. Often on rough roads and out in far-flung places, like Norway and Sweden, on rough dirt roads, but with decent tyres.'

His life as a cyclist started through exploring. As a child it was the best way to escape the small village where he grew up. Later on, it became a way to travel, and then cycling became a means of transport. And when mountain bikes appeared, his cycle tours got a bit more adventurous. This is why, for Rory, gravel cycling combines the first 10 years of becoming a touring cyclist, on skinny tyres, with the early days when he turned into a mountain bike racer, on narrow handlebars.

'Gravel is the term, but it's off-road riding. It's rough stuff.'

Rory grew up in West Sussex, a region that will always have a special place in his heart. When he started mountain biking it was not only a

way to define himself, but also to explore – there was so much more to explore in the area than just the well-known South Downs Way. And this is exactly where he thinks modern gravel bikes play the most important role. Gravel bikes encourage people to travel more, just like in his 'old' touring days.

For Rory gravel biking is as much about discovering the local area as it is about those bigger adventures. Rory is a big fan of the Rough-Stuff Fellowship; gravel cycling has a lot of parallels with this movement, where any bike can be used to explore the expansive tracts of land that Britain has to offer.

'As an engineer, Mike Hall had a great head for detail that helped him achieve so much in his big races. A mild manner hid his fiercely competitive nature on the bike. He also had a very generous outlook

YOU'LL FIND MANY HOUSES BUILT OF FLINT IN WEST SUSSEX.

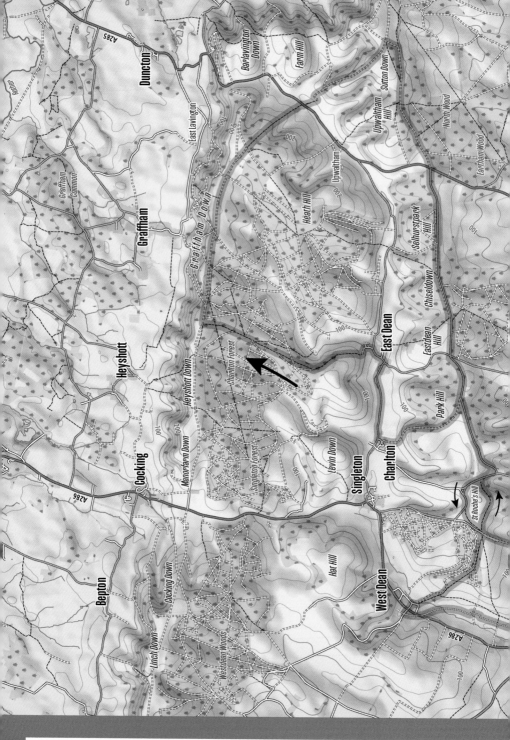

ON THE SOUTH DOWNS WAY NEAR UPWALTHAM.

on life and the TransContinental Race is a befitting legacy to the man that inspired a community of cyclists to take up adventures.'

Rory has a long connection with gravel and ultra-endurance cycling in Britain. In his role as Marketing and Senior Brand Manager he supported British ultra-endurance legend Mike Hall over his career: from his first ride on the Tour Divide in 2011, then winning the inaugural World Cycle Race in 2012 to him winning the Tour Divide in 2016, with a record that still stands today.

ABOUT RORY'S ROUTE

While Rory now calls Brighton his home, his favourite places to ride are around the ancient Roman city of Chichester – the area where he first started mountain biking. Defined by its open countryside, majestic woodlands, pubs, flint buildings and thatched roofs, there is a lot to explore. The trails aren't always straightforward – this route wouldn't have the signature of a former mountain bike champion if it didn't have the odd section to test your skills on drop bars, especially in wet conditions.

ROUTE DESCRIPTION

Chichester is the only city in West Sussex. It started as a Roman then an Anglo-Saxon settlement, and was a major market town in Norman and medieval times. The city retains some of the street plan as laid out by the Romans. Chichester Cathedral's spire, which rises above the green copper roof of the cathedral, can be seen for miles around. It is the only English medieval cathedral which is visible from the sea and can also be seen from many vantage points when cycling this route. In the past it was said that Chichester was small enough for the city's entire population to fit inside the cathedral at once.

The route starts at Chichester railway station and follows South Street into the city centre. There are plenty of options for getting a snack in the centre, although a short detour to the Canal Centre (which is passed near the end of the route) is highly recommended for coffee and pastries. At the Chichester Cross, an elaborate market cross standing at the intersection of the four principal streets, the route takes a left towards the cathedral and joins Sustrans National Route 2. The cathedral is an outstanding example of a typical English cathedral, but it does have the more unusual features of a free-standing medieval bell tower and double aisles. It includes both Norman- and Gothic-style architecture and is well worth a visit.

From the cathedral the route continues across the Westgate Roundabout and then on Westgate to the start of the Centurion Way, a cycling route that follows the old Chichester to Midhurst railway line. Fishbourne Roman Palace, the largest Roman house in Britain, is a short detour from the start of the Centurion Way. This section ascends gradually, although it is hardly noticeable, towards the South Downs. The route is traffic-free and mainly sealed, but some gravel sections remain as well. The path quickly enters the hidden woodland at Brandy Hole Copse, a local nature reserve; look out for sweet chestnut, oak and hazel trees and, in spring, bluebells can be spotted.

A little further north, where the Roman road from Silchester to Chichester crosses the route, is a wonderful sculpture by David Kemp – the *Chichester Road Gang* shows a pack of spade-wielding workers and a ganger in a bowler hat. After passing through Lavant on quiet roads, the route rejoins the old railway line to West Dean, where the Centurion Way currently finishes. Some steps need to be negotiated to leave the cycle path to reach the village of West Dean; with its whitewashed pub, thatched cottages, village store and cafe, this makes a great first stop on the route.

The route passes a bridge over the River Lavant and follows the Monarch's Way, passing near West Dean College, a centre for the study of conservation, arts, crafts, writing, gardening and music. Just outside the village the route starts climbing more

EXTRA CARE IS NEEDED ON CHALK ROAD.

steeply on a well-surfaced section of doubletrack, but some sections can be trickier. Sturdy tyres are recommended for this route, as the flint found on many paths of the South Downs breaks and chips into sharp-edged pieces. The route climbs past the Westside Plantation to pass The Trundle, an Iron Age hill fort built on top of an earlier Neolithic structure, situated on St Roche's Hill. This Neolithic site was discovered in 1925, when an archaeologist obtained an aerial photograph of The Trundle, which clearly showed additional structures inside the ramparts of the hill fort. The route traverses the southern side of the hill fort on a grassy path, with great views towards Chichester – you can easily spot the cathedral from here.

The route connects to Racecourse Road on a number of small trails and follows the road past Goodwood Racecourse. It follows Chalk Road, a gravel path at the edge of the racecourse, into a woodland, descending into Charlton. Extra care is needed on this section, as the path has deep ruts in some places. The chalky path can also become extremely slippery in wet conditions. However, in dry conditions this is fantastic gravel riding – some of the best in Britain. The route enters Charlton on Chalk Road, and then takes a right at The Fox Goes Free, a great countryside pub. For some relaxed riding the route follows Charlton Road to East Dean, passing the Gnarly Tree – this sustainable clothing shop is situated in an old fuel station and is well worth a stop. The parish church, pub and most of the houses are built of flint, and the village pond is the source of the River Lavant.

At the edge of the village the route leaves the main road and climbs steeply at first, and then more gradually, on a bridleway towards Eastdean Wood. East of Heyshott Down the route meets the South Downs Way. The South Downs Way, which follows old routes and ways along the ridges and chalk escarpment of the South Downs, is undoubtedly one of the most popular long-distance paths in England and is a great choice for off-road cyclists. One of the 16 National Trails in England and Wales, this 160-kilometre route is the only National Trail to lie entirely within a national park.

When you meet the South Downs Way you will reach the highest point of the route. As a reward for the steep climb, you can enjoy beautiful views over the area. The riding here is great too, but expect some muddy sections at times as well. The route undulates along the top, before a great descent follows. At the bottom of the valley, where the South Downs Way crosses the A285, the Cadence Cafe, at Cadence's Upwaltham Hub, provides another great rest stop. The cafe is nestled in a picturesque valley next to a beautiful rural campsite. It's the perfect stop along the South Downs Way to refuel, relax and take in the incredible views over the national park.

CHALKPIT LANE.

Its sandwiches, named after cycling legends, are great and the coffee is fabulous.

The route follows the South Downs Way up to Sutton Down, where it leaves the long-distance trail and follows a bridleway on the edge of a woodland to Upwaltham Hill. This part of the route can be muddy. Especially on a hot day, the woodland here provides some welcome shelter, before the route rejoins tarmac at Selhurst Park Road. There is a short off-road section just after Selhurstpark Hill, which provides some fabulous gravel riding in the woodland; you can continue along the road as an alternative. Just after Eastdean Hill the route overlaps with the outbound route and passes the Goodwood Racecourse once again. The Trundle is passed on its northern edge on a grassy bridleway, after which the outbound and return route meet. The views from here towards Chichester are again stunning, and what follows is one of the most fun descents in the route.

Following Chalkpit Lane, the route descends

DISTANCE **49km/30 miles** 〉 ASCENT **590m/1,936 ft** 〉 GRADE **Challenging** 〉 START/FINISH **Chichester railway station** 〉 START/FINISH GRID REF **SU 859043** 〉 BIKE-FRIENDLY PUBLIC TRANSPORT **At the start** 〉 HIGHEST POINT **234m/768 ft** 〉 TERRAIN **Fast-flowing riding with some technical sections; challenging in wet conditions** 〉 RECOMMENDED TYRES **Schwalbe G-One Bite**

BEST TIME TO RIDE

| JAN | FEB | MAR | APR | MAY | JUN | JUL | AUG | SEP | OCT | NOV | DEC |

SINGLETRACK **10%**   PATH **40%**   CYCLE PATH **15%**   ROAD **35%**

CHICHESTER CATHEDRAL.

from the South Downs back into the valley on a fabulous section of singletrack. As on other parts of the route care is needed, especially in wet conditions. Make sure that you watch out for other path users as well while enjoying the descent. The route continues on through East Lavant on Lower Road and Fordwater Road, then crosses the River Lavant and joins Fordwater Road again heading into town. The route is on tarmac all the way to the finish from here, passing Havenstoke Park and Oaklands Park. After a roundabout the route passes Priory Park, which is worth a quick detour. The park, which hosts the Guildhall and Chichester Castle, is bordered to the north and east by part of Chichester's medieval city walls, which are built upon Roman foundations. Following quiet and busier roads through the city centre, the route's last recommended stop is the picturesque basin of the Chichester Canal, where the heritage centre and cafe provide a perfect end to a great day on the bike.

OTHER ROUTES NEARBY
> Centurion Way
> South Downs Way
> Sustrans National Route 2

WHERE TO EAT
> West Dean Stores & Tea Room, West Dean
> The Fox Goes Free, Charlton
> Cadence Cafe, Upwaltham Hub, Littleton Farm
> Canal Cafe, Chichester

BIKE SHOPS
> Hargroves Cycles, Chichester (**T** 01243 537 337)

WHERE TO STOP
> Chichester Cross, SU 861048
> Chichester Cathedral, SU 860048
> Fishbourne Roman Palace, SU 840047
> Brandy Hole Copse, SU 852065
> *Chichester Road Gang*, SU 856076
> The Trundle, SU 877110
> Gnarly Tree, SU 901129
> City walls at Priory Park, SU 863051
> Chichester Canal Basin, SU 859041

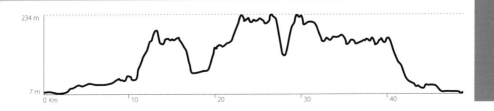

SOUTH DOWNS
21 MINT SAUCE GRAVEL
51KM   JO BURT

This route is a fast-flowing rollercoaster through Sussex, which provided years of inspiration for the famous Mint Sauce cartoons.

ABOUT JO
Gravel riding for Jo in three words
fun; bouncy; tongue-out

'I've got 30 years of pictures that I can show you of what cycling is like, but I am most famous for drawing the sheep on a mountain bike that's based around Sussex.'

Jo Burt is possibly best described as 'that bloke that does the sheep'. An illustrator, cartoonist, writer and cat owner, he loves drawing bikes and sheep and is well known for his iconic *Mint Sauce* cartoon strip in *Mountain Biking UK*, inspired by the landscape of the South Downs, which he calls home.

He started doing cartoons for the Mountain Bike Club, a UK organisation that ran races and sent out a photocopied newsletter in the early days of the UK mountain bike scene. He sent them some cartoons on spec – luckily, they liked them and put them in the newsletter. So he did some more, and it continued like this for a time. Jo then asked Max Glaskin from the Mountain Bike Club if he knew of any 'proper' magazines that might like his cartoons. *Mint Sauce* featured in *Bicycle Action* in 1988 and in *Mountain Biking UK* about 18 months later. After more than 30 years, *Mint Sauce* is still going strong.

When he is not drawing bikes, Jo rides them or writes about them. Or he enjoys eating after a bike ride. What bike he rides doesn't really matter, although in recent years he's developed a love for long road rides into the far distance, with just a toothbrush and a spare pair of socks for company.

'When I was 18 my dad gave me some money that I was supposed to invest in something. I went and bought a mountain bike with it.'

Jo learnt to ride a bike when he was about five, and hasn't stopped enjoying it since. From those early days in the car park of his

grandparents' pub, he went on to own a succession of second-hand bikes as a kid. Then he got 'a bit more serious' with his 'green Dawes light-tourer, sports-bike thing'. This was when Jo lived in the far reaches of the suburbs. A bike was simply a way of getting around and seeing friends.

When he started to cycle more as a hobby, he saw an advert for a mountain bike in a cycling magazine. About the same time, his dad gave him £500 for his eighteenth birthday. And while his dad was hoping he'd invest it wisely, he spent most of it on a top-of-the-range Saracen mountain bike.

'When gravel bikes turned up and they were comfier, more capable bikes, with brakes that worked, it was a natural swap to get one as soon as possible.'

Jo has been seen riding his Kinesis Tripster AT a lot, and has also now illustrated two sets of

DESCENDING NEAR STEYNING.

Steyning

Bramber

Upper
Beeding

Castle
Town

Steyning
Round Hill

Steyning
Bowl

Botolphs

Annington
Hill

Coombes

Beggars Bush

Old
Shoreham

SUSTRANS NATIONAL ROUTE 223.

bar tape for drop-bar bikes. He loves how capable gravel bikes are, and certainly rides them as if they were mountain bikes. In his eyes there'll be refinements on gravel bikes in the future, like suspension forks, lighter bike frames and improved tyres and gearing. The main reason he rides a gravel bike? They are super adaptable.

'Cycling is a lot like life. You can adapt all the cartoons to things that happen in your life and in cycling.'

If you ever see a sheep riding a gravel bike in the South Downs, you'll know who's responsible!

ABOUT JO'S ROUTE

There are quite a few sheep around the South Downs, and this route served as inspiration for many of Jo's cartoons. There is a huge variety of riding in this part of Britain, from the chalk to the beautiful woodlands, all intercepted by gravel paths and lots of small country roads. Jo is someone who learnt mountain biking in the early days, and some parts of this route are on the more technical side, especially when ridden in the wet. But the route also features many really nice and fast-flowing sections, and plenty of great places to stop, from nice cafes to fancy restaurants. It'll give you a real flavour of the country that inspired *Mint Sauce*.

ROUTE DESCRIPTION

The route starts at Shoreham-by-Sea railway station and follows Sustrans National Route 2 for a short distance. Just before the River Adur,

the route passes La Patisserie Shoreham, which will provide you with tasty coffee and pastries to help you tackle the many climbs to come.

After a short section on High Street, the route follows the Downs Link (Sustrans National Route 223) along the banks of the River Adur on a former railway line. This makes the first part of the route mostly flat, riding on a very smooth gravel path along the river. The Shoreham Toll Bridge, which crosses the river shortly afterwards, is not only the last of its kind in Sussex, but also one of the last of its kind anywhere in the world. After being closed and left to rot in the 1990s, it underwent a major refurbishment in 2008, which aimed to extend the life of the bridge for a further 30 years. The bridge is a popular local

A MORE TECHNICAL TRAIL.

landmark and, as it has been designated a bridleway, well used by people on foot, bike and horseback. It is also a popular spot for local fishermen.

The route continues on the Downs Link until it reaches the Steyning Bypass. You can either cross the busy road directly or, as is shown in the GPX file, take a short detour and cross the road via an underpass. The route follows a cycle path to a roundabout and heads west on Maudlin Lane and Sopers Lane to Steyning Bowl. This part of the route follows the Monarch's Way, a long-distance trail which traces the protracted route taken by King Charles II during his escape after being defeated by Cromwell in 1651.

The tarmac roads become a concrete path which climbs steeply uphill with beautiful views into the valley and over the surrounding hills of the South Downs. The route meets the South Downs Way at Titch Hill. A very popular choice for walkers and cyclists alike, the 160-kilometre South Downs Way is a bridleway for its entire length and follows the old routes and drove roads along the chalk ridges and escarpment of the South Downs. The route follows a singletrack trail parallel to the road first, and a wide gravel path once it crosses the road. The route

continues to climb, but much more gradually, until it flattens out above Steyning.

A bridleway on the right leads off the South Downs Way into a woodland. Care is needed on this section; the track continues on the edge of the woodland towards Steyning Round Hill and past a chalk pit heading towards Steyning. The route follows a number of roads downhill into the town. Steyning has plenty of opportunities to eat or stock up on supplies – there are a couple of supermarkets, plenty of bakeries and a few pubs in the centre of the town.

The route crosses the Steyning Bypass then shortly afterwards it turns right on to Roman Road and joins the Downs Link again to reach the remains of Bramber Castle, built in the late eleventh and early twelfth centuries. Little survives of the original structure, as subsidence on a large scale led to the ruin of the castle during the sixteenth century, and much of the stone was later used to construct the bridge and other buildings in the village. The most prominent remaining feature is the gatehouse tower, which still stands to almost its full height.

The route continues into Bramber, passing St Mary's House, a fifteenth-century timber-framed house on

APPROACHING DEVIL'S DYKE.

a site connected to the Knights Templar. There are charming gardens too, with some impressive topiary figures and a secret garden. The house and gardens are open to the public in summer and there is a tea room in the grounds.

After crossing the River Adur the route continues into Upper Beeding. If you need a bit of extra food before you tackle the toughest climb of the route, there is a handy petrol station in the village. After a few more residential streets, the route joins the Monarch's Way again and climbs steeply on a rutted gravel path. This is the most difficult section of the route – it might be a hike-a-bike section for some. At the top, the route crosses the South Downs Way and continues to climb on the Monarch's Way towards Beeding Hill.

After a nice descent on a fast gravel track another climb follows, as the route follows a bridleway on the left to Freshcombe and Summersdeane Farm on Truleigh Hill, where it rejoins the South Downs Way for a while. The South Downs Way descends on a wide gravel track to Edburton Hill, a great place to soak up the views. The landscape up here is open

and sparse. Rudyard Kipling famously described the Downs as being 'whalebacked' – looking at Perching Hill from this viewpoint you can imagine what he meant. A short climb follows, past the site of Edburton motte and bailey castle, which is believed to date from the immediate post-Conquest period. If you have time, you can stop to inspect the earthworks and interior area of the castle. A descent to Perching Hill follows.

While following the South Downs Way seems tempting, the route continues on a gravel track to the west of Perching Hill, right past Perchinghill Barn. Nearby is the site of a Downland medieval hamlet; the cultivation terraces are said to have survived until Victorian times. This is a remote place: just sheep, pylons, a rusting barn, big modern pastures and a slim fragment of the old Downland pastures where the steepness of the slopes halted the plough. The area has a wealth of old Downland pasture species, including orchids, spring sedge and devil's-bit. The path descends past Tenant Hill to Mile Oak Farm, which hosts a cafe and farm shop. From here, a climb to Cockroost Hill follows, after which the route

DISTANCE **51km/32 miles** 〉 ASCENT **858m/2,815 ft** 〉 GRADE **Challenging** 〉 START/FINISH **Shoreham-by-Sea railway station** 〉 START/FINISH GRID REF **TQ 218053** 〉 BIKE-FRIENDLY PUBLIC TRANSPORT **At the start** 〉 HIGHEST POINT **206m/676 ft** 〉 TERRAIN **Fast-flowing riding with some technical singletrack sections; challenging in wet conditions** 〉 RECOMMENDED TYRES **Schwalbe G-One Bite**

BEST TIME TO RIDE

| JAN | FEB | MAR | APR | MAY | JUN | JUL | AUG | SEP | OCT | NOV | DEC |

SINGLETRACK **20%**   PATH **35%**   CYCLE PATH **20%**   ROAD **25%**

continues on the Sussex Border Path to Fulking Hill, the peak immediately west of Devil's Dyke.

Devil's Dyke, which became a major local tourist attraction in the late nineteenth century, is a deep, dry, v-shaped valley; it is now a popular viewpoint and walking area. Where the South Downs Way crosses the road, you'll reach the highest point of the loop at 206 metres. The descent that follows gives way to great views over Devil's Dyke, before the route leaves the South Downs Way to the right and descends on a bridleway across the Dyke Golf Club. After the golf course a short section on the road follows, and then a bridleway descent. Above the Brighton and Hove Golf Club, the route joins the Monarch's Way again into the Benfield Valley.

A short climb towards the Brighton and Hove Bypass is followed by a fun descent on a bridleway into Portslade Village, and another climb on the Sussex Border Path on the western edge of Mile Oak. From here, the route follows a gravel track parallel to the bypass, then continues on a number of different roads to cross the bypass at the roundabout at Holmbush Centre. The route follows a byway to Erringham Farm, which marks the last climb. From here, it's downhill on the road, passing through Mill Hill Nature Reserve on the northern outskirts of Shoreham-by-Sea. This nature reserve is one of the best areas in Sussex for observing butterflies; it also boasts an impressive 160 species of flowering plant, with secondary woodland, chalk grassland and scrub to enjoy. More roads follow to return to Shoreham-by-Sea railway station. If you want to finish the ride in proper Jo Burt style, there are loads of places nearby to eat; Teddys of Shoreham is Jo's personal favourite.

A STEEP CLIMB ON THE MONARCH'S WAY.

OTHER ROUTES NEARBY
> Downs Link (Sustrans National Route 223)
> Monarch's Way
> South Downs Way
> Sussex Border Path
> Sustrans National Route 2

WHERE TO EAT
> La Patisserie Shoreham, Shoreham-by-Sea
> Steyning Tea Rooms, Steyning
> Mile Oak Farm Shop and Cafe, Portslade
> Devil's Dyke, Poynings
> Teddys of Shoreham, Shoreham-by-Sea

BIKE SHOPS
> Giant Shoreham, Shoreham-by-Sea (T 01273 463 579)
> M's Cycles, Shoreham-by-Sea (T 01273 567 591)
> Ebike Sussex, Shoreham-by-Sea (T 01273 596 368)

WHERE TO STOP
> Shoreham Toll Bridge, TQ 207059
> Steyning Bowl, TQ 162095
> Bramber Castle, TQ 185106
> Edburton Hill, TQ 232110
> Edburton motte and bailey castle, TQ 238110
> Medieval village of Perching, TQ 245104
> Devil's Dyke, TQ 264111
> Mill Hill Nature Reserve, TQ 212072

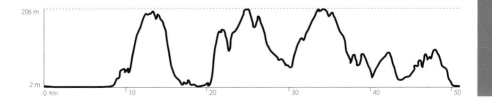

ISLE OF PURBECK

22 JURASSIC GRAVEL

51KM   CHARLIE HOBBS

White chalk cliffs provide the perfect backdrop to one of the longest running gravel events in Britain – the Dorset Dirt Dash – and this stunning ride on the Isle of Purbeck.

ABOUT CHARLIE

Gravel riding for Charlie in three words
bikes; beers; brothers

'The Dorset Dirt Dash was invented; we had gravel and people would know how to use these bikes.'
          Most people still know, and possibly will always know, Charlie Hobbs as 'Charlie the Bikemonger'. He started with an online bike shop; next he moved into his own physical shop in Swanage; he then sold his business in 2018. While he is no longer selling bikes, he still organises gravel events and works for Britain's much-loved mountain bike magazine, *Singletrack*. In fact, his Dorset Dirt Dash was either the first, or one of the first, gravel events in Britain.

For him, the gravel bike boom started with the Salsa Warbird. Charlie was one of the first dealers to sell these gravel bikes in the UK. After selling a few, he created the Dorset Dirt Dash – to give people the opportunity to ride gravel bikes where they should be ridden. His home trails around Swanage were perfect for this. Back in those days, only two events existed in the US, so in 2013 he started his own event. And little has changed: the route is almost the same. But just as gravel cycling has grown, the event has also grown significantly. From 30 guys and some chicken stew with stinging nettle and gin dumplings cooking on a fire, it has grown to 250 people – still riding bikes and sitting around a fire to share stories.

'Gravel cycling is just riding your bike in the countryside; you don't actually need to be on a gravel bike.'

Having started cycling more than 30 years ago, Charlie has experienced most of the innovations in the bike industry first-hand.

He was, and still is, an avid singlespeeder, so it doesn't come as a major surprise that he thinks that modern full suspension bikes are 'way over-biked', especially in an area like the Purbeck Hills.

'You're better off on a gravel bike. You can still get kicks on basic trails. We've almost gone all the way around in a 30-year circle; we're back to rigid bikes in the Purbecks.'

And in 10 years' time? With the experience of a former shopkeeper, he thinks that gravel bikes will become the norm. Mountain bikes aren't that practical, as they are always going to be slower on the roads. As an everyday bike, a gravel bike is much more fun. As more bikes are sold, they will eventually also become more accessible, and move from niche to mainstream. And eventually events will follow that trajectory as well.

OLD HARRY ROCKS.

Sandbanks

Ferry

South Haven
Point

Gravel Point

Brand's
Bay

Studland Heath

Rempstone Heath

Studland
Bay

Godlingston
Heath

Studland

Handfast Point

B3351

Brenscombe Hill

Ballard Down

Woolgarston

Kingswood Down

Ballard
Point

Purbeck Hills

Ulwell

100

40

rman's
Cross

A351

20

Swanage
Bay

Langton
Matravers

Acton

Peveril
Point

Swanage

100

100

Durlston Head

ON THE PRIEST'S WAY NEAR SWANAGE.

ABOUT CHARLIE'S ROUTE

In the past, this ride would have been described as a classic 1990s mountain bike ride – enjoyable without suspension and on V-brakes. Three decades later, the Jurassic Coast is still a special place to ride bikes, but gravel bikes have taken the spot of the 1990s mountain bike.

Normally the Earth is stacked up in layers. Here those stacks have moved and tilted, creating visible folds of rock and fascinating geology. You can see these folds in the rock, along with some amazing dinosaur footprints, in Purbeck.

For Charlie, who grew up in Bournemouth, a much bigger town than Swanage, this is where the West Country starts, and the countryside becomes wild. The ride offers a taste of everything that he loves about this area: beautiful coastline, lots of coves and cliffs and massive views. And there are places like Corfe Castle and Swanage – proper Enid Blyton country. This route takes you through a brilliant place to live, and a brilliant place to visit.

ROUTE DESCRIPTION

The Isle of Purbeck is not an island in geographical terms, but a peninsula, bordered on three sides by water. It became known as an 'island' because, as the land is low lying, in the past it would have been extremely boggy and tricky to cross in winter. The Purbeck Hills, which are a ridge of chalk from the Cretaceous period, extend along the peninsula from Ballard Down in the east through Corfe Castle and almost to East Lulworth. The Purbeck Hills form part of the Southern England chalk downlands, which also

REMPSTONE HEATH – SANDY BUT BEAUTIFUL.

include Salisbury Plain and the South Downs. The riding here is similar to these areas.

This section of the British coastline is part of the Jurassic Coast – a hugely distinct and appealing landscape with globally significant geology. In 2001, it was announced by UNESCO that the Jurassic Coast was to be a World Heritage Site, due to the exceptional universal value of its landforms, rocks and fossils. It is England's only natural World Heritage Site. This ride is on the eastern edge of the Jurassic Coast, while **23 A taste of the East Devon Trail** (pages 203–211) explores its western side in East Devon. The whole loop is situated in the Dorset Area of Outstanding Natural Beauty, the fifth largest in England, with over 80 per cent of the UK's mammal species living here.

Among the stunning natural beauty of the area

there are a number of Iron Age, Roman and Saxon archaeological sites here to explore. The small settlements in Purbeck grew during the Victorian era, partly due to a rise of tourism. In particular, Swanage became an important seaside resort.

The route starts at the Shell Bay Ferry Terminal, where a chain ferry which crosses the entrance of Poole Harbour from Sandbanks arrives. The ferry service operates from 7.00 a.m. to 11.00 p.m. every day, with shorter operating hours on Christmas Day. The route follows Sustrans National Route 2 from the ferry, heading south-west on a road, passing Studland Bay, a vast area of sandy beaches and heathland. Where Sustrans National Route 2 takes a right turn, the route continues straight ahead on a path that climbs gently towards Knowl Hill, and then follows a bridleway on the left into a woodland.

BEAUTIFUL TRAIL THROUGH A WOODLAND NEAR THE FINISH.

The route continues on Wadmore Lane and meets Ferry Road, on which it continues to Studland. There are a number of pubs here: the route passes the Bankes Arms, which has a large outside seating area and offers accommodation. The route follows lanes through the village. The Norman parish church was built in around 1180; it is largely unchanged from that time. At the edge of the village, the route follows England's longest waymarked walking route, the South West Coast Path. The bridleway crosses a beautiful woodland and continues on a wide path across the cliffs of Ballard Down, leading to Handfast Point. The scenery here is outstanding on a good day. You can see the boats leaving and arriving in Poole Harbour while marvelling at Old Harry Rocks, three chalk formations rising from the sea, including a stump and a stack. They mark the most eastern point of the Jurassic Coast. The path leading up here isn't a wide gravel path as such, but a number of singletrack lines running in parallel. The path to the Old Harry Rocks viewpoint can get extremely busy in summer, so extra care is needed while riding here.

The route continues on the South West Coast Path, climbing gradually along the edge of the cliffs from Handfast Point to Ballard Point, with stunning views over the English Channel. Just before Ballard Point the route follows a bridleway on the right, waymarked as the

Purbeck Way, another long-distance walking route. The climb to Studland Hill will test your legs for the first, but not the last, time on this route. More amazing views follow as you head across Ballard Cliff towards Swanage. Shortly after Studland Hill, there is a technical singletrack descent from Ballard Down. The surface here is very loose, so be prepared to get off the bike and push for some sections. The route continues on a singletrack trail through a woodland and meets a road at Whitecliff Farm. From here, roads are followed into Swanage. The town, which was originally a fishing village and small port, prospered in the Victorian era,

MEANDERING ACROSS THE HIGHEST POINTS OF THE PURBECK HILLS.

first as a quarrying port and later a seaside resort. It remains a popular tourist resort, with many thousands of visitors flocking to the sandy beaches during the peak summer season, so expect things to be busy.

The route continues on Shore Road along the sandy beach, with great views toward the chalk cliffs of Ballard Down on one side of the bay, and Swanage Pier on the opposite side. In summer, part of the shore road is closed for cycling, so you'll have to walk with your bike for about 300 metres. There is an abundance of pubs and cafes in town, and the Swanage Railway is a well-loved attraction for all ages.

The route follows Kings Road through town, and then starts climbing again on a number of residential streets. It picks up the Priest's Way, which follows in the footsteps of a medieval priest on a great, newly-surfaced gravel track. The route passes across open fields, weaves between quarries and enjoys some spectacular views. Only a stone's throw off the

path are the Spyway Dinosaur Footprints, nestled alongside a working quarry and easily accessible on a short walking path. These incredible footprints were made by Jurassic giants, over 140 million years ago.

After Eastington Farm, the route continues on a bridleway to reach a road, which is followed into Worth Matravers to one of Dorset's most famous pubs, which also hosts a Fossil Museum. The much-loved Square and Compass was established in around 1776 and is a Mecca for locals and visitors alike. It sells a range of local ales, but is best known for its traditional, home-pressed cider, made by the owner, as well as pies and pasties. The pub also hosts a buoyant calendar of live music, poetry and performance.

From here, the route continues on a road to meet the B3069 into Kingston. This short section is part of a Dorset Council cycle route – the Purbeck Ride. In Kingston the route continues on a small road to the left, following the Hardy Way, a route named after

WATCH OUT FOR OTHER PATH USERS.

author Thomas Hardy which travels 349 kilometres through Dorset and Wiltshire. At a car park the route follows a wide gravel track through Polar Wood to Swyre Head, at 203 metres the highest point of the Isle of Purbeck (and the route). The hill commands vast views, including east to the Isle of Wight, west past the Isle of Portland to Dartmoor, as well as north across the Purbeck Hills to Poole Harbour. A long downhill on a wide gravel path to Kimmeridge follows, passing Smedmore Hill. The last section, just before the track meets the road, should be ridden with care, as it is steep and loose. The route continues to Blackmanston Farm, from where the route climbs uphill once again. It then turns left on to another road, again following the Purbeck Ride, and continues to climb on the road past Steeple. The route passes the border of the Lulworth Ranges, a military firing range which includes the 'ghost village' of Tyneham. The village was requisitioned in 1943 (supposedly a temporary measure), but was formally placed under a compulsory purchase order by the

British Army in 1948. The village is accessible when the Lulworth Ranges are open to the public; times and dates can be found online.

The route turns right to climb on a section of singletrack on to the ridge and passes Grange Arch, also known as Creech Folly. This folly dates from the eighteenth century and was built by Denis Bond, who owned Creech Grange, a local manor house. Before the trees of the surrounding woodland grew to obscure it, Grange Arch could be seen from the impressive rooms on the south side of Creech Grange. Its aim was to impress visitors by showing them the extent of their host's land and by demonstrating his cultural sophistication.

The route continues on a wide, grassy track along the ridge to Ridgeway Hill, one of the highest points of the Purbeck Hills. From here the route descends to Bare Cross and climbs again to Knowle Hill, following the Hardy Way once again. The route descends again and offers great views towards Corfe Castle, one of the biggest tourist landmarks in Dorset. The castle,

DISTANCE **51km/32 miles** › ASCENT **685m/2,247 ft** › GRADE **Challenging** › START/FINISH **Shell Bay Ferry Terminal** › START/FINISH GRID REF **SZ 036867** BIKE-FRIENDLY PUBLIC TRANSPORT **Poole railway station (8km from the route)** › HIGHEST POINT **203m/666 ft** › TERRAIN **Challenging, especially in high winds as the route is exposed. Some sections are rocky and loose, others are sandy** › RECOMMENDED TYRES **Schwalbe G-One Bite**

BEST TIME TO RIDE

| JAN | FEB | MAR | APR | MAY | JUN | JUL | AUG | SEP | OCT | NOV | DEC |

SINGLETRACK **25%**   PATH **25%**   ROAD **50%**

which dominates the surrounding landscape, has had various functions over the centuries: a Saxon fortress, a Norman stronghold, a royal palace and a family home.

A short detour takes you into the village of Corfe Castle, which can become very busy in the peak summer season but has a brilliant bakery. The route follows the A351 to a roundabout and continues on a single-track road to Norden Common. This, almost flat, part of the route follows vast stretches of heath. The route passes the small settlement of Scotland and joins Sustrans National Route 2 on a gravel track on the right. It continues on a mixture of paths across heath and through woodlands. Some parts can be sandy, but this is mostly very relaxed off-road riding through beautiful scenery. Diverting from Sustrans National Route 2, the route follows a bridleway across Rempstone Heath to Newton Bay and rejoins Sustrans National Route 2 to return to the ferry.

OTHER ROUTES NEARBY

> Dorset 330
> Dorset Council cycle routes (including the Purbeck Ride)
> Dorset Dirt Dash
> Priest's Way
> Sustrans National Route 2

WHERE TO EAT

> Bankes Arms, Studland
> Tawny's Wine Bar, Swanage
> The Salt Pig, Swanage
> Square and Compass, Worth Matravers
> Corfe Castle Village Bakery, Corfe Castle

BIKE SHOPS

> Wareham Cycleworks, Wareham (T 01929 556 601)
> Cyclexperience (bike hire), Corfe Castle

WHERE TO STOP

> Studland Bay, SZ 034835
> Old Harry Rocks viewpoint, SZ 054824
> Spyway Dinosaur Footprints, SY 987781
> Fossil Museum at the Square and Compass, SY 975776
> Swyre Head, SY 934785
> Grange Arch, SY 913818
> Corfe Castle, SY 959823

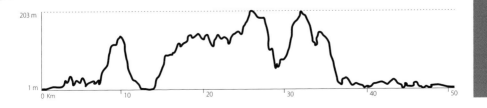

EAST DEVON
23 A TASTE OF THE EAST DEVON TRAIL
77KM KATHERINE MOORE

A gravel route that features demanding riding and rewarding stops in equal measures, in one of the most green and beautiful parts of England. Binoculars are a must too, as the route offers multiple opportunities to enjoy the wildlife along the route.

ABOUT KATHERINE

Gravel riding for Katherine in three words
community; nature; escapism

'I think there is this really new community, that is a complete mixed bag of people in the best way possible. It has this rebellious, alternative streak to it, which I really like. There are no rules about what you have to wear or ride. Any bike is a gravel bike if you have the confidence.'

Based between Devon and Bristol, Katherine Moore describes herself as writer, journalist and guide. We met for the first time in person at Gritfest in Wales, which, as an event, stands for Katherine's interpretation of gravel riding. For her, it is this new thing. It doesn't have any history; it doesn't have anything attached to it. It is our opportunity to create something completely new, and there is no stigma, or anything else, attached to it. For Katherine, gravel is amazingly inclusive and also a fantastic way of travelling.

'Gravel is a misleading term around these parts. It's multi-terrain riding. It's really varied, and really beautiful.'

She has travelled extensively across Britain and knows the gravel scene in England like no other journalist. Katherine normally has multiple hats on: working as freelance editor for Komoot and creating her own routes. When we met to ride this route, a shortened version of her own East Devon Trail, she had just finished her role as editor at **ADVNTR.cc**, a gravel cycling and bikepacking community.

'You gotta take the rough with the smooth, quite literally.'

In Katherine's opinion there really is 'proper' gravel in England, you just have to know where to look (despite the weather, which can often be rather wet, especially in the South West).

'There's a theory behind it. When you see people that you can relate to doing something, you're more likely to want to do it yourself. And I think there are some amazing women in the gravel scene. You don't have to be the fastest or go the furthest or whatever, it's just about enjoying it and sharing the love of riding and riding off-road. Hopefully that encourages more people to do it.'

While she loves watching the big endurance races and following women's progress in them, riding them isn't the

DISUSED RAILWAY LINE THROUGH HARPFORD WOOD.

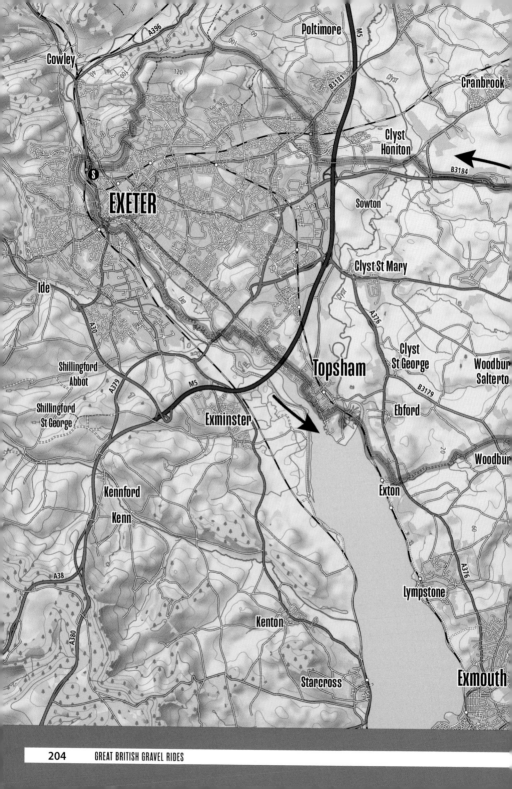

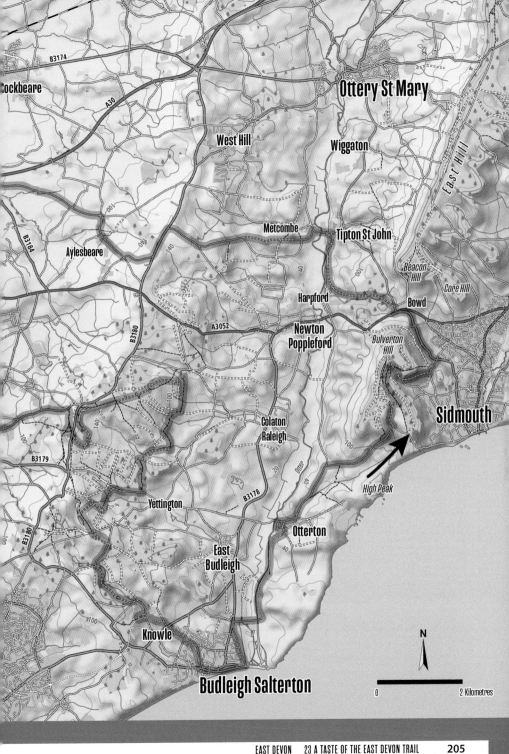

IT RAINS A LOT IN DEVON, BUT YOU'LL BE AMAZED BY THE BEAUTIFUL FORESTS ON THIS ROUTE.

most tempting thing for her. There is this massive synergy between photography and videography and the riding itself, and this is exactly what makes Katherine tick. It is not the big miles and the endless nights of sleep deprivation; it is the creative side of riding and documenting it that makes her cycle, and she also sees that as the side that makes gravel riding so cool. Cool in a creative way, as it brings us more beautiful journals and films and encourages more women to cycle too.

'More non-cyclists getting into gravel riding would be my dream.'

Mountain bikers, road cyclists, or total beginners – the nice thing about gravel riding is that people are coming into it for the first time. Katherine loves the inclusive nature of the sport, the escapism of being out in nature, and sharing all that with her friends.

While there are some amazing women in the gravel scene – Katherine being one of them herself – she also makes sure that they get the column inches they rightly deserve.

ABOUT KATHERINE'S ROUTE

Close to Bristol by train and her home by bike, this route is a shorter variation of Katherine's East Devon Trail, a 185-kilometre bikepacking route through East Devon. The trail showcases the best of this lesser-known corner of Devon and the wide variety of habitats it boasts: freshwater marshes, lowland heath, green agricultural field networks, steep cliffs, pebbled beaches and sleepy woodlands.

It's no accident that the East Devon Trail is punctuated by a

weather forecasting organisation for the United Kingdom, is based in Exeter, and the city's cathedral is well worth a visit.

The route crosses the train tracks over the River Exe and then follows a cycle path along the Exeter Flood Relief Channel, at times following the route of the Tour de Manche, a 700-kilometre cycling route linking Devon and Dorset in England to Brittany and Normandy in France. This section of the route offers beautiful riding along the banks of the River Exe. The route passes Exeter Quay, once a thriving port, now a stunning place for a bite to eat or an early coffee stop. You can often enjoy exhibitions at the Custom House. The route continues along the river, passing through Riverside Valley Park. The cycling here offers excellent river views, with the floodplain meadows giving way to the wilder estuary.

Crossing the Exe at Countess Wear, the route joins Sustrans National Route 2 into Topsham. (An alternative to reach Topsham is to continue on the cycle path along the western bank of the river until Topsham Lock Cottage, from where a ferry runs across the River Exe to the landing in Ferry Road in Topsham.) Route 2, named after Sustrans National Route 2, offers everything a cyclist wants: great coffee, bike service, bikes to hire and accommodation. This makes it a perfect alternative start and finish if you are visiting the area.

Formerly an important seaport and connected by rail to Exeter, Topsham is notable for its scenery, architecture and the nearby nature reserves, including RSPB Bowling Green Marsh on the Exe Estuary, which is the next point of interest on this route. One of Katherine's favourite spots, it offers an excellent bird hide for viewing the wading and migrating birds.

The route continues on a great traffic-free path between Topsham and Exton, and then follows quiet roads through Exton, where it leaves the Exe Estuary. A track, which is rough in places, links to the village of Woodbury, from where the route follows quiet lanes. A long, steady climb up to Woodbury Common follows, perfect to enjoy the pretty village and thatched cottages as you wind your way up the hill. It links up to the golf course near Woodbury Castle. The route follows an alternative to the steeper top of

number of nature reserves, which encourage you to pause a while. If you own some, binoculars are a must on the packing list, as there are a few hides to watch birds from along the route; this is one of Katherine's favourite activities on bikepacking trips.

ROUTE DESCRIPTION

The route starts on the forecourt of Exeter St Davids railway station. Exeter, after playing a key role in Roman Britain, became an important religious location in the Middle Ages and afterwards a wealthy centre for the wool trade. But by the early twentieth century the city's fortunes were in decline. Suffering severe damage in World War II, much of the city centre was rebuilt, and the city is nowadays a booming business hub again. The Met Office, the main

HAWKERLAND BRIDLEWAY WILL TEST YOUR GRAVEL SKILLS.

Castle Lane, along a rutted, and often wet, bridleway. After this, a sharper climb up to the car park opposite Woodbury Castle follows. Woodbury Castle is an Iron Age hill fort, now covered in beech trees, which sits high on stunning heathland. Visitors are free to roam among the earthworks; interpretation boards dotted around explain the importance of the fort and the archaeology of the site. The castle is free to access and a fascinating place to explore.

Woodbury Castle lies within the Pebblebed Heaths Conservation Area, home to a variety of bird, animal and plant life. From the top, incredible views out over the estuary can be enjoyed on a clear day. Besides being a training ground for the Royal Marines who are based nearby, the common features a network of expansive fire roads, twisting singletrack, wooded trails and even some man-made jumps if you are looking for 'rad' riding.

As the route continues across the wide, pebblebed trails on Woodbury Common, you'll notice the purple signs and foxglove symbols of the East Devon Way. Also, look out for Royal Marines who might be out on training exercises. After a short and fast downhill section through woodland, the route follows gravel paths and more singletrack through Crook Plantation. After a short section on tarmac, it passes the 'sheep dip', an obstacle which consists of two pools connected by two underwater tunnels, used by the Royal Marines for training purposes.

The route enters the former Dalditch Camp and passes a bank which once formed the backstop for military target practice. When you get closer, the bunkers where people would hold up the targets

A QUIET LANE NEAR VENN OTTERY COMMON.

from are still visible. The route then passes through the centre of the old quarry, with lakes on either side of the track and more views to the coast on a clear day. Various birds, including Canada geese and tufted ducks, can be observed in the water. Extra care is needed here, as this area in particular is a popular route for walkers, entered by gates at either end. The route crosses a road, proceeds on a track and then rejoins tarmac for a short while. Continuing on more gravel paths and small roads, Dalditch Farm is an interesting next stop. It's worth checking out all the metalwork on its side, from the postbox to wacky drainpipes.

Just north of Budleigh Salterton, the ride joins Sustrans National Route 2 for a short section, and then continues on roads into the small town. Budleigh Salterton, almost at the halfway point of

the route, is perfect for a quick stop. The town lies to the west of the mouth of the River Otter; the estuary includes a grazing marsh and a reed bed. The estuary is a Site of Special Scientific Interest and a haven for migratory birds. The cliffs and pebble beach are part of the Jurassic Coast World Heritage Site, which is further explored in **22 Jurassic Gravel** (pages 193–201). The beach is great for a stop to enjoy a takeaway coffee and crab sandwich from Tea & Tittle Tattle. The route follows Granary Lane out of town and rejoins Sustrans National Route 2 along the River Otter.

For those looking for an afternoon tea, Otterton Mill is a brilliant stop-off point near the river. The glorious old red brick mill houses a farm shop and cafe, so there's plenty to choose from here. You can also get your snacks and drinks to take away and sit alongside the river next to the car park, which

BUDLEIGH SALTERTON.

is lovely in the sun. From here the route continues along Sustrans National Route 2 on Peak Hill Road, before it ventures off-road once again shortly before Sidmouth. The technical climb from the last corner on Peak Hill Road can be wet in places. Running alongside the Otterton Brook, the riding through this steep-sided valley between twisted trees feels more like Exmoor than East Devon.

Next up is Mutter's Moor, another one of the pebblebed heaths of East Devon and home to nightjars and Dartford warblers. On a brilliant stretch of wide, sandy and stony bridleway, travelling between the heathland moor and forest plantation through trees, you can enjoy spectacular views of the town of Sidmouth and the English Channel.

After a short section of tarmac on the western edge of Sidmouth, the route joins Sustrans National Route 248 into Tipton St John on a flat off-road section that winds through Harpford Wood. This old railway line is well drained and sheltered, so it stays rideable all year round. From Tipton St John, the route follows a great gravel road west across the fields. This includes a climb and quite a few puddles in wet conditions; an alternative is to take the lane to the south instead.

The route soon joins a quiet lane and passes the small nature reserve at Venn Ottery Common, perfect for another slice of the East Devon pebblebed heath. Be aware that the boggy tracks and footpaths can get very wet underfoot, especially in winter. Despite being relatively small, around 40 different species of birds breed here, and four of the six species of British reptiles are also present: common lizards, slow worms, grass snakes and adders. Keep an eye out for

DISTANCE **77km/48 miles** 〉 ASCENT **1,057m/3,468 ft** 〉 GRADE **Expert** 〉 START/FINISH **Exeter St Davids railway station** 〉 START/FINISH GRID REF **SX 912933** 〉 BIKE-FRIENDLY PUBLIC TRANSPORT **At the start** 〉 HIGHEST POINT **193m/633 ft** 〉 TERRAIN **Wide gravel paths on pebblebed heaths combined with relaxed river path cycling. Some sections on technical singletrack, which require grippy tyres** 〉 RECOMMENDED TYRES **Schwalbe G-One Ultrabite**

BEST TIME TO RIDE

| JAN | FEB | MAR | APR | MAY | JUN | JUL | AUG | SEP | OCT | NOV | DEC |

SINGLETRACK **5%**   PATH **25%**   CYCLE PATH **15%**   ROAD **55%**

WOODBURY COMMON.

nightjars on summer evenings, as well as stonechats and Dartford warblers as they perch in the gorse bushes. From here, the route follows more lanes to Aylesbeare on the northern side of the East Devon pebblebed heathlands.

Shortly after Clyst Honiton, Redhayes Bridge provides a segregated cycle and pedestrian route across the M5 motorway. The bridge, as well as having an elegant and interesting design, re-establishes a route that was cut off when the motorway was originally constructed. The route passes Pinhoe and climbs up to Beacon Hill, and shortly after Stoke Post follows a bridleway towards Stoke Woods. Located to the north of Exeter, the woodland hosts some of the largest and oldest trees in the area. From here, the route follows roads and cycle paths back to Exeter St Davids railway station.

OTHER ROUTES NEARBY
> East Devon Trail
> Exe Estuary Trail
> Sustrans National Route 2
> Sustrans National Route 248
> Tour de Manche

WHERE TO EAT
> Route 2, Topsham
> Tea & Tittle Tattle, Budleigh Salterton
> Otterton Mill, Otterton

BIKE SHOPS
> Route 2, Topsham (T 01392 879 160)

WHERE TO STOP
> RSPB Bowling Green Marsh bird hide, SX 971876
> Woodbury Castle, SY 032872
> Remains of Dalditch Camp, SY 038849
> Budleigh Salterton, SY 064817
> Venn Ottery Common, SY 066916

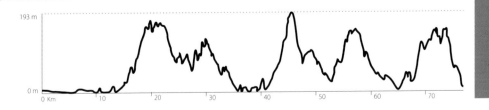

WALES

24 TWMPA GRAVEL TOUR

76KM   ANDY DIX

From narrow lanes to wide open hilltop tracks with stunning views, this loop takes you on a demanding ride in Powys.

ABOUT ANDY

Gravel riding for Andy in three words
childlike; exhilarating; liberating

'Rob was writing a book about an ash tree and approached me with a commission to build a piece of furniture from the tree that he had felled for the project.'

Both Andy Dix's story and my own story with bikes are closely connected to Robert Penn. His book *It's All About the Bike: The Pursuit of Happiness on Two Wheels*, which documents Rob's worldwide search for the perfect custom bike, was one of my biggest inspirations when I took up cycling. An ash tree that Rob cut down for his book *The Man Who Made Things Out of Trees* inspired the idea of Twmpa Cycles. Andy, a furniture maker based in Hay-on-Wye, was commissioned to produce something from the tree. As Rob's passion is bikes, Andy was thinking about making a wooden frame. But time was against him, so the idea got parked and he produced a writing desk for Rob instead. But when the pandemic started, Andy picked up the bike idea again and built his first wooden bike.

'The reason why we make wooden gravel bikes: because wood is the perfect material to make a gravel frame from.'

In September 2020 he launched his first bike, the Twmpa GR 1.0, which is perfectly suited to the local terrain. His bike design was inspired by the plethora of back roads and small lanes, which often lead to forest roads, and on to and over hills. One thing leads to another, and he realised that he wanted to produce a bike that allowed him to knit all those different things together. A bike which is the perfect tool for Powys.

'I found that the bikes that we build, the bike that I have here, have just been the perfect escape machine during lockdown.'

The first and successive lockdowns gave Andy the opportunity to get to know the local neighbourhood like the back of his hand. As this was the case for many, he saw the rapid rise in the popularity of gravel bikes in Britain as an opportunity to start his own brand. The back roads in Wales often deteriorate and become gravel tracks, so a gravel bike seemed most suited to ride on the roads and terrain around his local area. Being locked down there led to endless opportunities for Andy to explore, escape and slow down, and to discover all the intricate details of the green lanes of Powys and the lesser-visited areas.

'Twmpa is where a lot of the riding I do takes place, and a lot of the testing on bikes. It's been an area where I tried my best to break the prototypes, and it has become the place that has given the bikes their name.'

His goal is to establish Twmpa as a genuine competitor to other gravel bikes. For him it's easy to view wood as a novelty product, because there are very few wooden gravel bikes out there.

PREVIOUS PAGE LUSH, GREEN COUNTRYSIDE – TYPICAL FOR POWYS (ROUTE 24).
OPPOSITE THE DESCENT TOWARDS LLEWELYN'S CAVE.

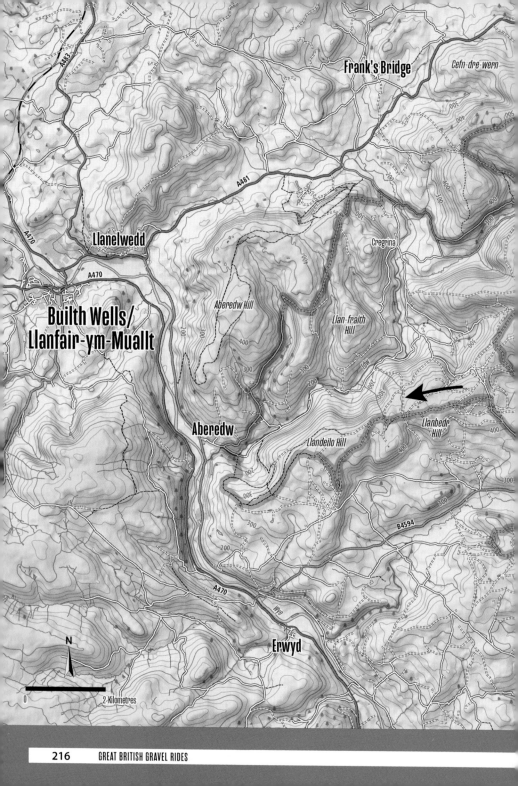

Frank's Bridge

Cefn-dre-wern

A481

Llanelwedd

Cregrina

A470

Builth Wells/
Llanfair-ym-Muallt

Aberedw Hill

Llan-fraith
Hill

Llanbedr
Hill

Aberedw

Llandeilo Hill

B4594

N

A470

Wye

Erwyd

0   2 Kilometres

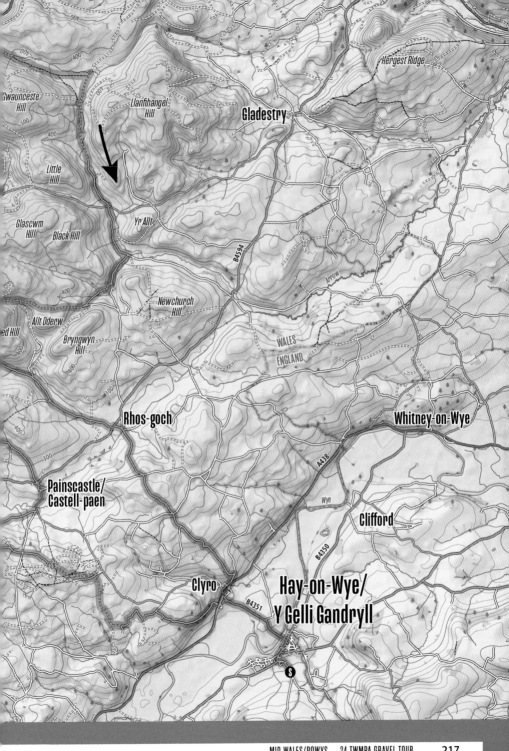

GRASSY TRAILS WITH TWMPA, THE MOUNTAIN WHICH GAVE ANDY'S BIKES THEIR NAME, IN THE BACKGROUND.

But the reason he makes gravel bikes is not to make novelty bikes: it's because he believes that wood has particular properties, such as absorbing vibrations, that makes it well suited for bike frames.

'Riding gravel roads anywhere invites exploration. It invites you to discover the less obvious types of off-road riding available. Every time I ride there is a new discovery.'

And as mountain biking has been around for such a long time, Andy embraces the novelty that is still attached to gravel riding. While most areas have been well-explored for mountain bikers, the great thing about gravel riding is that it opens his eyes to areas that he otherwise would not experience. Especially in Wales, which has masses of open country and a very low population density.

And his plans for the future? Other models, like a touring bike or a hub-geared city bike, and a beautiful and practical ebike, which has just been launched. Of course, all made out of wood.

ABOUT ANDY'S ROUTE

Circling around Andy's local area, this route is an exhilarating mix of the various types of terrain that gravel bikes enable you to explore, from narrow lanes to wide open hilltop tracks with stunning views. At times, the riding will push you to the edge of what's possible, both uphill and

downhill. But with a good dose of handling skills and good legs, this route is one of the most scenic in the book.

ROUTE DESCRIPTION

Hay-on-Wye has become world famous for its large number of second-hand and antiquarian bookshops. The Hay Festival, an annual, 10-day literary festival held in May or June, was described by Bill Clinton in 2001 as 'the Woodstock of the mind'; it has become a prominent festival in British culture. The concept of the 'book town', a small rural town or village in which second-hand and antiquarian bookshops are concentrated, was initiated by Richard Booth in Hay-on-Wye in

LANE NEAR LLOWES COMMON.

the late 1970s. He also declared Hay an 'independent kingdom', crowned himself as monarch with the title of Richard Cœur de Livre, and made his horse prime minister. As you might imagine, this publicity stunt gained him extensive news coverage.

Twmpa, a mountain forming part of the substantial north-west escarpment of the Black Mountains, lies about 7 kilometres south of Hay. It gives its name not only to Andy's bikes, but also to this route. At 690 metres in height, it is clearly visible on a good day from various points on the route. The loop starts at Drover Cycles in Hay, which offers not only excellent refreshments in their cafe, but also bike hire, sales and service. The route follows a very short section of Sustrans National Route 42 into Hay, and then crosses the River Wye on the main road and climbs gradually out of town. At Clyro, the route leaves the B4351 and then crosses the busy A438 to continue on a small lane towards Llowes Common. For those not used to cycling on Welsh lanes, extra care and attention is needed on these very narrow single-track roads; they are often lined on both sides by tall hedges. The route climbs steadily uphill and, once the tarmac ends, climbs further on a track.

After another short section on tarmac, the route enters The Begwns. This small, National-Trust-owned upland area is spanned by a number of public footpaths and bridleways and offers spectacular, panoramic views over the surrounding countryside. There are a number of small pools in the area, and the route passes one of them. These pools offer a good opportunity to spot dragonflies. The riding here is dominated by well-compacted singletrack trails and wider tracks, which make for fantastic gravel riding.

The gravel tracks are succeeded by another section on tarmac, and shortly afterwards you descend on gravel first, then on a quiet road, towards Painscastle. The next steep climb starts just before the village, which sits in the wide valley of the Bachawy, a small tributary of the River Wye. Little else, apart from the massive earthworks, remains of the castle that gives the village its name, but the pub

CHAT AT THE VILLAGE PUB IN ABEREDW.

is a welcome stop for refreshments. The route climbs on tarmac almost all the way to the top of Llanbedr Hill. The route leaves the road again and continues on a wide track. This is again ideal for gravel cycling, taking you through open country, with empty hills rolling into the distance. A descent to Byrgwm Pool is followed by another gentle climb. Further wide tracks provide more fun; the descent towards Llewelyn's Cave is a hoot, with an abandoned house right next to the route before it joins tarmac.

Back on roads, the route climbs gently towards Aberedw, but then takes a right-hand turn just before the small village. If open, the village pub is worth a small detour for refreshments. If it is closed, an ancient spring just opposite the pub provides a good opportunity to fill up water bottles. Sadly, local people do not attribute any mystical powers to the water, which would be helpful to tackle the next bit of the route, as the climbing continues. Once the road runs out at Blaenmilouchaf, a steep climb on a gravel track is rewarded with more amazing views across the valleys. The route traverses the top of Aberedw Hill then descends on wide and rocky gravel trails into the next valley, to join Sustrans National Route 825 for a short section before continuing on to Glascwm.

While this short stint provides some time to relax, the next climb is steep, rocky and likely to push any gravel rider to the limits. The work is once again rewarded with fantastic views, and the route reaches its highest point at 506 metres near Gwaunceste Hill. Descending on a mix of singletrack and gravel trails, the route crosses Sustrans National Route 825 near

DISTANCE **76km/47 miles** 〉 ASCENT **1,807m/5,928 ft** 〉 GRADE **Expert** 〉 START/FINISH **Drover Cycles, Hay-on-Wye** 〉 START/FINISH GRID REF **SO 230419** 〉 BIKE-FRIENDLY PUBLIC TRANSPORT **Hereford railway station (34km from the route)** 〉 HIGHEST POINT **506m/1,660 ft** 〉 TERRAIN **Exposed, open moorland with at times technical and rocky paths and singletrack trails** 〉 RECOMMENDED TYRES **Schwalbe G-One Ultrabite**

BEST TIME TO RIDE

| JAN | FEB | MAR | APR | MAY | JUN | JUL | AUG | SEP | OCT | NOV | DEC |

SINGLETRACK **15%**   PATH **30%**   ROAD **55%**

DUSTY TRAILS IN THE BEGWNS.

Cloggau. It continues on tarmac and fords a river between Upper Glasnant and Lower Glasnant, before another steep off-road climb will test the legs once again, traversing Red Hill. At Hondon, the route joins a road to Rhos-goch and climbs one last time towards Clyro Hill. Once at the top, Hay is clearly visible in the valley, and it's downhill all the way from Clyro. After a very short section on the busy A438, you follow the outward route back to Hay.

OTHER ROUTES NEARBY
› Gospel Pass
› Sustrans National Route 42
› Sustrans National Route 825

WHERE TO EAT
› Drover Cycles Cafe, Hay-on-Wye
› The Cosy Cafe, Hay-on-Wye
› Shepherds Parlour, Hay-on-Wye
› The Seven Stars Inn, Aberedw

BIKE SHOPS
› Drover Cycles, Hay-on-Wye (T 01497 822 419)

WHERE TO STOP
› Hay Castle, SO 229423
› The Begwns, SO 168442
› Painscastle Castle, SO 167461
› Cradle Rocks, SO 116477

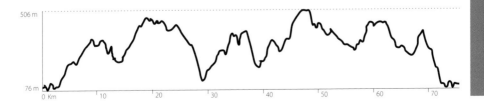

25 A GRITFEST IN THE CAMBRIAN MOUNTAINS

59KM   MATT PAGE

Inspired by the early gravel adventures of the Rough-Stuff Fellowship, this route combines rich cultural history, vibrant natural beauty and fabulous gravel-riding-friendly forest tracks.

ABOUT MATT

Gravel riding for Matt in three words
openness; speed; freedom

'It's nice to organise something again.' Matt Page's own event successes are impressive. He has won the UK 24-hour Solo Championships, the European Singlespeed Championships and the European 24-hour Solo Championships, and he came second in the 2016 Celtman! Extreme Scottish Triathlon, to name just a few. He is a coach, mountain bike leader and regular writer for cycling magazines. Matt is not only interested in winning events, but is also brilliant at organising them.

With the pandemic temporarily bringing a pause to what he loves most, Matt simply loved running Gritfest, a 2-day gravel enduro in the Cambrian Mountains of Wales, again in 2021.

'In Wales and in most of the UK we've got a difficulty with races, where you can't legally race. I wanted to try and find a way that you can get a race, but stay within the boundaries of what we've got. The only way you can do that is timed stages and an enduro format.'

And that's exactly what his flagship gravel event, Gritfest, is all about. It started in 2018 – the concept worked, and people enjoyed it. It pleases the people who want to race, but also the rest of the riders, who just want to relax and enjoy the views. And there are plenty of views to enjoy.

'A lot of the mountain biking I was doing was more gravel anyway. I was doing long distances and doing some forest and fire roads, so I guess I've been gravel riding since 2000.'

Like other riders in this book, Matt thinks that gravel riding has existed long before gravel bikes have. He got his first gravel bike about a decade ago, and since then the whole scene has not only got bigger, but also much better.

'For me, it's not a true gravel event if someone on a mountain bike wins, because that means it's too technical and wider tyres are too much of an advantage.'

The first Gritfest Matt organised had roughly a 50–50 split between mountain bikes and gravel bikes, and also a fair few cyclo-cross bikes and narrower tyres. Gritfest in 2021 was a very different affair, with around 80 per cent gravel bikes. For him, the event should be won on a gravel bike; that's ultimately what Matt wants to happen, and how he chooses the routes. It needs to be on terrain that's fastest on a gravel bike.

GRAVEL AND LUSH FORESTS AT GRITFEST NEAR PUMSAINT.

BEAUTIFUL WOODLAND ON THE ROAD TO ABERBOWLAN.

'You're able to explore more than you would on a road bike, and travel a little but further than you would on a mountain bike.'

For Matt, the forests and the open landscapes of Wales are perfect to explore. Not unlike other parts of the UK, but much more accessible, as it is closer to major cities like London and Birmingham. And perfect for holding an event that people enjoy, just as much as Matt enjoys organising it.

ABOUT MATT'S ROUTE

The Cambrian Mountains are a remote and tranquil area, so sparsely populated that this part of Wales has been described by writers in past centuries as the 'Green Desert of Wales'.

Matt's favourite route formed the riding on day 2 of the 2021 Gritfest. One of the things that sets the event apart from others is the stunning location, which has attracted cyclists for many decades. For Matt this route is the 'truest' gravel you can find in Britain. Most of the tracks in this route are wide and pretty smooth, and all set in the stunning scenery of one of the most beautiful, colourful and varied landscapes in the southern part of Britain.

Gritfest follows in a long tradition of off-road cycling, which dates back to the days before the inauguration of the famous Rough-Stuff Fellowship on 29 May 1955. From the 1933 cover of *The CTC Gazette*, the official magazine of the Cyclists' Touring Club (which was founded 1878), we learn that the moorland and valley roads of the Upper Towy Valley were as popular back then with cyclists looking for peace and quiet as they are now.

ROUTE DESCRIPTION

The Cambrian Mountains sit between their better-known neighbours, the Brecon Beacons National Park and Snowdonia National Park. In the 1960s an attempt was made to designate

CLIMBING TO PEN RHIWIAR.

the area as a national park; sadly, this ultimately failed. But many decades later the Cambrian Mountains are still one of the most special parts of Wales: they form a largely unspoiled and peaceful landscape with an abundant cultural history, stunning natural beauty and fabulous forest tracks for gravel riding.

This route starts in the village of Cilycwm, north of the town of Llandovery. The route follows a road on the western side of the Upper Towy Valley, passing Cwm-y-Rhaeadr, meaning 'Valley of the Waterfall' in Welsh. This remote woodland and picnic area with dramatic waterfalls is popular with mountain bikers.

The road follows the Afon Tywi (River Towy) upstream, passing another woodland. The Towy Bridge Inn at Rhandirmwyn Bridge is a great first stop and has a nice outdoor seating area next to the river. The Grade-II-listed steel bridge opposite the pub is a scarce example of a Warren truss bridge. It was constructed using lightweight prefabricated components, making it convenient for use in the

remote Upper Towy Valley. It is also notable as an example of road transport improvements in rural Wales.

At the next fork the route follows the road on the right. As soon as the tarmac stops, the climbing starts. The route ascends on a gravel track out of the valley, with beautiful views across the lush, green landscape. The higher you climb, the steeper it gets, but your hard work is rewarded with more stunning views. As the route leaves the woodland it flattens out, then continues to climb more gradually across the upper reaches of the hills. It enters another woodland and reaches its highest point of 413 metres at Pen Rhiwiar. The gravel track continues to undulate through the forest, and then descends towards Bwlch-y-rhiw. Not directly on the route but just a short ride in the opposite direction is Bwlch-y-rhiw Chapel, one of Wales' oldest Baptist chapels.

The route descends on a road that runs parallel to the Afon Cothi to Cwrt-y-Cadno (the fox court), another small village. The village is situated on an important crossroads on the route which drovers took from Ceredigion to Smithfield Market in England. The cattle were shod to protect their hooves; water and pasture were available for the herd in the village. At the beginning of the nineteenth century, Cwrt-y-Cadno was home to Dr John Harries, an extraordinary man who was considered by locals to be a wizard; he is said to have been able to cure illness, predict the future and calm evil spirits.

It's easy to predict what is to come from here – more hills! However, superpowers are not needed. There are some steeper sections as the route climbs on the road to the right towards Llwyn-diried Farm. It then takes a left at the farm to continue on a road. Shortly afterwards, the route joins a gravel track on the left and continues along this for a while. There are some short climbs in this section, before the route descends to Pumsaint. At 33 kilometres into the ride, this is a great place to stop for lunch, with less distance and climbing remaining from here to the finish.

Pumsaint (spelt Pumpsaint on Open Street Maps) is a sleepy Carmarthenshire village with an award-winning pub (the Dolaucothi Arms won the BBC Countryfile Country Pub of the Year in 2019), which forms part of the extensive estate of Dolaucothi, owned by the National Trust. Not far from the village are the Dolaucothi Gold Mines, the only known Roman gold mines in Britain. The name Pumsaint is Welsh for 'Five Saints'. There is a small standing stone near the gold mines – legend has it that the stone is associated with five saints, who used to lay their heads on the stone. However, it turns out that, in reality, the standing stone was used as an anvil in the Roman period for crushing gold ore. Similar technology has been found in Spanish gold mines dating from the Roman period.

If you're not into gold mines or Roman history, or don't have the time to visit the Dolaucothi Gold Mines, you can spot a mining tower and buildings from the road while you are climbing steeply through a beautiful woodland. Once past the mine, the route descends to Caio, another village which lies at the confluence of the Afon Annell and the Nant Frena.

The next part of the route offers more fantastic gravel riding as it climbs into Caeo Forest; this working conifer forest, which was planted by the Forestry Commission in the twentieth century, spreads out over the uplands high above the village of Caio. The route descends and climbs again as you head through this extensive man-made landscape. There are a number of large log piles in the forest – which are great for photo opportunities – and there are nice views across the surrounding countryside too. A long descent takes you out of the woods

DISTANCE **59km/37 miles** 〉 ASCENT **1,241m/4,072 ft** 〉 GRADE **Expert** 〉 START/FINISH **Cilycwm** 〉 START/FINISH GRID REF **SN 752402** 〉 BIKE-FRIENDLY PUBLIC TRANSPORT **Cynghordy (6km from the route)** 〉 HIGHEST POINT **413m/1,355 ft** 〉 TERRAIN **Hilly, at times very exposed, but with well-surfaced, rideable paths** 〉 RECOMMENDED TYRES **Schwalbe G-One R**

BEST TIME TO RIDE

JAN	FEB	MAR	APR	MAY	JUN	JUL	AUG	SEP	OCT	NOV	DEC

PATH **60%**   ROAD **40%**

CAEO FOREST.

and on to the road to Aberbowlan. In summer, this section feels like an amazing 'tunnel' through a beautiful woodland. If you are stretched for time, taking the road from Caio to Aberbowlan cuts out the section through Caeo Forest.

Taking a left at Aberbowlan, the route follows a road and climbs uphill again. This is the last large climb of the route: at Blaen-dyffryn the road becomes a track and starts descending. The route passes another beautiful woodland – be prepared for some muddy sections and puddles here. The track descends around the slopes of Pen Lifau into the valley of the Afon Dunant towards Cwm-Dunant. From here, a final section on the road gives you plenty of opportunities to marvel at the lush hills of the 'Green Desert of Wales' on your way back to Cilycwm, where you can celebrate with a nice pint.

OTHER ROUTES NEARBY
> Cwm Rhaeadr mountain bike route (red)
> GB Divide
> Sustrans National Route 43
> Sustrans National Route 82

WHERE TO EAT
> Towy Bridge Inn, Rhandirmwyn
> Dolaucothi Arms, Pumsaint
> Neuadd Arms, Cilycwm

BIKE SHOPS
> None in the local area

WHERE TO STOP
> Cwm-y-Rhaeadr, SN 765422
> Rhandirmwyn Bridge, SN 768447
> Bwlch-y-rhiw Chapel, SN 730464
> Cwrt-y-Cadno Welsh Calvinistic Methodist Chapel, SN 692442
> Dolaucothi Gold Mines, SN 664403
> Caeo Forest, SN 681402

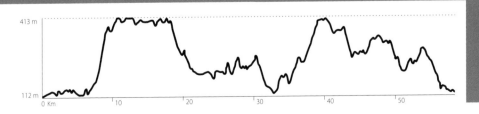

BONUS ROUTE

26 DEER ISLAND GRAVEL
20KM MARKUS STITZ

Immerse yourself in the beautifully rugged landscape that inspired George Orwell, one of Britain's most celebrated novelists, with stunning coastal views and a Scottish single malt never far away.

ABOUT MARKUS' ROUTE
Gravel riding for Markus in three words
freedom; nature; challenge

I found it hard to choose a particular trail or region for my favourite route, as the choice is so vast. While researching this book during the spring and summer of 2021, I left selecting this route to the last minute. But when I toured the Inner Hebrides to map a new bikepacking route, this loop on Jura clearly stood out.

There are a few things that are unique about gravel riding in Scotland, and this route on the Isle of Jura features them all. You'll get a very real sense of the remoteness of large stretches of the Highlands, although the route doesn't take you that far away from the nearest cafe or resupply point.

The route starts at the charming ferry terminal in Feolin, which is nothing more than a slipway, a few parking spaces and a waiting room. The nicely decorated and well-maintained waiting room hinted at the sense of community that can often only be found on these remote islands. It also provided shelter from the gusting winds and frequent rain showers that are as typical for this part of Scotland as the whisky is.

Jura is also one of the few places on the west coast where you might see an eagle. I was lucky enough to spot one of these majestic animals on this ride. While only small, the woodland at the start of the route with its gnarly and windswept trees is a fine example of the type of native woodlands which once could be found in many more places in the Highlands and Islands.

The views across the Sound of Islay are fabulous on a clear day. You'll be able to see Colonsay in the distance, which is my favourite Hebredian island, but sadly much more difficult to get to for a spontaneous trip.

You can spot the whitewashed buildings of the distilleries lining up on Islay on the other side of the sound. Caol Ila Distillery, with its name painted in big black letters on the outside of the warehouse, and Ardnahoe Distillery, with its traditional cupola, are clearly visible from the trail that meanders along the rugged coast.

The tracks that form this route are characteristic of much of the gravel riding I learnt to enjoy and embrace in Scotland, which has been my home for over a decade now. It's hard to find big gravel 'highways' with smooth surfaces that go on for miles on end. Most of the gravel riding in Scotland is a mixed bag: rough, rutted tracks that are a challenge to ride, but with views to die for. With the very rapidly changing weather you can ride in perfect sunshine in one moment, find yourself in the middle of a heavy downpour in

PREVIOUS PAGE THE PAPS OF JURA (ROUTE 26).   **OPPOSITE** FINEST GRAVEL WITH BEINN A'CHAOLAIS IN THE BACKGROUND.
ABOVE © NILS LAENGNER

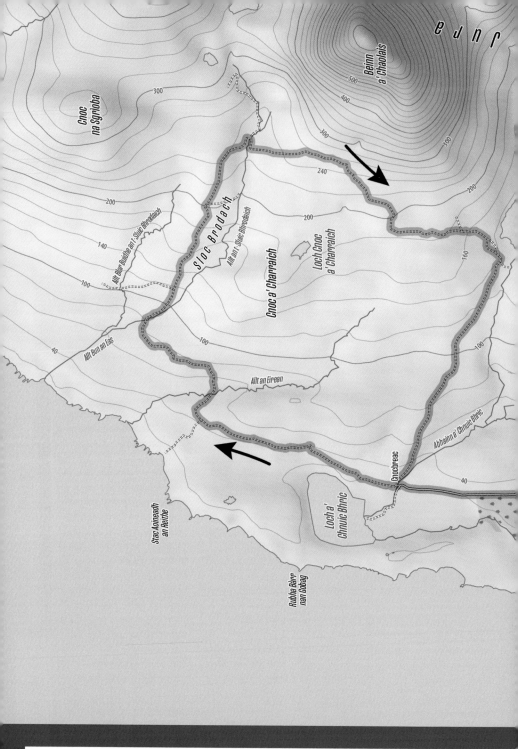

Jura

Beinn
a' Chaolais

500

400

300

Cnoc
na Sgriaba

300

240

200

200

160

Sloc Brodach

Allt Gleir Bodha an t-Sluic Bhrodaich

Allt an t-Sluic Bhrodaich

Cnoc a' Charraich

Loch Cnoc
a' Charraich

200

140

100

160

Allt Bun an Eas

40

100

100

Allt an Eirean

100

Abhainn a' Chnuic Bhric

40

Cnocbreac

Loch a'
Chnuic Bhric

Stac Aoineadh
an Nerithe

Rubha Barr
nan Gobag

A SHORT BUT WORTHWHILE DETOUR FROM THE ROUTE – JURA DISTILLERY AT CRAIGHOUSE.

the next, and marvel at the rainbows over the majestic mountains soon afterwards.

This was exactly the experience I had when I rode this loop on Jura, and it's worth sharing!

ROUTE DESCRIPTION

Feolin itself is nothing more than an anchoring place for the ferry and starting point for the only road on Jura, officially classified as the A846, which is actually more than it deserves in some places. The Ferry House is the only dwelling at Feolin and used to be the home of the ferryman in earlier days.

The Isle of Jura is not always the easiest place for an impromptu visit, since it doesn't have a direct ferry link with the mainland all year. From April to September a small passenger ferry operates a service from Tayvallich on the mainland to Craighouse on Jura. At other times, you'll need to first travel to Islay by ferry from the mainland, then take the ferry from Islay to Jura. It's a very short crossing to Jura from Islay across the Sound of Islay, the fast-flowing channel that separates these two beautiful Inner Hebridean islands.

Starting at the port at Feolin, there is only a very short section of tarmac right at the start of the route on 'The Long Road'. The route turns left at the Ferry House, from where a great gravel road with a few small river fords leads into the Inver Estate. As the gravel road undulates towards Inver Cottage, it offers great views of the rugged coastline of Jura and over to Islay, where a few distilleries are visible on the other side.

Where the gravel track leaves the coast, it passes through a short stretch of Atlantic woodland, the only section of this type of woodland on Jura. Climbing on a very smooth gravel track out of the woodland, the Paps of Jura dominate the view. The highest of the three is Beinn an Oir. The 'Mountain of Gold' is the only Corbett in the group at 785 metres. Beinn Shiantaidh, the 'Sacred Mountain', stands at 757 metres to the east of Beinn an Oir, while Beinn a' Chaolais, the 'Mountain of the Sound', stands to the south-west and is the smallest of the three at 733 metres. Corra Bheinn, the 'Steep Mountain', stands at a height of 573 metres to the north-east of Beinn Shiantaidh and, while not considered to be one of the Paps, is part of the same group of mountains.

The island of Jura is largely

GRAVEL HEAVEN ON THE ISLE OF JURA.

comprised of Dalradian quartzite; this hard metamorphic rock forms the uneven surface of the Paps. During a period of intense volcanic activity in the early Palaeogene period (around 56 million years ago), particularly on the western half of the island, the quartzite has been penetrated by a sheet of linear basalt rock. These dikes are most noticeable on the west coast, as erosion of the surrounding rock has exposed them. The west coast also has some internationally important raised beaches.

The route passes Cnocbreac next. Once a small settlement, nowadays there is nothing left to indicate that people once lived here. As stated on a sign on the estate, many islanders have connections to Cnocbreac. The population of Jura roughly halved during the time of the Highland Clearances, although evictions were not on the same scale that other places in Scotland experienced. There's a loch to the left, which is a short detour off the route.

From Cnocbreac, the track gets rougher and gradually climbs while heading north. The views across the Sound of Islay on a clear day are stunning, with Colonsay and Oronsay visible in the distance. Both golden eagles and white-tailed sea eagles can be seen on the island, and there is an abundance of red deer which roam the countryside. It's very unlikely that you won't spot deer on this ride, and while the chances of spotting an eagle are lower, it's not too unlikely. Ignore the track that branches off to the left where the route turns inland – continue climbing more steeply on the rocky track. The riding here becomes more technical, but most of the route is rideable on a gravel bike. Some sections might require pushing, depending on your riding ability and track conditions.

After another section parallel to the coast, the track takes a 90-degree turn to the right – this is where the steepest section of the route begins. Beinn an Oir

dominates the view to the left, and Beinn a' Chaolais towers above towards the right of the track. While this route is relatively short, it gives you a real sense of the remoteness of the very sparsely populated stretches of the Highlands and Islands of Scotland. On a clear day, make sure to stop to soak up the views in all directions from here. From where another track branches off to the left, the going gets really tough. Good bike handling skills are needed when bouncing over the chunkier rocks. The route fords the Allt an t-Sluic Bhrodaich then turns to the south. After around another 1 kilometre you reach the

DISTANCE **20km/12 miles** ⟩ ASCENT **329m/1,079 ft** ⟩ GRADE **Straightforward** ⟩ START/FINISH **Feolin, Jura** ⟩ START/FINISH GRID REF **NR 441692** BIKE-FRIENDLY PUBLIC TRANSPORT **At the start** ⟩ HIGHEST POINT **260m/853 ft** ⟩ TERRAIN **Remote and exposed open moorland with a more gentle section along the coast** ⟩ RECOMMENDED TYRES **Schwalbe G-One Bite**

BEST TIME TO RIDE

| JAN | FEB | MAR | APR | MAY | JUN | JUL | AUG | SEP | OCT | NOV | DEC |

PATH **100%**

HUMANS ARE OUTNUMBERED BY DEER ON JURA.

route's highest point at 260 metres. While the riding on the rough track is still demanding, it's all downhill from here to Inver Cottage.

From Lochan Gleann Astaile a very smooth gravel 'highway' leads down to the coast. The existing lochan was raised to become storage for a large hydropower scheme, one of the largest privately developed hydropower schemes in the UK. You'll notice the difference in riding compared to the rougher estate tracks. From Cnocbreac, the route follows the outward route back to the ferry port at Feolin.

OTHER ROUTES NEARBY
> Bikepacking Argyll's Islands

WHERE TO EAT
> Port Askaig Hotel and Stores, Port Askaig, Isle of Islay
> The Antlers Bistro Restaurant, Craighouse, Isle of Jura

BIKE TOURS
> Kayak Wild Islay (fatbike tours), Port Ellen, Isle of Islay, www.kayakwildislay.co.uk

WHERE TO STOP
> Atlantic woodland, NR 443714
> Cnocbreac, NR 449731
> Lochan Gleann Astaile, NR 469721

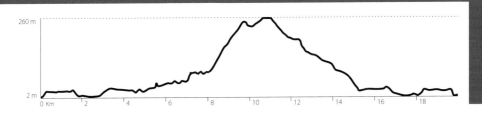

APPENDIX

READING LIST

Bikepacking: Exploring the Roads Less Cycled,
   edited by Stefan Amato
Great British Bike Rides, by Dave Barter
Endurance, by Mark Beaumont
Cycling Touring Guides (various editions and books),
   by Harold Briercliffe
Where There's a Will, by Emily Chappell
Pennine Bridleway, by Hannah Collingridge
Escape by Bike, by Joshua Cunningham
The Drove Roads of Scotland, by ARB Haldane
The Rough-Stuff Fellowship Archive, by Mark Hudson
Further Adventures in Rough Stuff, by Mark Hudson
Bikepacking Aotearoa, by The Kennett Brothers
The West Kernow Way, by Guy Kesteven
Bikepacking England, by Emma Kingston
The Scottish Glens (various books),
   by Peter D. Koch-Osborne
Gravel Cycling, by Nick Legan
Riding Out, by Simon Parker
It's All About the Bike, by Robert Penn
Roads Were Not Built for Cars, by Carlton Reid
1001 Cycling Tips, by Hannah Reynolds
Big Rides: Great Britain & Ireland, edited by
   Kathy Rogers and Markus Stitz
Scottish Hill Tracks, produced by the Scottish Rights
   of Way and Access Society
22,000 Miles, by Richard Seipp
Gravel Rides Scotland, by Ed Shoote
Wild Cycling, by Chris Sidwells
Lost Lanes (various books), by Jack Thurston
Tough Women Adventure Stories, edited by Jenny Tough

WEBSITES

ADVNTR is an online resource for all things
   adventure cycling in the UK, www.advntr.cc
Bikepacking.com is a great online resource for
   routes, inspiring stories and gear reviews from
   around the world, www.bikepacking.com
Bikepacking Scotland, which I run, is a free resource
   for bikepacking and gravel routes in Scotland,
   www.bikepackingscotland.com

The Cateran Ecomuseum offers gravel routes
   in Eastern Perthshire and Angus,
   www.cateranecomuseum.co.uk
Cyclingtips has inspirational stories and gear
   reviews, www.cyclingtips.com
Cycling UK (previously named the Cyclists' Touring
   Club) has championed the cause of cycling for
   more than 140 years. Their website includes useful
   information and route descriptions,
   www.cyclinguk.org
The Geograph® project aims to collect
   geographically accurate photographs and
   information for every square kilometre of Great
   Britain and Ireland, www.geograph.org.uk
Gravel Cyclist offers more information about gravel
   cycling, mainly from a US perspective,
   www.gravelcyclist.com
Gravelfoyle is a great resource for ideas around
   Aberfoyle, www.gravelfoyle.com
Gravel Union is a website and community for gravel
   cycling in Britain, www.gravelunion.cc
Heritage Paths lists and maps historic routes in
   Scotland; it is run by the Scottish Rights of Way and
   Access Society, www.heritagepaths.co.uk
Pannier.cc, run by Stefan Amato, offers plenty of
   wonderful visual inspiration for your adventures,
   guided rides and a shop, www.pannier.cc
Perthshire Gravel Trails offers gravel and
   bikepacking routes in Highland Perthshire,
   www.perthshiregravel.com
Rail&Trail offers day and multi-day gravel routes
   on Scotland's Adventure Coast in Argyll,
   www.railandtrail.co.uk
The website of the Rough-Stuff Fellowship has
   information on the club, how to join, route
   descriptions and GPX files to download,
   www.rsf.org.uk
For any technical questions relating to a bike,
   Sheldon Brown's website is a gold mine:
   www.sheldonbrown.com
Sustrans are the custodians of the National Cycle
   Network, a UK-wide network of traffic-free paths

PREVIOUS PAGE AN OLD PACKHORSE BRIDGE IN YORKSHIRE (ROUTE 13).

LATE SUMMER IN EAST ANGLIA (ROUTE 16).

for everyone, connecting cities, towns and countryside, **www.sustrans.org.uk**

The Draft offers cycling blogs with a fresh perspective on training, travelling and racing, **www.yellowjersey.co.uk/the-draft**

The Radavist are a group of individuals who share a love of cycling and the outdoors, **www.theradavist.com**

Visit East Lothian has a number of gravel routes on their website, **www.visiteastlothian.org**

EVENTS

With the rise of gravel cycling in Britain there are new events appearing regularly; here is a list of new and established events.

> **Battle on the Beach** (South Wales; April)
> **Dirty Reiver** (Northumberland; April)
> **Dorset Dirt Dash** (Dorset; May)
> **Gritopia** (Scottish Borders; May)
> **Gritfest** (Mid Wales; June)
> **Outsider Gravel Grind** (Scottish Borders; July)
> **GBDURO** (Land's End to John o' Groats; August)

> **Raiders Gravel** (Galloway; August)
> **Dukes Weekender** (Trossachs; September)
> **King's Cup** (Suffolk; September)
> **Dunoon Dirt Dash** (Argyll and Bute; September)

GUIDED GRAVEL RIDES

Esther Tacke and Warren Saunders (see **10 Raiders gravel** (pages 87–93)) from **Galloway Cycling Holidays** offer day and multi-day trips on gravel bikes, **www.gallowaygravelholidays.com**

Stefan Amato from **Pannier.cc** (see **15 Pannier gravel** (pages 131–137)) offers group gravel bikepacking weekends and bikepacking tours, **www.pannier.cc**

Naomi Freireich (see **02 In search of gravel on the Monega Pass** (pages 13–19)) and Jaimi Wilson (see **12 Lakes gravel** (pages 107–113)) are part of the **School of Rocks**. This is a woman-led community, founded by Eleanor Jaskowska, which offers a toolkit to empower everyone to find joy in off-road cycling by organising a curriculum of rides over six-week terms, **www.instagram.com/theschoolofrocks**

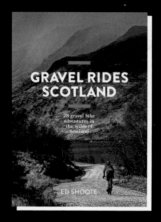
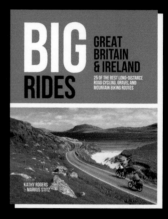